Central to the debate about access to higher education, and about how to develop the educated workforce vital to economic development, are America's open-access, low-cost community colleges that enroll around half of all first-time freshmen in the United States. Can these institutions bridge the gap, and how might they do so? The answer is complicated by their multiple missions—as gateways to four-year colleges, and as providers of occupational education, community services, and workforce development, as well as of basic skills instruction and remediation.

To enable today's administrators and policy makers to understand and contextualize the complexity of the present, this history describes and analyzes the ideological, social, and political motives that led to the creation of community colleges, and that have shaped their subsequent development. In doing so it fills a large void in our knowledge of these institutions.

The "junior college," later renamed the "community college" in the 1960s and 1970s, was originally designed to *limit* access to higher education in the name of social efficiency. Subsequently leaders and communities tried to refashion this institution into a tool for increased social mobility, community organization, and regional economic development. Thus, community colleges were born of contradictions, and continue to be an enigma.

This volume examines the institutionalization process of the community college in the United States, casting light on how this educational institution was formed, and for what purposes, and how has it evolved. It uncovers the historically conditioned rules, procedures, rituals, and ideas that ordered and defined the particular educational structure of these colleges. It focuses on the individuals, organizations, ideas, and the larger political economy that contributed to defining the community college's educational missions, and that have enabled or constrained this institution from enacting those missions. The author also sets the history in the context of contemporary debates about access and effectiveness, and traces how these colleges have responded to calls for accountability from the 1970s to the present.

Community colleges hold immense promise if they can overcome their historical legacy and be re-institutionalized with unified missions, clear goals of educational success, and adequate financial resources. This book presents the history in all its complexity so that policy makers and practitioners might better understand the constraints of the past in an effort to realize the possibilities of the future.

The Author: J. M. Beach has been a teacher and educational administrator in K-12 and postsecondary education for over fifteen years. He has variously been a lecturer at Oregon State University and the University of California, and an instructor at several community colleges in Southern California. Outside of higher education, Beach has been a teacher and school administrator. He is a poet and holds advanced degrees in English, history, philosophy, and education. Email at jmbeach@jmbeach.com or browse through his research on his website at www.jmbeach.com

GATEWAY TO OPPORTUNITY?

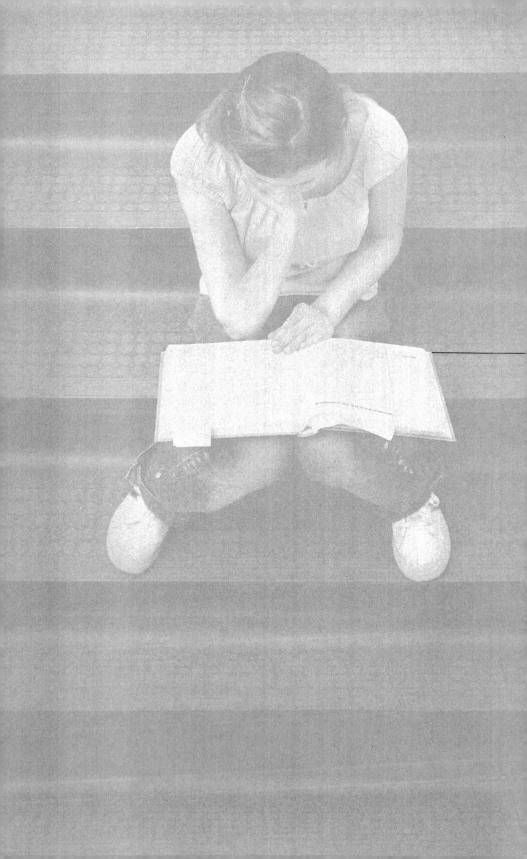

GATEWAY TO OPPORTUNITY?

A History of the Community College in the United States

J. M. Beach

Foreword by W. Norton Grubb

1996–2011 15TH ANNIVERSARY

Stylus
PUBLISHING, LLC.

STERLING, VIRGINIA

Published by Stylus Publishing, LLC
22883 Quicksilver Drive
Sterling, Virginia 20166–2102

Library of Congress Cataloging-in-Publication-Data
Beach, J. M. (Josh M.)
    Gateway to opportunity? : a history of the community
college in the United States / J.M. Beach ; foreword by W.
Norton Grubb.—1st ed.
        p. cm.
    Includes bibliographical references and index.
    ISBN 978-1-57922-451-6 (cloth : alk. paper)
    ISBN 978-1-57922-452-3 (pbk. : alk. paper)
    1. Community colleges—United States—History.
2. Community college students—United
States—History.   3. College students—Conduct of
life—History.   I. Title.
    LB2328.15.U6B43   2010
    378.1'5430973—dc22   2010017525

13-digit ISBN: 978-1-57922-451-6 (cloth)
13-digit ISBN: 978-1-57922-452-3 (paper)

Printed in the United States of America

All first editions printed on acid free paper
that meets the American National Standards Institute
Z39-48 Standard.

Bulk Purchases

Quantity discounts are available for use in workshops
and for staff development.
Call 1-800-232-0223

First Edition, 2010

10   9   8   7   6   5   4   3   2   1

This book is dedicated to community college students, faculty, counselors, staff, and administrators.

A special dedication to Tim Wollman, community college student *extraordinaire*.

The genius of the United States . . . always most in the common people . . . these are unrhymed poetry . . . flesh shall be a great poem . . . A great poem is no finish . . . but rather a beginning.

—WALT WHITMAN, "Preface," *Leaves of Grass*, 1855

CONTENTS

ACKNOWLEDGMENTS

Tthis book grew out of my own experiences with the community college. I began higher education as a community college student, and later I became a community college instructor. The ethical tenor of this book was greatly influenced by conversations with my students. Finally, I studied the community college as a university researcher. The need for this book grew out of the persistent neglect of historical and philosophical issues in the field of higher education. In writing this book I am indebted to many colleagues. Thanks are extended to John Levin for his critical comments at an early stage of this project. Thanks to Rick Wagoner, Rob Rhoads, Jose Santos, and Ken Meier for insightful dialogue. Thanks also to Elizabeth Cox, Carrie Kisker, and colleagues at California Community College Collaborative (C4). Special thanks to Art Cohen for his foundational contributions to community college scholarship and for reviewing an early draft of this manuscript. Special thanks also to Norton Grubb for reviewing this manuscript and writing the foreword. This project was inspired in large part by the breadth and depth of Grubb's research on education in general and the community college specifically. Finally, special thanks to John von Knorring, president and publisher of Stylus. His vision and support in getting this book into print is much appreciated.

Many parts of this book were first presented at various conferences, and I would like to thank my colleagues for their critical comments. Some sections were previously published as "A Critique of Human Capital Formation in the United States and the Economic Returns to Sub-Baccalaureate Credentials" in *Educational Studies* (2009).

The American community college is an endlessly fascinating institution—perhaps more so to those of us outside the college than to the administrators, faculty, and other staff who actually work in community colleges. Most of them are too busy or too preoccupied by daily requirements to sit back and contemplate the institution they work in. The gulf between researchers and practitioners (faculty, staff, administrative) is just as wide as it is in other areas of education. And that is too bad because real improvements in educational institutions rarely occur except through the concerted and collective efforts of people who work in these institutions, rarely through state and federal policies imposed on them from outside. So there's a crucial role for research and writing to highlight the issues that only education professionals can resolve, something I'll come back to at the end of this foreword.

J. M. Beach's *Gateway to Opportunity?* does a fine job of outlining the dilemmas community college administrators face now, the dilemmas they and historians and policy makers need to chew over. It asks us all to think long and hard about the educational institutions we create and why they seem so contradictory. To be sure, the notion of the community college as a *contradictory college*—in some ways behaving like high schools and in other ways like 4-year colleges and universities—is not a new idea since it was explored at length in Kevin Dougherty's *The Contradictory College* some years ago. But *Gateway to Opportunity?* adds a great deal to our understanding of this central fact.

One contribution is to clarify the many ways the dilemma of what the community college is and should be has appeared through the long debates over the 20th century. These debates have been crystallized most clearly in the discussion about whether colleges *cool out*, or sidetrack, certain individuals—working-class students, racial minority students, and immigrant students—from their aspirations of attending 4-year colleges, or whether they *warm up* aspirations and educational outcomes by persuading more students to go beyond high school. This is a debate that extends to many other educational practices, such as the creation of occupational programs first in high school and then in community colleges; other programs that might also be seen as tracking mechanisms, such as special education; and expansion of the underexamined regional universities in this country, which have been analyzed even less than community college have been. The debates in the specific case of community colleges have been pretty much decided by statistical evidence pointing to the dominance of warming up over cooling out, but still Beach's book points to many examples where cooling out is alive and well—particularly in the area of resources, which community colleges receive much less of, including money, than their higher-status cousins in higher education.

Beach has also incorporated racial and ethnic issues into his discussion on community colleges. As he points out, the community college world (like K–12) is as a practical matter divided into *urban* colleges—a euphemism for colleges dominated by working-class individuals and students of color with especially poor K–12 systems that leave students badly prepared for any kind of postsecondary education—and *suburban* colleges, more likely to have white and middle-class students with higher completion and transfer rates. So even the *people's college*, as supporters like to call the community college, hasn't solved the problem that plagues all of education: outcomes that are markedly unequal by class and race, at least in part because of the spatial policies that have segregated low-income and racial minority students in cities. This is of course not the fault of community colleges, but the consequences for inequality among colleges is severe and won't disappear until we as a country recognize and try to moderate the vicious circle of location and low-quality schooling.

This book also clarifies a series of dilemmas colleges face, though several of them are really endemic to U.S. education as a whole. One might be called the dilemma of comprehensiveness. Over time community colleges have taken on more and more purposes, or missions, starting with the transfer mission; provision of occupational education, various community services, workforce development for specific employers; and sometimes economic development and technology transfer for small businesses. Its mission now extends to developing and providing a system of basic skills instruction or remediation that threatens to overwhelm its other missions. As community-serving institutions, colleges have been called upon to provide these and other services, and the dilemma is whether one institution can do all of them well. But comprehensive educational institutions are a general phenomenon in the United States. The high school is similarly comprehensive, and its extracurricular activities help make it look like "the shopping mall high school," as one analysis put it; it would be easy to write a parallel account of the "shopping mall community college." Our research universities have become "multiversities," as Clark Kerr named them, again providing a wide variety of academic and nonacademic offerings. And for community colleges, on the low end of the ranks in postsecondary education, this is unlikely to stop. Several states have transformed their technical institutes into comprehensive community colleges, and another movement is under way to allow colleges to grant baccalaureate degrees, both ways of gaining higher status. So the dilemma of comprehensiveness is unlikely to go away.

Another dilemma that Beach touches on is one that affects students. For at least a century, various supporters of education have preached what I call the Education Gospel—the belief that expanding levels of schooling (and especially vocationally oriented schooling) can address all manner of individual and social problems. For students, this means they need to go as far in their schooling as they can, not because they enjoy education for its own sake but to get ahead—or, more defensively, so at least they do not fall behind others who are getting more schooling. Currently this has become most obvious in the notion of *college for all*, the idea that everyone needs to be prepared to go to college. And community colleges are the most obvious (and cheapest) place to expand higher education. But this means that colleges are full of students who don't necessarily want to be there and who don't act like the diligent, hard-working students of the academic ideal. Becky Cox has explored this dilemma in *The College Fear Factor: How Students and Professors Misunderstand One Another*. Based on ethnographic research in one community college, she found that students fear being exposed as ignorant, and they undermine their own learning by the stratagems they devise to avoid being caught and hide their problems from instructors. This dilemma could be defused somewhat through careful discussion between faculty and students about what college is supposed to be about, but the Education Gospel is unlikely to go away anytime soon— indeed, it appears to be gathering strength in the rhetoric of policy makers and educators.

A third dilemma that Beach confronts is the problem of resources. In virtually all states, community colleges constitute the bottom rung of a tripartite system of postsecondary education, with elite research universities at the top, regional universities (the old state colleges) in the middle, and community colleges on the bottom, open to all and costing less than the others in tuition and opportunity. But this also means they receive lower levels of funding per student even though they have students with more complex needs and less parental support than those in 4-year colleges, public or private. Community college instructors teach more classes than their peers in 4-year colleges, and there are many more part-time or adjunct professors who don't have the time necessary to put into instructional improvement. Resources such as counseling and guidance, assistance for learning disabilities, and tutoring and mentoring are in short supply. All these problems are especially acute in California, which Beach uses as an extended case study, somewhat unfortunately since California is in much worse shape than most states, though it might be a harbinger of the future of other states. California's inability to adequately fund its schools and community colleges has created many more students with inadequate academic skills, and at the same time instructors and administrators are exhausted by the additional roles they have to play. Many schools and colleges in California have lost the capacity to reform themselves since there is no slack or free time or psychological resources to do much more than keep up with the flood of students and the pressure of daily obligations. And, like the other dilemmas of the community colleges, this is likely to get worse before it gets better. The movement toward accountability in higher education, like its counterpart in K–12 education, is likely to increase the pressures on colleges without giving them the capacity to meet these new goals.

There are still other dilemmas that community colleges might face. One that I think is particularly important but gets little mention in *A Gateway to Opportunity?* is the dilemma of instruction, the subject of a book I wrote a decade ago with several colleagues titled *Honored But Invisible: Teaching in Community Colleges*. College administrators pride themselves on running teaching institutions, but as institutions they do little to improve the quality of teaching. The result is that instructional approaches are idiosyncratic, with some excellent instructors and practices (such as learning communities and integrated courses) but with many more faculty teaching in conventional behaviorist ways. And certainly regarding basic skills, which colleagues and I are now examining in a number of colleges, most teaching is conventional, dreary, remedial instruction, involving teaching elementary reading, writing, and math through drill and repetition to students who have failed to learn with these methods in many years of earlier schooling—small wonder that basic skills programs are so unsuccessful in getting students to college-level course work. My own contention is that it is impossible to understand what happens in educational institutions without understanding what happens in classrooms, but far too many administrators, policy makers, and researchers fail to do this.

The portrait that emerges from these dilemmas might lead a cynical observer to call the current situation the exhaustion of education. Many community college students are exhausted, combining employment and family life with schooling they don't find particularly enjoyable. Instructors and administrators are often too exhausted to engage in serious reform, teaching is too often mediocre, and policy makers seem mentally exhausted, at least in the sense that they keep on recycling old ideas (such as accountability) even when it is clear they don't work. The community college movement, which seemed so full of promise in the 1960s—with its vision of greater equity in higher education, the dedication of faculty to a teaching mission, the creation of a thoroughly nontraditional educational institution—seems to have crashed on the shoals of bureaucracy with webs of rules and regulations, conventional interest group conflicts, equitable visions in a highly inequitable society, and inadequate resources. In some sense community colleges, indeed, all public higher education, seem to be victims of their own success with too many students and too many impossible demands to cope with.

But this is too pessimistic. I am constantly impressed by the dedication of community college faculty to their students and to the vision of the community college as an equitable institution where students can pursue a variety of goals, not just the baccalaureate degree. I like to think that faculty and administrators could use *Gateway to Opportunity?* to think about the dilemmas of the college and to forge workable proposals and solutions. Of course, this is asking them to engage in the hard work of reform just as many individuals and institutions lack the resources to do this, so neither they nor any other group of educators can do this alone. It will require confronting each of the dilemmas of the colleges, examining which aspects colleges can improve and which require reforming other institutions (especially K–12) and the collaboration of policy makers—particularly in providing resources—and in recognizing that accountability without capacity building is a foolish approach. It will require confronting the deep-seated causes of inequality, only some of which can be overcome by improved instruction and more equitable educational resources. It will require examining such fundamental beliefs as the Education Gospel, college for all, and the ways we make educational policy in this country.

To take a historical perspective again, in many ways this country took a wrong turn in education after 1900, just as high schools were assuming their modern form and as the first community colleges were being founded. That direction was codified by the so-called administrative progressives with their emphasis on efficiency, uniformity, top-down control of institutions, instructional approaches that have come to be seen as conventional, quantification of inputs and outputs, and an approach to the diversity of students that stressed stratification of students and allocated the lowest-performing students to the worst-resourced tracks and institutions. Indeed, even though administrative progressives concentrated on the K–12 system, community colleges are in many ways perfect examples of their way of thinking: low-cost and therefore efficient institutions, enrolling large numbers of low-performing high school graduates in colleges with relatively few resources, conventional teaching, and top-down administration. Fortunately, there are glimmers of change in K–12 education and in some colleges following the *pedagogical* progressives such as John Dewey. These institutions place a greater emphasis on equity by allocating resources differently, focusing on effectiveness rather than efficiency, implementing real changes in instructional approaches and assessment, distributing leadership among faculty and administrators rather than exercising it in authoritarian ways, and providing a fuller roster of student support services. This is a much more powerful vision than the one emerging from the administrative progressives, particularly given the importance Americans have always placed on education. If followed consistently by all supporters of education, it could reshape community colleges as well as K–12 education as real gateways to opportunity rather than as barriers.

W. Norton Grubb
David Gardner Chair in Higher Education
University of California, Berkeley

The Institutionalization of Community Colleges

At the dawn of the 21st century some 30 percent of American adults had earned a bachelor's degree or higher, the highest percentage of Americans who earned a higher education degree in this country's history. However, higher education is still not equally available for all American citizens, and the returns from a college credential still bring differential earnings based on ethnicity, sex, and class. Access to institutions of higher education and the knowledge and economic returns of a college education are not for everyone. These luxuries continue to be restricted to a minority of the American population, although this educated minority has grown significantly over the past century.[1]

The State of the Union

It took the United States almost two centuries to grant all citizens full political rights, but at the start of the 21st century not all citizens have equal access to the political process nor equal claim to the educational tools needed for economic independence. Centuries of social and political struggle have enabled a large minority of American citizens to gain a measure of economic, educational, and political success, but the sacred principles articulated in the Declaration of Independence have yet to become a reality for *all* citizens, let alone the millions of immigrants and foreigners living in this country. Not all Americans are living free and equal in their pursuit of happiness, nor is the government (which was supposedly instituted *by and for* the people) equally responsive or just in protecting the rights and well-being of *all* citizens.[2]

It is unclear whether social, political, and economic conditions will improve for the majority of Americans in the 21st century, especially given the global economic collapse of 2008–2009, although the administration of President Barack Obama has taken some hopeful steps on this front. Will most citizens have increased access to and success in higher education? Will most citizens have increased access to and participation in the political process? Will most citizens experience a more just and equitable distribution of income? Will most citizens be able to rely on quality social services and safety nets, such as public schooling, affordable health care, and retirement benefits? And how much access will immigrants have to participate in American society, higher education, and the political process?

Or, will a resurgent class structure in American society be unveiled in the 21st century? Peter Drucker, an influential business guru, predicted in the 1990s that a new elite class of "knowledge workers" was beginning to form. With higher education credentials and specialized technological skills, these knowledge workers would one day foment a "new class conflict" in America. According to Drucker, this new sociopolitical order would not only be inevitable but also "right and proper" because those citizens privileged enough to become educated knowledge workers deserved to rule. Drucker's message was clear: American citizens must either scramble up the competitive ladder of success by earning college degrees and gaining technology-oriented skills, or they shall rightfully fall beneath a new class of technocratic elites.[3]

Drucker's version of the American Dream reformulates the mythic hope of meritocracy by turning the ideology of Americanism into a dystopic threat: Better yourself or else! It also blames the victims who for many reasons cannot seem to grasp the American Dream. For those citizens of the United States who hold sacred the democratic principles outlined in the *Declaration of Independence*, this dark and foreboding prophecy of a new elite betrays the very hope this nation supposedly embodies.

To make an accurate assessment of future social, educational, and political possibilities, the past must be revisited and understood to contextualize the complexity of the present. But complex understandings of history rarely inform public policy in this country. Even when policy makers are aware of history, rarely does historical knowledge affect the political process in which public policy is fought over, negotiated, and compromised. As Deborah Stone has argued, the policy-making process is about power and "the struggle over ideas," as politicians rhetorically dance through the many political fires of competing interests. Policy makers seek to control interpretations by framing, or spinning, present problems under the rhetorical guise of what is legitimate, what is feasible, or what is good. But rarely do policy makers consider the historical complexity of how the past has created the present. In polarized and heated political debates, history is valued only to the extent that it can be fashioned into a political tool. This usually results in the denial of history and the creation of politicized myths. The history used by policy makers is almost always a quasi-fictional political narrative shaped to gain legitimate power, thereby securing social, political, and economic resources.[4]

Higher education policy in the United States rests on two politicized myths: *socioeconomic meritocracy* and *equal access to higher education*. Yet upon close inspection of the historical record, neither narrative has much concrete validity. A look at the history of higher education in the United States and the changing dynamics of student access is a bleak tale until fairly recently. The historical record reveals some expansion of access and equity in terms of increasing amounts of postsecondary education for a broader swath of Americans, but inequality has remained constant. Traditionally underserved populations, such as the economically disadvantaged and non-white ethnic/racial minorities, still struggle to achieve equality of opportu-nity in American society and its institutions of higher education. Financial returns for postsecondary degrees are still lower for women and nonwhite minorities because regional labor markets continue to perpetuate a long his-tory of institutionalized discrimination. As the United States moves into a postindustrial knowledge economy in a highly globalized world, the issue of student access to higher education has become one of the most pressing political problems for those concerned with sociopolitical equity and eco-nomic development. The educational and economic success of the student and the economic development of the nation have become intertwined polit-ical issues. Can the United States keep its dominant economic position in the highly competitive world economy with only 30 percent of the American population holding bachelor's degrees? If the majority of U.S. citizens lack a higher education, can the United States live up to its democratic principles and preserve its political institutions?

At the center of these questions is the policy issue of *access* to higher education. Who has access to what forms of higher education at what cost? For most Americans, access is restricted to the open-access, low-cost Ameri-can community college. This institution enrolls about half of all first-time college students in the United States. Most students who enroll in commu-nity colleges have the goal of transferring to a 4-year college or university to earn a bachelor's degree, but the vast majority of these students will never earn any degree. Community colleges have been praised for almost a century as an efficient way to handle the vast surge of Americans looking for access to higher education and as an economical path for social mobility. However, it is unclear *if* this institution actually helps students, let alone *how* it might help. Scholars have never been able to completely agree on the mission of the community college, and therefore, have never been able to adequately determine what it is the community college is supposed to do, not to mention how it is supposed to do it.

The junior college, later renamed the community college in the 1960s and 1970s, was originally designed to *limit* access to higher education in the name of social efficiency. But students and local communities had other ideas. Grassroots movements were inspired by the democratic rhetoric of Americanism and the promise made by junior college leaders, and many communities tried to refashion this institution into a tool for increased social mobility, community organization, and regional economic development. Thus, the community college, much like the country itself, was born of contradictions, and it continues to be an enigma. Contradictions have been sewn into the very fabric of what has become a celebrated, yet beleaguered, institution of higher education. For the past century this institution has been seen by many as a promise. The community college has represented a meritocratic ladder to college and to the middle class. However, it has also earned itself a reputation as a less than legitimate institution of higher education: "a high school with ashtrays," "a halfway school for losers," "a self-esteem workshop," and "a place where old people go to keep their minds active as they circle the drain of eternity."[5]

What has this institution actually done? What is it doing today? And what will it do in the future? Unraveling the institutional complexity and contradictions of the community college is the central focus of this historical study. At the heart of this book are two current policy debates on the community college. The first is access to higher education as it relates to the American Dream of meritocracy and sociopolitical equality. This issue has been much discussed over the past century, especially in the wake of the mid-20th-century civil rights movement. Has the community college offered increased access to higher education and social mobility, or has this "semi-higher" institution been just a diversion keeping the economically disadvantaged and ethnic minorities from realizing the American Dream? The second concerns the effectiveness of educational institutions. Many in the policy community have stopped focusing on the issue of access and are instead asking new questions. What are the institutional missions of the community college, and has it ever effectively fulfilled its complex educational and economic functions to justify public expenditures? While policy debates over access and equity have had a much-documented history, the policy debate over institutional effectiveness has not received any historical attention; thus, some historical contextualization is necessary to better inform policy makers.

The Institutional Effectiveness Movement and Higher Education

Institutions of higher education in the United States were traditionally given wide latitude to demonstrate various outcomes that were largely assumed to be *practical* results of a college education. Institutional reputations, the popularity of individual scholars, apocryphal stories of the success of alumni, and the mythic aura that clings to stately college campuses all subtly reassured the public that colleges directly benefited individual students and society at large, even though no hard evidence was at hand to bolster such a claim.[6] As W. Norton Grubb and Marvin Lazerson pointed out, there was a "simple faith" that higher education had great value.[7] Until the 1970s there was no agreed-upon criteria for educational institutions, yet because of increased federal and state oversight of educational systems during the 1960s and 1970s, educational institutions were increasingly besieged by calls for institutional assessment, which was often framed in a "management by objectives" language of institutional efficiency and productivity.[8] This change of direction in educational policy made it seem as if educational programs were "being constantly under attack by hard-nosed evaluators."[9]

Since the 1980s federal and state governments, most powerfully symbolized by the actions of presidents and governors, have used the bully pulpit and the creation of educational commissions to galvanize widespread institutional reform centered on so-called evidence-based practice and accountability measures.[10] Other national interest groups, such as business lobbies and think tanks, have also played a strong role in framing policy issues by creating programmatic ideas that have influenced the rhetoric of state and federal officials.[11] The implementation of No Child Left Behind has become the paradigmatic symbol for the institutionalization of educational assessment legislation[12] and it has become a model of sorts for current and future reforms in higher education.[13] It is clear that educational institutions must produce accountability measures to prove their effectiveness so they are able to earn the right to limited public resources.

It was only a matter of time before this wave hit community colleges. Early discussions of institutional effectiveness in relation to public financial support of community colleges took place during the 1970s. James W. Thornton explained how the community college would be increasingly "required to justify its procedures and its expenditures by reference to output" and standardized objectives. Public policy surrounding community colleges was still embryonic until the 1980s because of a small and weak national policy-making community focused on this institution. But in the small circle of community college policy makers who became more vocal and visible to national politicians, the policy rhetoric seemed to shift. In fact, this shift was noticeable for all levels of education. Educational policy significantly changed during the Republican ascendancy of Ronald Reagan and George Bush during the 1980s, and a new politics of efficiency became the dominant logic, increasingly defining educational policy for the past thirty years. The new politics of efficiency focused primarily on how educational institutions should demonstrate quality, productivity, and accountability. By the 1990s *institutional accountability* and *performance measures* in community colleges were still policy buzzwords and not yet established facts.[14] In 1999 Grubb and associates noted there was still "no general pressure on community colleges to reform" because a "national wave of dissatisfaction (as there is for K–12 education)" had not yet occurred. But several publications since 1999 have helped to serve as catalysts for the community college accountability movement, including several scholarly works of criticism that were never intended to support accountability initiatives.[15]

By 2004 some influential reports were published on institutional assessment strategies for evaluating community colleges. The League for Innovation in the Community College published a report, *An Assessment Framework for the Community College*, that called for an assessment blueprint that would standardize "terms, processes, and procedures," which would supposedly improve the development of institutional effectiveness programs. The logic of this report was based on a business model of delivering a clearly defined product. According to this report, community colleges produced a product called *student learning*. The report assumed that student learning, like any other product, can be broken down into isolated parts and easily measured. Further, the report assumed that any measurable product can be easily improved through logical efficiency mechanisms. Improving student learning was merely a technical problem awaiting the proper experts to engineer a simple solution.[16]

Another influential report was released that same summer. An issue of *New Directions for Community Colleges* was devoted to assessment and student learning outcomes. The editors explained how community colleges were "under increased pressure to produce evidence of student learning and achievement" because older assumptions of "institutional effectiveness do not fully satisfy new demands for evidence of student learning." This echoed the language of another influential policy report, *Measuring Up 2000*. This document rated state systems of higher education by giving them report cards. It was no surprise that all states received a grade of incomplete for student learning outcomes because this was still a policy buzz phrase at the time and not an implemented accountability measure.

As early as 1999 Grubb emphasized the lack of student learning outcomes in community colleges, but over the next decade there would be a massive push to implement accountability measures.[17] By 2007 a monumental transformation had taken place. Forty-seven states, with the exception of Delaware, New York, and Rhode Island, adopted a performance reporting data system for community colleges for retention, graduation, transfers, and job placements, and 15 states had adopted some form of performance-based funding.[18] It seems clear that all postsecondary educational institutions in the 21st century will have to prove themselves worthy of public funds by paying the state in tangible dividends, such as student learning outcomes and other accountability measures.

Most scholars trace the origins of the institutional effectiveness movement to the 1970s and 1980s when a series of international fiscal and labor market crises constrained federal and state expenditures on education.[19] However, other scholars, mostly historians, trace this movement farther to the so-called progressive social, political, and educational movements of the late 19th and early 20th centuries. Before *accountability* became a policy buzzword in the 1970s, many progressive school reformers used the logic of scientific management and called for efficiency and standardization in education.[20] To truly understand the purposes and possibilities of the educational efficiency movement one must explore the long history of such political posturing.

Very little historical work has been done on the community college. While a substantial body of historical literature exists on early 20th-century social, political, and economic influences on American higher education, there is a remarkable absence of historical literature on the community college. Even later historical studies of higher education have devoted only a fractional amount of space to the subject of community colleges.[21]

This book is an attempt to historically contextualize the current institutional effectiveness movement in relation to the older policy debate over equity and access in two ways. First, it examines the institutionalization process of the community college in the United States. How was this educational institution formed, for what purposes, and how has it evolved? Second, it contextualizes the access and effectiveness debates on the history of this institution. Has the community college enabled greater access to and success in higher education and has it done so effectively? But before these questions can be adequately addressed, a discussion of institutional theory is required to define the subject's theoretical and methodological parameters.

What Is an Institution?

This study is an analysis of the creation, institutionalization, and politicized debate over the community college, a uniquely American institution that developed over the course of the 20th century. But to understand the community college as an institution, we need to understand the basic theory of human institutions.

The study of social institutions traces to the 19th century, deriving its origins from the disciplines of history, philosophy, political science, and sociology. Given this long and diverse history, usage of the term has varied greatly. Only in the last couple of decades has the concept of institutionalism gained wider currency and a more explicit definition. The growing importance of this concept was recognized with the 1993 and 2009 Nobel Prizes in economics.[22] Institutions are the self-evident and often taken-for-granted social structures, ideological and organizational, in particular human societies. The social structure of an institution can be described as the organized ideas and procedures that pattern particular social practices. These institutional procedures can also be described as the constituent rules of a social practice. The early historical sociologists, Karl Marx, Émile Durkheim, and Max Weber, each studied different social structures of constituting rule systems in Western society. They wanted to understand the underlying logic that established and maintained the modern world: the social, political, economic, and religious *rules, organizations, procedures, rituals,* and *ideas* that ordered societies. Later institutional theorists complicated older notions of institutions, which were often overly simplistic, by exploring the rich structures of diverse, overlapping, and often conflicting patterns of social practice.[23]

This study focuses specifically on the institution of the American junior college, which later became the community college. This study seeks to uncover the historically conditioned rules, procedures, rituals, and ideas that have ordered and defined a particular type of educational structure that has various objectives. Institutions are human creations, so to study institutions is to study the actions, ideas, and organizations of human beings. At the core of this study are those individuals, organizations, ideas, and the larger political economy[24] that have contributed to defining the community college's educational missions and have enabled or constrained this institution from enacting those missions: What have been the purposes of the community college? Who conceptualized these purposes and why? How has this institution been able to achieve these purposes? How have these issues changed over time?

Of course embedded in these questions are unexamined political assumptions: Who has the right or power to define this institution's mission? Who has the responsibility for supporting and enacting its roles? Finally, what criteria and whose values are to be used to judge this institution?

But deeper assumptions are embedded in all scholarly research and public policy. The taken-for-granted rationality of modernity claims that human individuals have enough knowledge and power to *control* society, the people in that society, and the institutions that define and structure that society. But this hypothesis is largely unproven, and important questions remain unanswered. For instance: How rational are human beings? How much do human beings control their psychological, social, and physical environments? Do human beings have the power to control and change social institutions?[25] Academic scholars on institutions have only begun to ask these questions, unearthing the grounding assumptions of modern rationality that have been debated by philosophers for centuries.[26]

We only briefly discuss these issues of rationality and social institutions. Examining these important assumptions would take a sustained, interdisciplinary study that far exceeds the more limited parameters of this book, narrowly focused as it is on the institutionalization of the community college. However, it is important to raise these issues because our understanding of human institutions, historical change, and the future of the community college rests upon our assumptions of individual and collective rationality, the power of human agency, and the human capacity for purposive social change.

The concept of social institutions hurdles a social-scientific dualism that has been unresolved for the past century. At the center of the social sciences is a central debate over how societies and social institutions are constituted and how they change. Societies and social institution can be seen, on the one hand, as the product of human design and the outcome of purposive human action. However, they can also be seen as the result of human activity, but not necessarily the product of conscious design. One of the paradigmatic examples of this dualism is language. From birth, human beings are taught to speak a particular language with predefined words and a predesigned grammar; however, individuals are also able to adopt new languages, create new words, and change the existing definition of words or grammatical structures. But is any individual or group of individuals in conscious control of any particular language? The obvious answer is no, but each individual has some measure of effect yet just how much effect is subject to debate. For the past quarter century or so scholars have rejected the idea that societies, institutions, and organizations can be reduced to the rational decisions of individuals, although purposive individuals do play a role. The new theory of institutions focuses on larger units of analysis, such as social groups and organizations "that cannot be reduced to aggregations or direct consequences of individual's attributes or motives." Individuals do constitute and perpetuate social structures and institutions, but they do so not as completely or as freely as they believe.[27]

The new institutional theory has focused mainly on how social organizations have been the locus of institutionalization, which is the formation and perpetuation of social institutions. While groups of human beings create and sustain social organizations, these organizations develop through time into structures that resist individual human control. Organizations also take on a life of their own that sometimes defies the intentions of those human beings directing the organization. While institutions can sometimes begin with the rational planning of individuals, the preservation and stability of institutions through *path dependent* processes (what we generally call *history*) are often predicated on ritualized routines, social conventions, norms, and myths. Once an institution becomes institutionalized, the social structure perpetuates a stickiness that makes the structure resistant to change. Individual human actors become enveloped and controlled by the organization's self-reinforcing social norms, rules, and explanatory myths, which are solidified through positive feedback mechanisms that transcend any particular human individual. These organizational phenomena shape individual human perception, constrain individual agency, and constitute individual action. As one institutional theorist argued, all human "actors and their interests are institutionally constructed." To a certain extent humans do create institutions and organizations, but more immediately over the course of history institutions and organizations create us. Many millions of individuals have consciously shaped the English language, but as a child I was made an English-speaking person without my knowledge or consent. It is perhaps more accurate to say that English allowed for the creation of my individuality than it is to say that my individual subjectivity shaped the institution of English.[28]

But if all human thought and action is constituted by previously existing institutions, do human beings really have any freedom to shape their lives or change society? This is actually a very hard question to answer and it remains at the center of long-standing debates. Durkheim and Talcott Parsons seemed to solidify a sociology that left no room for individual volition. Marx stressed human control but seemed to put agency in the hands of groups, not individuals. Weber discussed the possibility of individual agency, especially for charismatic leaders, but he emphasized how human volition was always "caged" by institutions and social organizations. Michel Foucault conceptualized human beings as almost enslaved by the various modern institutions of prisons, schools, and professions.[29]

Some neoinstitutional theorists have left open the possibility of individual rationality and freedom. Human agency is occasionally defined as the mediation, manipulation, and sometimes modification of existing institutions. Human beings can also *refuse* institutionalized norms and procedures, highlighting another type of agency. Humans can also *exploit contradictions* between different institutional structures and use one institution to modify another. Ronald L. Jepperson argued there can be "degrees of institutionalization" as well as institutional "contradictions" with environmental conditions. This means that certain institutions can be "relative[ly] vulnerab[le] to social intervention" at particular historical junctures. Jepperson is one of the few institutional analysts who conceptualize a theory of human action and institutional change that allows for deinstitutionalization and reinstitutionalization. But Jepperson does not validate rational choice theories of individual agency. He argued instead that "actors cannot be represented as foundational elements of social structure" because their identity and "interests are highly institutional in their origins." However, this position does not disavow institutionally mediated individual choice and action. As Walter W. Powell argued, "Individual preferences and choices cannot be understood apart from the larger cultural setting and historical period in which they are embedded," but individual actors have some freedom within institutional environments to "use institutionalized rules and accounts to further their own ends." Roger Friedland and Robert R. Alford contended that "the meaning and relevance of symbols may be contested, even as they are shared." "Constraints," Powell paradoxically said in one essay, "open up possibilities at the same time as they restrict or deny others."[30]

Anthropologist Sherry B. Ortner has developed a more comprehensive theory of human agency that allows individuals more power to consciously participate in and shape and modify institutions. She described the individual agent in a relationship with social structures. This relationship can be transformative for both parties: Each acts and shapes the other. While the individual is enveloped by social structures, there is a "politics of agency" in which individual actors can become "differentially empowered" in the layered "web of relations" that make up the constraints of culture. Individuals can act through a process of reflexivity, resistance, and bricolage. Humans use an awareness of subjectivity and negotiate their acceptance and refusal of the status quo. Through this process, humans can re-create existing social structures by reforming traditional practices and also by introducing novel practices. Ortner conceptualized the process of agency as the playing of "serious games," using a metaphor originally employed by analytical philosopher Ludwig Wittgenstein. She argued forcefully that existing cultural structures and social reproduction is "never total, always imperfect, and vulnerable," which constantly leaves open the possibility of "social transformation" to those who dare to act out against the status quo.[31]

Traditionally, social scientists have assumed an inflated notion of rationality, agency, and control for human individuals. Neoinstitutional theory has sought to correct these fallacies. But traditional social science has assumed these same qualities for social organizations as well: societies, political states, and economic corporations. Structural functionalist sociologists, using classical organizational theories, often conceptualized modern society as a highly structured and rationalized field populated by various bureaucratic organizations with specific and clearly defined social functions. It was assumed that social organizations were driven by rationalized processes, efficient technologies, and controlling managers. Organizations were seen as a totalizing social structure that "use[d] human beings to perform organizational tasks." Organizations were also seen as insulated structures, which were clearly differentiated and autonomous from the larger society.[32]

Later organizational theorists, still embracing a structural functionalism, pointed out how organizations were only quasi rational and largely constrained by other social structures. These new organizational theorists also pointed out that the functions of an organization were often *loosely coupled* or in conflict with its actual operations. Organizational actors could be "limited in their knowledge and in their capacities," and thus, merely subjectively rational. This meant that individuals, even corporate managers, were not in complete control of themselves, let alone their organizations. This led some organizational theorists to describe social organizations as anarchical because nobody seemed to be in complete control, but yet the organization did seem to function because it was not falling apart.[33] Organizations also came to be seen not as isolated entities but as connected to and influenced by other organizations and larger social structures such as the state or the regional economy.[34]

The new institutionalism took this quasi-rational and constrained line of analysis even further. New research has shown that social organizations are more often structured by "the myths of their institutional environments" than they are by the functional "demands of their work activities." This insight is especially apt for the study of community colleges. In fact, the supposedly functional technology of modern organizations in the postindustrial West have come to be seen as not very functional and not very efficient. Instead of an objective system of rationality, organizations are now seen to be ordered by myths of rationality that codify various institutional rules based on the authoritative normative design and isomorphic power of rationalized bureaucracies. Thus, neoinstitutional theorists argue that organizations are driven by social legitimacy and survival within an institutional environment instead of rationality and productivity, especially organizations such as schools and churches that operate in highly institutional environments. Paul J. DiMaggio and Walter W. Powell argued, "Organizations compete not just for resources and customers, but for political power and institutional legitimacy, for social as well as economic fitness." Under such circumstances, managers do not necessarily control production or efficiency but instead are often ceremonial figures who preside over a loosely coupled organization driven by the assumption that everyone is acting in good faith.[35]

Recent scholarship has also emphasized how organizations and institutions are structured within an organizational ecology. Looking at the wider sphere of organizational ecology allows researchers to understand how individuals and social organizations are interconnected in a dense social web. Interdependent social groups interact with each other to mutually shape the physical and social environment, which in turn affects the evolution of organizations, organizational forms, and institutionalized practices and norms.[36] Organizations are mutually influenced by a host of social sectors, including nation-states, geographical regions, local governments, other organizations, and micro social groups, such as the family and peer networks.[37] In each sector are diverse "clusters of norms" and organizational typologies that institutionally define and constrain individual and organizational actors, and a host of institutional norms and forms are continually reified and perpetuated across a diversely populated social and organizational landscape that slowly changes through time. Because societies are characterized by such

diversity of social sectors, each with their own institutions and norms, different institutions can be "potentially contradictory," which can allow for social
conflict and social change through time as institutions develop in relation
with the institutional and physical environment.[38] However, it is still unclear
how institutions *change* and what change actually means. Theorizing the
nature and extent of institutional change is an unresolved issue. Institutions
are seen as stable social structures outside the control of rational agents who
seem to slowly adapt to internal and environmental conditions through an
incremental process, although some evidence suggests that rapid changes can
occur in short periods because of environmental shocks.[39]

The Community College: A Contradictory Institution

Only four major historical sociological studies focused on the institutionalization of community colleges in the United States.[40] Only one of these studies
used the theory of institutions as an analytical framework. These studies have
mostly investigated the early formative stages of the junior college in the early
20th century. Conceptually, these studies trace *communities of practice* that
have become ritualized, institutionalized, reproduced, and contested through
time, but most of these studies do not follow the community college from its
origins in the 19th century to its contradictory state in the 21st century. Nor
have many of these studies focused on how this institution has evolved in
relation to external sociopolitical-economic environments.[41]

Of these four historical works, only Steven Brint and Jerome Karabel
attempted to trace the institutionalization of the community college into the
latter half of the 20th century, but their study only went as far as the 1970s
and early 1980s. Their focus on vocationalism, however, precluded a larger
analysis of the contested institutionalization of the community college in
relation to other historical trends in the United States. Brint and Karabel
also did not discuss racial segregation and the mid-20th-century civil rights
movement, nor did they analyze the late-20th-century movement for educational standards and institutional evaluation. A deeper methodological issue
has also not been fully explored: To what extent do university scholars exercise (and continue to exercise) a primary power over defining, legitimizing,
and reforming institutional discourse and practice? The scholarly literature
on the community college (and the actual impact this literature has had on
practice) is perhaps the most revealing phenomenon defining this institution.
Thus, the discourse of university scholars is the most important and immediate source for a history of the institutionalization process of the community

college, but no one has historicized the past century of academic scholarship on this institution.

The American junior college, later turned *community* college, is used in this book as a case study for understanding the formation and historical evolution of an institution of higher education. This case study draws upon the seminal work of Brint and Karabel, and it seeks to extend their basic thesis, with modifications, into the 21st century. This study seeks to address the larger issues of access to higher education and social mobility, while addressing the more particular issue of the institutional purposes, institutional effectiveness, and the role of the community college in the larger political economy. As already mentioned, this study focuses on the political assumptions about who has the right or power to define this institution's mission, who is responsible for enacting its roles, and how this institution is supposed to be valued and judged. And this study attempts to address the much larger and more theoretical issue of whether particular human actors or groups have been able to control the contours of this institution.

The basic narrative of the institutionalization of the community college is a muddle of mixed motives and competing actors. It involves external social control and internal organizational anarchy. While this institution was formed with clear purposes in mind, it soon became apparent that this institution was not operating as planned, nor was it efficient at achieving its stated missions. Between 1920 and 1940 junior college leaders went through an intense identity crisis as they debated the purpose of junior colleges and the placement of these institutions between secondary and postsecondary education systems. Were junior colleges extended secondary schools or separate *junior* colleges? Were junior colleges primarily supposed to prepare academically talented students for entry to a 4-year university, or were they also supposed to train less-talented vocationally oriented students for local labor markets? And were junior colleges only responsive to universities and labor markets by training and credentialing postsecondary students, or were they also supposed to be responsive to local community needs, which might include noncredentialing purposes such as offering literacy, citizenship, and general community education classes? Arguably a measure of consensus over these questions among junior college leaders, federal and state educational authorities, and the general public did not congeal until the publication of the President's Commission on Higher Education report in 1947.

The report, *Higher Education for American Democracy,* seemed not only to legitimate junior colleges by arguing that half the American population could benefit from 2 years of postsecondary schooling, but it also seemed to sanction a broad comprehensive mission for these institutions by suggesting a new name and thereby a new institutional identity: the community college. Until the publication of this report, junior college leaders had debated whether the primary function of the institution was to keep its traditional mission as a conduit for student transfers to 4-year universities, or whether it should adopt new missions, such as offering terminal occupational and semiprofessional programs. Most junior college leaders liked the latter of these two options because it would increase the legitimacy of the institution within already established systems of secondary and postsecondary education. There were also calls for expanding the institutional mission to incorporate adult education, such as literacy and citizenship classes, and also programs that would meet diverse local needs.

However, not everyone at the time saw the community college in such lofty democratic and egalitarian terms. From the start, university officials promoted junior colleges because of their value as a *screening service* to divert many postsecondary students from the selective and resource-limited universities. State legislators also promoted junior colleges as a less-expensive form of higher education for the masses that would allow a cost-effective means to democratize access to higher education while also creating an institution that would filter out the unprepared or disadvantaged majority from actually earning a college degree. University of California, Berkeley, sociologist Burton R. Clark famously called this the *cooling-out* process.[42]

Clark's thesis was extended in an internationally acclaimed book published in 1989: Brint and Karabel's *The Diverted Dream: Community Colleges and the Promise of Educational Opportunity in America, 1900–1985*. Brint and Karabel argued that education in the United States has always been a "hierarchically differentiated" system structurally connected to the labor market and class. But the American educational system has also been relatively open and democratic compared with Europe and Asia, especially in the 20th century. Most Americans have seen it as a ladder of opportunity and a means of upward mobility. The institution of community colleges offered an "egalitarian promise," but at the same time it also reflected the constraints of the capitalist economic system it was embedded in. Part of the reality of that system is an optimistic society that generates more ambition than it can structurally satisfy, which creates a need for an elaborate and often hidden tracking system to channel students into occupationally appropriate avenues largely based on their socioeconomic origins.[43]

From its beginnings the community college has had the contradictory function of opening higher education to larger numbers of students from all socioeconomic backgrounds while operating within a highly stratified economic and educational system, which created a need to "select and sort students." This cooling-out function (or *the diversion effect*) caused ever-increasing numbers of lower-class and ethnic minority students in higher education to be diverted into more modest positions at the lower end of the labor market. As Burton Clark once admitted, "for large numbers failure is inevitable and *structured.*" Brint and Karabel argued that not only do community colleges help "transmit inequalities" through their sorting function, but they also "contribute to the legitimization of these inequalities" by upholding meritocratic rhetoric that often blames the victim for failing to succeed in a structurally rigged class system:

> The very real contribution that the community college has made to the expansion of opportunities for some individuals does not, however, mean that its *aggregate* effect has been a democratizing one. On the contrary, the two-year institution has accentuated rather than reduced existing patterns of social inequality.[44]

The majority of students who enrolled in junior colleges during the first half of the 20th century were middle-class high school graduates who wanted to earn their bachelor's degree and enter a white-collar profession. Working-class high school students either dropped out of high school early to get a job, or they waited until earning their high school diploma to enter the workforce. Very few working-class students entered junior colleges. However, the point of Brint and Karabel's study remains substantial: Junior college leaders in conjunction with community business leaders actively tried to manipulate junior college student aspirations by engineering more and more occupationally oriented terminal programs. They also encouraged this route more passively by neglecting a pedagogically appropriate curriculum and adequate student support services geared toward less–academically prepared students. Many junior college students tended to either drop out or settle for a terminal occupational certificate. By the 1970s the community college became the point of entry for new student populations who were older and more economically disadvantaged. But this institution did not have the resources to help serve these new populations. About 75 percent of low-achieving students dropped out during their first year in urban community colleges. Critics pointed out that it was not an accident that the lowest-achieving students in secondary and postsecondary schools have historically been, and continue to be, the economically disadvantaged, ethnic/racialized minorities, immigrants, the disabled, and dislocated low-skilled workers.

Despite the transfer mission's remaining a primary emphasis for most community colleges throughout the 20th century, the apparent manipulation of institutional purposes by community college leaders, state governments, and the business community has remained constant if not intensified. Later scholarship on the community college has demonstrated that community college administrators have increasingly adopted an ideological stance of neoliberalism over the past couple of decades, which has directed them to focus on efficiency, productivity, and marketplace needs. This has led to a much larger array of occupationally oriented terminal programs. Some have claimed these occupational offerings may be crowding out academic transfer-oriented programs and leading community colleges away from an institutional climate focused on *higher* education.

A look at the history of higher education in the United States and the changing dynamics of student access does reveal some expansion of access and equity in terms of increasing amounts of postsecondary education for a broader swath of Americans. It seems fairly certain that the community college offers opportunities that would otherwise not be available to many students. However, traditionally underserved populations such as the economically disadvantaged and many racialized minorities still struggle to achieve equality of opportunity in American society and its systems of higher education. As the United States moves into a postindustrial knowledge economy in a highly globalized world, the issue of unequal student access to higher education remains a prominent and pressing political problem, and it has become intertwined with the issue of outcomes in educational and economic success of the student and the economic development of the nation. However, the policy community seems more preoccupied with the politicized issue of institutional accountability to justify public expenditures in a fiscally constrained economic environment. Because of the recession of 2007–2009, the politics of constrained budgets will mostly likely only get worse over the short term. But policy makers must not lose sight of the equally important issue of access and social mobility, because the United States remains an inequitable class-based society.

The open-access mission of the community college was forged in an environment of sociopolitical inequality, educational elitism, and restricted educational and financial resources. Community colleges were designed to be underfunded and marginalized institutions in hierarchical state systems of education. While access to community colleges was open to all, no provisions were made to ensure the success of students in community colleges nor access to the more advanced and economically rewarding levels of the higher education system. In fact, it was assumed that a great many students enrolled in community colleges would be drawn away from higher education and redirected to terminal, lower-status, and lower-paid vocational careers.

Since more and more students have been clamoring for a university education because of economic conditions that heavily reward university credentials, the notion of community colleges as holding pens for the under-privileged has been increasingly examined by scholars over the past quarter century. Increased awareness of its institutional past has led many state educational officials and community college administrators to curtail older institutional policies of benign neglect that allowed large numbers of students to fail, cooling out their ambitions. Most state officials and community college administrators now promote more equitable and just policies to open up state systems of higher education and increase student success. However, the past cannot be ignored. New policies enacted ex nihilo cannot be expected to work because the inequalities and injustices of the past still powerfully constrain the present.

Community colleges hold immense promise if they can overcome their historical legacy and be reinstitutionalized with unified missions, clear goals of educational success, properly trained faculty, sufficient numbers of support staff, and adequate financial resources. However, despite the good intentions of the policy community, the future is not certain. Institutions are path dependent. Past organizational structures constrain future possibilities. Institutional actors are restricted by incomplete knowledge, bounded rationality, and limited power. Educational institutions are also limited by the micro-level abilities and motivations of their students and the macro-level economic opportunity of regional, state, national, and global labor markets. Thus, institutional structures are incredibly resistant to change and notoriously difficult to redirect.

Can an educational institution that was "born subordinate" as the lower-level holding pen for the university and the feeder for lower levels of the labor market overcome its own legacy and develop into an effective, meritocratic, and democratizing institution? This study does not provide easy answers because none exist. Instead, this book tries to illuminate the parameters of this question by looking at the past. The historical trajectory of this institution in all its complexity is discussed in this book so policy makers and education professionals might better understand the constraints of the past in an effort to realize the possibilities of the future.[45]

Chapters 1 and 2 examine the institutionalization process of the community college in the United States over the 20th century by providing a historical narrative of its formation by a diverse set of actors, including professors of higher education, educational administrators, state officials, local communities, community college faculty, and students. How was this educational institution formed, by whom, for what purposes, and how has it evolved over the past century? Attention will also be paid to the social, political, economical, and organizational ecology surrounding community colleges to demonstrate how this institution and its changing missions have been shaped by its environment. Chapter 3 explores all these issues in the more localized context of a single state, California, that created some of the earliest junior colleges and was the first state to create a community college system. It has led the way in expanding access and formulating institutional accountability measures. California also represents a cautionary tale of how constrained fiscal resources can cripple student access and institutional efficiency.

This book also explores and contextualizes two major policy debates over the community college: equitable access to higher education and the institutional effectiveness of community colleges. Has the community college enabled greater access to and success in higher education during the 20th century, and has it done so effectively? Finally, this book addresses the complex issues of institutional identity and institutional change. On the one hand, social institutions are stable structures that resist the control of rational agents, and they seem to slowly adapt to internal and environmental conditions through an incremental process. However, there is also evidence that rapid changes can occur to institutions over short periods of time because of external shocks caused by the social, political, and economic environment. The final chapter addresses all these issues in relation to those who have a stake in the future of the community college.

THE CREATION AND INSTITUTIONALIZATION OF JUNIOR COLLEGES IN THE UNITED STATES, 1900–1980s

The open-access comprehensive community college is a uniquely American invention. This institution began with a simple purpose: to prepare high school graduates for delayed entry into a 4-year university. Over the years, however, the community college has acquired a diverse set of missions. It is now responsive to the needs of local residents, local businesses, state systems of secondary and postsecondary education, and state and regional economies, not to mention the myriad needs of many different types of students. But the community college did not begin as a comprehensive institution of higher education, nor will it necessarily keep such a diverse set of missions as it evolves further in the 21st century.

To understand the current role and future possibilities of the community college within the ever-expanding yet highly stratified landscape of higher education in the United States, it is important to get a sense of its history. How did the community college acquire such a comprehensive and complex (and some also argue conflicting, contradictory, ambiguous, and paradoxical) set of missions? And why have these diverse missions come to be the distinctive feature of this institution? One scholar and education practitioner has argued that the emblem of the community college should be the hermit crab because this institution seems to be destined always to borrow its shell from the landscape surrounding it, lacking a permanent form of its own. The early 20th-century junior college, and its midcentury counterpart, the rechristened multipurpose community college, has always been an institution in flux, constituted and revised by the expectations and rationalizations of university officials, state policy makers, and junior college administrators, but very responsive to its social and economic environment and the needs of its constituency. While the junior college turned community college has largely been an overdetermined institution, it has still shown a remarkable ability to break free of established policy to try to be, as some critics have derisively mocked, *everything to everyone.*[1]

An Aristocracy of Talent: The Origins of Higher Education in the United States

Institutions of higher education in America grew out of the older European tradition of Catholic seminaries and liberal arts colleges, and they still reflect and perpetuate traditional elitist notions that are at odds with the democratic principles this country supposedly upholds. The main purpose of medieval and early modern institutions of higher education was to train clergy who would spread the word of God and Christian cultural discipline across the world. These institutions also trained a literate bureaucracy who would become the political functionaries of ecclesiastical and monarchical courts.[2] The first college in the Americas was named Harvard, after a wealthy bene- factor, and it was built in the small town of Cambridge in the Massachusetts colony. Harvard College carried forward the older European educational traditions into the new world.[3] By the time the United States of America became an independent country there were nine religious colleges that were privately run but subsidized with public funds.[4] In relation to the broader ideological current of a Protestant-republican-Americanism,[5] colonial col- leges began to differ from earlier European models of higher education by developing a more practical orientation that went beyond the mere training of courtiers and clergy. American colleges became institutions not only for the transmission of elite cultural mores and the consecration of clergy, but also for the training of political leaders and doctors—preparing what Jeffer- son once called an "aristocracy of talent."[6] Thus, the college in the young republic of the United States intertwined aristocratic culture with a particu- lar American brand of noblesse oblige.[7]

As a bastion of privileged elites, American institutions of higher educa- tion up until the middle of the 19th century were intensely local, highly religious, and discriminatory. By 1848 there were 113 small colleges, mostly founded by various Protestant denominations, especially Presbyterians, Methodists, and Baptists. Only 16 colleges were state-funded public institu- tions.[8] These colleges enrolled a small population of Protestant wealthy white young men,[9] although four colleges did enroll women before midcentury.[10] Most American colleges were located in the East and Midwest until the late 19th century, and the northeastern establishment remained the center of the American intellectual world until at least the mid-20th century. Eastern colleges were formative in the socialization of wealthy American gentry— those who would become the center of the eastern political, economic, and educational establishment. This liberally educated gentry class actively excluded many groups from full participation in the social, political, economic, and educational opportunities America had to offer.[11]

While there was much support in the early 19th century for Republican-Protestant, open-access, publicly funded "common" primary schools in the East and Midwest,[12] it was not until the late 19th century that somewhat egalitarian public institutions of secondary and postsecondary education began to flourish. Public colleges and universities did not become permanently secure until the second Morrill Act of 1890 that institutionalized steady state funds for higher education. By the late 19th century, practically oriented and publicly open state systems of public higher education began to emerge in places such as Wisconsin and California, and similarly oriented private universities also emerged, such as the University of Chicago and Johns Hopkins University. These institutions refashioned a more democratically oriented, progressive, noblesse oblige ideology as they broadened their student base to include a larger swath of ambitious middle-class Americans, especially white Protestant women. According to the educational leaders of the time, these institutions also began to develop a new national-oriented Americanism, rationalized professional standards, depoliticized civil service training, and a Protestant-infused mission focused on efficiently engineering social problems in the name of public good.[13]

As this institutional transformation was proceeding in the late 19th century, a demographic transformation was also developing. Slowly, very slowly, more and more Americans were gaining upward social mobility, political representation, and economic stability, and more young adults were gaining access to higher education. However, it would take over a century for the divergent, and sometimes conflicting, progressive sociopolitical projects[14] to open American society and its systems of education to a majority of citizens. Only 5 percent of the 19- to 22-year-old population was enrolled in an institution of higher education in 1910. A more diverse array of white middle-class Protestant men were the first to break into exclusive American colleges after the Civil War (excluding the few Roman Catholic colleges that exclusively served Catholic men, a largely Irish population). White middle-class

Protestant women took advantage of coeducational public institutions, and by 1880 women constituted about one third of all American college students.[15] By the turn of the 20th century other predominantly white religious groups, such as reformist Protestant sects, Jews, and Catholics, were allowed greater access to mainstream institutions of higher education, but there were often implicit, if not explicit, discriminatory quotas that limited particular ethnic and religious groups to a certain percentage of the total student population. Only belatedly in the second half of the 20th century did the most disadvantaged Americans gain access to some form of higher education: non-white ethnic and racialized minorities, the working class and poor, and the physically and learning disabled. Up through the first half of the 20th century, higher education was too expensive for most American families, and the typical college student was often an upper-class white man between the ages of 17 and 21.[16]

Educational Innovation: The Creation of Junior Colleges, 1900–1940s

The institution of a lower-division, state-sponsored college for semiprofessional training actually had its origins in what was known as the normal school. Normal schools predated high schools as institutions of secondary education meant to train teachers for public primary schools. This type of institution was spreading across America because of the common school movement. While normal schools were created with a very specific purpose in mind (training public elementary school teachers), many normal school students saw these institutions as a vehicle for social mobility. Normal schools were seen by many students as institutions of higher education that were more accessible than college because of geographical proximity, lower cost, and easier admission policies. Thus, normal school students began to demand and enroll in more liberal arts classes rather than teacher training courses. Evidence suggests that in some states only a relatively small percentage of normal school students actually went on to a career in teaching. David F. Labaree called normal schools the first "people's college" because these institutions offered an avenue into higher education for many Americans who might not otherwise have been able to go to college.[17]

The junior college, like the normal school, was spawned by educational reformers who wanted to make the American educational system more rational, efficient, and accommodating to the growing number of high school graduates who would be looking for a postsecondary education. Ray Lyman Wilbur, president of Stanford University in 1927, justified the junior college as an open institution that would allow new generations of students to "try out" higher education "without great economic disadvantage and without leaving home after high school graduation." He further explained,

> The large student mortality in the freshman and sophomore years of the great universities has been mortifying and humiliating to thousands of our youth. The junior college offers the opportunity for students to find out more about their own interests and capacities, and helps them through the preparatory stages if they know that they want to [go into a profession]. . . . It [also] provides for those who have neither the capacity to profit by university instruction nor the necessary financial backing the chance to round out their education by two years of work of college grade. . . . While serving as a trying-out place for the youth of the country, the junior college, by relieving the university of the elementary work of the first two years, can set the American university free to carry out its own great purposes.[18]

The junior college began as an idea: a 2-year university preparatory institution to be housed in high schools, or in some cases in separate facilities near or on university campuses. This idea can be traced to 1852 in the work of Henry P. Tappan, president of the University of Michigan. There is also some evidence of early 2-year colleges on university campuses in 1835 at Monticello College, and in 1858 at Susquehanna University. Some scholars have pointed to Lewis Institute in Chicago, formed in 1896 as the first private junior college. The first public institution to be named a junior college in the United States was Joliet Junior College in Illinois, which was created in 1901 as an annex to the Joliet public high school. This innovation was the work of William Rainey Harper, president of the University of Chicago, which had been founded in 1890, and J. Stanley Brown, principal of Joliet High School. They both contributed to the creation of Joliet Junior College, although the term *junior college* seemed to have been the sole creation of Harper who used it "for lack of a better term, to cover the work of the freshman and sophomore years."[19]

These two educators conceived the junior college as an additional two years of secondary schooling housed in the high school. This institution would further prepare students for college by offering a curriculum compatible to the first two undergraduate years of study in a university and leading to the newly established *junior certificate*, the precursor to the associate's degree. Harper was one of the first of a new breed of college presidents who wanted to reinvent higher education in the United States along the lines of the German research university. However, many thought this reorganization of the American college as a university would necessitate the curtailment or abolishment of the undergraduate curriculum so that university faculty could focus exclusively on specialized, professional, research-oriented disciplines. Thus, Harper's work in establishing junior colleges was part of his larger vision for a new American high school (modeled after the German *gymnasia*) to accompany the new American research university. The college preparatory high school in conjunction with the junior college would take over the first year or two of undergraduate general studies. This would prepare students to enter a university, which would be strictly for specialized professional study and disciplinary research.[20]

In the early 20th century, the growth of junior colleges increased steadily as more and more American students were entering and graduating from public high schools. The junior college was the product of a movement to reorganize the America secondary school population, and it was accompanied by another new institution, the junior high school. Both of these new institutions were conceptualized and initiated by educational leaders in universities who wanted a more rational and efficient system of education. Progressive educational leaders such as Alexis F. Lange, a professor at the University of California and the head of the California Commission on Readjustment of Courses of Study, envisioned a reorganization of secondary education into three levels: the junior high school, the senior high school, and the junior college.

The comprehensive coeducational public high school was itself a relatively new innovation by the mid-19th century. It finally became nationally legitimated and began to enroll a sizable portion of the elementary student population by the 1880s. Over the course of the 19th century, high schools changed from private, selective, tuition-based college preparatory schools to public comprehensive schools offering not only a college preparatory curriculum but also a wide range of classes focusing on manual skills, occupational training, literacy, and citizenship. The national population of students enrolled in a high school in 1890 was only around 202,963 pupils, but this number rapidly grew to 1,645,171 by 1918—a growth of 711 percent. Between 6 to 7 percent of the 14- to 17-year-old population was enrolled in high schools in 1890. In 1900 over 11 percent of this population was enrolled. This number increased to over 30 percent in 1920, although the percentage of black and foreign-born students attending high schools during this time was roughly half the rate of native-born white attendance. By 1930 over 51 percent of the 14- to 17-year-old population was enrolled in high schools, almost 4.5 million students.[21]

Because of increased high school enrollments, American junior colleges also had impressive growth rates over the course of the 20th century, with several large growth spurts during the 1920s, the late 1930s and 1940s, and then the 1960s. In 1910 there were only 25 junior colleges in the United States, but by 1927 there were 325 colleges in 39 states with 35,630 students. In 1927 junior colleges were clustered primarily in the South (with a majority of private institutions), the Midwest (with a mixture of private and public), and California (with a majority of public institutions). By 1939 there were 575 colleges in 45 states, although the average size of each college was only a couple hundred students. In 1970 there were 1,091 colleges in all 50 states, and by the 1980s the median-size public junior college averaged almost 3,000 students. Private junior colleges outnumbered public colleges until the late 1940s, but after that private colleges began to wither and numbered only 20 percent of all 2-year colleges by the early 1970s. In 1922 there were about 20,000 enrolled junior college students nationally. Eighty-seven years later in 1989 about 50 percent of all students started their postsecondary education by enrolling in a 2-year college, and by 1991 almost 47 percent of ethnic minority students in postsecondary education were enrolled in 2-year colleges.[22]

From the late 1910s to the 1930s, as junior colleges expanded and flourished, university presidents, university professors, and newly certified junior college administrators (who were newly trained in lately developed university courses on higher education) began to identify themselves as part of a national junior college movement. This small group of university-educated men began to debate the educational parameters of this new institution to define its future. In 1917 a regional body called the North Central Association of Colleges and Schools was the first junior college organization to establish accreditation standards for admissions policies, faculty qualifications, and funding. The first national organization of junior college leaders began to form in 1920 at a conference in St. Louis brought together by the leadership of the U.S. commissioner of education, Philander Claxton. The American Association of Junior Colleges (AAJC) was dedicated to creating and articulating a national "institutional identity" along with uniform purposes for the growing junior colleges. It went from 34 members in the first preliminary conference in St. Louis to 236 members by 1929. In 1922 the AAJC defined the junior college as "an institution offering two years of instruction of strictly collegiate grade." However this narrow definition would be expanded just 3 years later to include "the larger and ever-changing civic, social, religious, and vocational needs of the entire community."[23] This organization's professional organ, *Junior College Journal*, first appeared in 1930 and was published by Stanford University Press. It became an important outlet for junior college leaders in their effort to wrestle over the present and future missions of a new educational movement.[24]

The leaders of the junior college movement were political and educational progressives, and the junior college was an institution embodying progressive ideology. Progressives believed in a white Anglo-Saxon middle-class meritocracy that supported the capitalist system. Progressive sociopolitical reformers engineered the expansion and centralization of federal and state governments by remaking the state as a rational bureaucratic system of social services that would mollify the worst extremes of working-class and immigrant poverty while keeping intact the hierarchically structured system of racial and economic privilege. Progressives used social-democratic rhetoric to talk about a classless and apolitical society run by enlightened experts, but behind this rhetoric were class-based and race-based assumptions guiding a politicized vision of a white, middle-class, Protestant, rational bureaucratic, capitalist, individualistic, and meritocratic society governed by an educated and professional elite. The ideological ends of pan-Protestant Americanism and scientific rationalism inspired the progressive quest to engineer the perfect society. Every institution would be rationally defined and reorganized into a coherent whole, and thereby it was assumed they would all effectively serve the public good.[25]

The scientific management of schooling was a progressive method to guide educational reform. To create a rational public school system, new institutions would be created, such as high school, junior high school, junior college, and kindergarten. However, despite the progressive belief that all public goods could be unified in a perfect society, the new rationalized system of American education was designed with contradictory purposes. New institutions, such as the junior college and the high school, would offer increased educational equality and meritocratic opportunity, while also structuring a socially efficient and hierarchically tiered system that would constrain the social mobility of lower-class, nonwhite, and immigrant students. These institutions were created not only to educate but also to sort students into predetermined social classes based on economic status, race, and gender.[26]

This contradiction was readily apparent in the California model of education. In the early 20th century educational progressives in California engineered what they thought would be a rationally efficient and meritocratic system of education. The California model consisted of a hierarchically arranged system of educational institutions. The bottom rung, the elementary school, was open to everyone. In fact students were being *compelled* to enroll for their own good and the good of society, as elementary school (and later high school) became compulsory. The pinnacle of the system was the university, which was only open to the best and brightest students (and, it went without saying, the most advantaged), the future leaders of America. Progressive intellectuals saw the junior college as an institution that would allow expanded access to postsecondary schooling, while also limiting that education to terminal-vocational pursuits and thus offering a structurally limited opportunity to students in a hierarchically organized society.

However, taking progressive democratic rhetoric seriously, students wanted to exploit the junior college as a vehicle for social mobility via access to the baccalaureate degree. Junior college leaders recognized this important function but didn't feel it was appropriate for the majority of junior college students. Progressive leaders did their best to rhetorically institutionalize the junior college as more than just a preparatory school for the university to differentiate at least two curricular tracks. They emphasized vocational training as an easier (and more appropriate) route to the middle class for the majority of students. Thus, there was an ideological gap between the expansive democratic rhetoric of the junior college vision and the social-efficiency programming of junior college curriculums. This gap institutionalized a "loosely coupled" educational organization and there was often conflict over the ends of education between students, teachers, and administrators.[27] This ideological conflict, in turn, allowed students and the broader community to use this newly formed institution for their own socioeconomic purposes[28] through a grassroots "politics of agency."[29] But junior college leaders never ceased to define and promote the tracked vocational mission for this institution.

Alexis F. Lange, professor of English and later dean of the Department of Education at the University of California, Berkeley, was one of the most influential of the early junior college leaders. In 1918 he gave what would become a very famous oration on the newly institutionalized, but still ambiguous, junior college. In "The Junior College—What Manner of Child Shall This Be?!" Lange asked what lay behind the "scholastic camouflage" of the

name *junior college*. He answered that the junior college would be a preparatory institution at the top of the secondary school hierarchy. And yet his
audience was given an intimation of an institution that promised much more
than mere educational efficiency. Lange phrased his thesis in such grandiose
and quasi-religious language he almost sanctified the junior college as a
sacred institution that would "cultivate the consciousness of organic one-
ness." The junior college would be an agent of "preparedness and progress,"
and it would require the faith of all Americans to fulfill the prophesy that
the high school would become "the people's college." The junior college at
the top of the secondary system would consummate the holy blessing of
educational reform, and it would become a finishing school for vocational
education so that the nation would have new cadre of enlightened mechanics
and clerks.[30]

Leonard V. Koos, professor of education at the University of Minnesota
and later at the University of Chicago, was another one of the most prominent first-generation junior college leaders. He surveyed two decades of literature on the reorganization of secondary and postsecondary education and
the development of the junior college to produce the first scholarly book on
the subject in 1925, *The Junior-College Movement*. Koos conceptualized the
junior college as an "isthmus" connecting elementary and secondary education to higher education and advanced professional training. He noted that
most people considered the primary mission of this new institution as "offering two years of work acceptable to colleges and universities" so that junior
college students could transfer to these more advanced institutions and earn
their bachelor's degree. However, Koos emphasized that the junior college
was much more than just a university preparatory school. It was also a finishing school for high school students that would "round out" the education
of young adults "who will not, cannot, or should not 'go on.'" As such it
would prepare these students for an occupation in a newly designated (but
somewhat imaginary) segment of the labor market called the "semi-profes-
sions." Koos was very focused on reorganizing, rationalizing, and "standard-
izing" the American educational system to promote efficiency. The junior
college allowed a more articulated and differentiated transition between high
school and the university: "It will permit the consummation of the secondary school, will assure the small college an unquestionable function in the
educational system, and will encourage the university to differentiate its
activities from those of the lower schools" while also being "highly service-
able to the local community."[31]

The junior college was meant to more rationally separate the wheat from the chaff in the middle and upper-middle class "literate white native-born" student population. This group made up 90 percent of the college population in the United States during the first two decades of the 20th century. Since more and more students were graduating from high schools and demanding increased access to higher education, a crisis of legitimation was taking place because aristocratically minded university officials were concerned with the accompanying quality of students. Koos and many other educational leaders were concerned that "biological *heredity*" passed on fixed "physical *and mental traits*" [italics added] not only between races, but also within races, and these biological "endow[ments]" established "definite limits on the possibilities of training." Most junior college leaders up until the 1930s saw the college-going population as a mix of deserving and undeserving students. Only a select few were really capable of advanced university-level work, but the "democratic assumptions" of the country demanded that a larger percentage of the "literate white native-born" population had a right to some kind of postsecondary education. So the junior college would be the newly established institution that would enroll the "flood of 'inferior' candidates for higher education—many of whom, although deserving of some extent of opportunity beyond the present high-school level, are not warranted in aspiring to a full traditional college or university course."[32]

The early scholarship of Koos was later eclipsed by Walter Crosby Eells who became another influential junior college leader during this formative period. Eells was a professor of education at Stanford University and editor of the *Junior College Journal*. Eells's scholarship would define the field of junior colleges for over two decades, and his work would be widely used to train upcoming generations of junior college administrators in university education programs. Eells produced a textbook on junior college in 1931, *The Junior College*. This book superseded Koos's earlier treatment and went on to become the defining text on the subject of junior colleges for over a decade. Eells delivered a very detailed analysis of the junior college, but given that his subject was but a "young institution" (the majority of the 450 junior colleges in the 1930s were less than 10 years old), he did not say much that had not already been said before. On the whole, Eells brought nothing substantially new to the discussion of the junior college, as his argument was essentially the same as Koos's, which of course was the basic argument of all early junior college leaders until the 1940s: The transfer function was important, but because of the fact that the majority of all junior college students will not and should not go on to a university, junior colleges needed to organize more fully trade and semiprofessional terminal programs that would meet local and regional labor market needs.[33]

Alexis F. Lange, Leonard V. Koos, and Walter Crosby Eells were all a part of the intellectual vanguard of the junior college movement that was composed of university presidents, professors of education, and junior college administrators. Many of the university presidents and professors were not only connected to state departments of education but were also purposely training a generation of junior college administrators and instructors. These leaders shared a common progressive ideology that informed their social, political, and educational outlook. As a whole this group was greatly affected by the Bureau of Education's report *Cardinal Principles of Secondary Education*, which was published in 1918. This report argued that schools could be consciously controlled by educational and political leaders, and these institutions should be efficiently used as a socializing function to promote national "cooperation, social cohesion, and social solidarity." According to John H. Frye, junior college leaders were preoccupied with a vision of "order, hierarchy, and efficiency," which they used to promote the junior college as a terminal institution for semiprofessional education in a calculated effort to allow universities to become more selective research-oriented institutions for advanced professional training. However, junior college leaders' vision of terminal education was at odds with the general public's aspiration for social mobility. Thus, there was a lurking contradiction at the heart of this new educational enterprise. This ideological contradiction would eventually expose many other unresolved issues, the culmination of which would lead to the first important debate over the parameters of this institution.[34]

By the second decade of the junior college movement, the self-proclaimed leaders of the junior college began to go through an intense identity crisis revolving around the purpose of junior colleges and the central placement of this institution between secondary and postsecondary education systems. The expansive institutional myth of the junior college was colliding with a complex and contradictory educational landscape littered with a vast array of overlapping educational institutions. There was no national blueprint for education, and most states negotiated ad hoc arrangements that were mostly organized and administered locally. Thus, junior colleges did not have a concrete and settled institutional space in the messy environment of local educational politics. Junior college leaders balked at the uncertainty of many "loosely coupled" educational institutions haphazardly federated into local school districts, so they strove to create more rationally organized state systems of education.[35]

But where would junior colleges logically fit in the institutional landscape of the times? Some junior colleges were built out of secondary schools, some were built out of universities, some were built out of normal schools, and some were independent mostly private organizations, and of these, some were nonacademic technical institutes. From the beginning, junior colleges combined an erratic mixture of curricula: college-level transfer, college preparatory, remedial, and technical/vocational. Such diversity caused much uncertainty: Which institutional model should dominate? Were junior colleges "just glorified high schools"? Or were they separate junior "colleges"? Were junior colleges primarily supposed to prepare academically talented students for entry into a 4-year university? Or were they also supposed to train less-talented vocationally oriented students for local labor markets? And were junior colleges only responsive to universities and labor markets by training and credentialing postsecondary students? Or were they also supposed to be responsive to local community needs, which might include noncredentialing purposes such as literacy classes, citizenship classes, and general community education classes? Would junior colleges define their own agenda? Or would they simply take orders from universities and state departments of education? Edmund J. Gleazer Jr. argued that early junior college history was marked by "a discernible search for institutional freedom to determine its program and to look to the community as the arbiter of the suitability of its programs rather than the universities."[36]

But junior colleges were not the only educational institution with this predicament. In the early 20th century, most educational institutions were negotiating new institutional boundaries. Elementary schools, junior high schools, high schools, junior colleges, adult education schools, normal schools, state colleges, private colleges, and newly built research universities were all experiencing an institutional identity crisis as they tried to secure their own unique programmatic niche. They all tried to reconcile conflicting ideological rationales with comprehensive curricula in a confusing institutional environment that was becoming more rationally organized on a statewide basis. For most of the 20th century, every American educational institution was torn by contradictory purposes and mutually incompatible goals because they were all trying to promote inclusiveness while also protecting exclusiveness. These institutions were trying to foster greater opportunity, while also limiting opportunity through greater stratification. All

American institutions of education have had a "confusing array of functions," which corresponds to the chaotic paradox of American history. This country has always rhetorically celebrated individual equality and economic mobility while also constraining various social groups based on hierarchies of class, gender, religion, and race. Like the social and political experiment of America itself, conflicting ideals were never resolved so much as folded into the very fabric of American educational institutions. From the beginning, the junior college, like other educational institutions, was consecrated with a complex and conflicting mission. It would be an agency for democratization of higher education while it also sorted out the multitude into a hierarchically segmented labor market.[37]

Arguably a measure of consensus over institutional identity among junior college leaders, federal and state educational authorities, and the general public did not congeal until the publication of the President's Commission on Higher Education report (also called the Truman Commission's Report) in 1947.[38] However, the parameters of this consensus had been firmly solidified in the minds of the leaders of the junior college movement by the 1930s. This consensus was cogently presented to policy makers and the general public in an influential monograph published by the AAJC in 1941 titled, *Why Junior College Terminal Education?* This report was a product of the Commission on Junior College Terminal Education, which was directed by Walter Crosby Eells, and it included such notable figures as Aubrey A. Douglass, Leonard V. Koos, George F. Zook, Byron S. Hollinshead, Leland L. Medsker, and Rosco C. Ingalls. The basic message of this monograph was not new. In fact, Eells basically reformulated his argument in favor of terminal education that he had made a decade earlier in *The Junior College*. He explained, "It would be unwise and unfortunate if all of these [junior college students] tried to enter a university and prepare for professions which in most cases are already overcrowded, and for which their talents and abilities in many cases do not fit them." As Eells had admitted in 1931, there was a powerful stigma attached to terminal education, thus, junior college leaders would need to conduct "missionary work" to make this new institutional mission successful. This 1941 report represented the culmination of a decade's worth of such missionary work.[39]

The commission defined *terminal education* as a degree completion program that combined general "social citizenship" education with vocational education for a semiprofession. However, the term *semiprofession* was never adequately defined by the commission. A semiprofession was "more than mere occupational training," similar in quality and type to professional training, but because it was only a 2-year program, the training would lead to an occupation that would be less prestigious and with less pay than a professional career. In essence the commission argued that semiprofessions were whatever the "judgments of experts" said they were, based upon the existing needs of the hierarchically organized labor market. This sleight of hand was an attempt to defend the managerial "adjust[ment]" of students to existing "social and economic conditions," where they would be placed according to the economy's need. In essence students would be prepared by the junior college to assume whatever role the economy dictated, and that job, however unskilled it really was, would be transformed into a semiprofession. In practice, terminal semiprofessional programs were basically training in a low- to midskilled vocational field with a few liberal arts courses thrown in to make the worker a good citizen, at least on the transcript. It's no wonder that few students, less than a third nationally, enrolled in these terminal programs.[40]

The engineering of semiprofessions and the push for expanding terminal education in junior colleges had become national priorities by the 1940s because there were some 600,000 "idle young men," a lingering pool of unemployed from the upheavals of the Great Depression. These idle youth were not in the labor force because of a "scarcity of employment," and they were not in an institution of higher education because of a scarcity of capacity. Edward F. Mason called these idle youth a "liability to any country," and he used the embryonic logic of human capital theory to argue that these idle youth were a wasted national asset (not to mention a threat, as many conservatives still feared a Communist revolt of the underemployed masses). According to the commission, the junior college had an obligation to solve the crisis of idle youth by surveying the "actual employment needs and opportunities" in local communities and then offer semiprofessional programs to meet those needs. It was clear that the United States did not have the economic infrastructure to employ its increasing population, hard hit by a decade of economic uncertainty and retrenchment. But instead of arguing for increased investment in the economy to produce more jobs (a position that Franklin D. Roosevelt liberals had been experimenting with), junior college leaders instead wanted to send the hordes of idle youth back to school to keep them out of the labor market, therein to strategically prepare them for the limited amount of jobs that would become available as the economy opened up. Thus, the junior college was praised not so much as democracy's college, but as capitalism's college: Transfer the brightest junior college students to the university and keep the untalented majority in school and out of the labor market long enough to adequately "adjust" the individual to a tightly constrained and inequitable economic order.[41]

A Reformation: The Reinstitutionalization of Community Colleges Due to Increasing Student Access, 1950s–1960s

The Truman Commission's Report, *Higher Education for American Democracy*,[42] seemed not only to legitimate junior colleges by arguing that half of the American population could benefit from 2 years of postsecondary schooling, but the report also seemed to sanction a broad comprehensive mission for these institutions by suggesting a new name, and thereby a new institutional identity: the community college.[43] Until the publication of this report, junior college leaders had debated whether the primary function of the institution was to keep its traditional mission as a conduit for student transfers to 4-year universities or whether it should adopt new missions, such as offering terminal occupational and semiprofessional programs. Most junior college leaders leaned toward the latter of these two options because it would increase the legitimacy of the institution within already established systems of secondary and postsecondary education. The Truman Commission legitimized an expanded institutional mission, which would incorporate academically oriented general education, vocational education, adult education, and also responsiveness to local community needs.[44]

Of course the concept of the community college had been established long before 1947. In 1936 Byron Holinshead discussed the notion of a community college because he believed that junior colleges should be separate and distinct postsecondary institutions that primarily served the local needs of the community. However, servicing the community took some emphasis away from the traditional transfer function and gave more importance to meeting the diverse needs of the local community through noncredit and terminal programs. Because of a unique blend of state government and university support, California was the center of the fastest-growing community college movement, and schools in this state served as a model that pulled many junior college leaders toward the idea of separate comprehensive postsecondary institutions that would be responsive to community needs. A Santa Monica College faculty member, Sheldon Hayden, published an article in 1939 titled "Junior College as a Community Institution" in which he celebrated the comprehensive community-oriented mission of junior colleges as a democratic imperative. He also linked this new institutional conception to the educational programming being done in California.[45]

George F. Zook, who was later chair of the Truman Commission, argued in 1941 that junior colleges should become "the cultural leaders on a broad front in the communities in which they are located." Zook wanted junior colleges to "represent the highest expression of intellectual, esthetic, and cultural life in the community." Later Zook and the Truman Commission sanctioned the notion of and the name community college. It would be an institution to promote democracy, social mobility, and economic development. But after the publication of the Truman Commission Report, the most influential booster of the community college, Jesse Bogue, spread the gospel of a community-oriented institution of higher education. In 1950 Bogue published his inspired work, *The Community College,* in which he argued that the most important mission of this new institution was "service primarily to the people of the community." Later, the Carnegie Commission on Higher Education in its report *The Open Door Colleges* (1970) also reiterated this endorsement of the people's community college. As Kenneth Meier argued, "The emergence of the community college ideal transformed the junior college from an upward extension of secondary education emphasizing terminal and transfer education to an expansive social and educational movement supporting democratic progress."[46]

One of the most important scholarly reviews and evaluations of this newly rechristened institution was a widely influential work published in 1960 by Leland L. Medsker, vice chairman of the Center for the Study of Higher Education at the University of California, Berkeley. Medsker documented the growing prestige of the comprehensive junior college, which was increasingly branded community college. The name change was because of the fact that this institution not only offered a transfer-oriented academic curriculum but also functioned as "a major role in the educational, cultural, and civic activities in the community." The early junior college had been a democratizing agency. It helped open up access to higher education in the 20th century through the convenience of greater geographical proximity and through low tuition, which enabled more and more Americans in lower socioeconomic classes to attend a postsecondary institution. The junior college also offered a salvage function for those students who were not able to finish their high school education. These students could attempt to complete a secondary education with the possibility of going on to college. The total American student population enrolled in postsecondary institutions rose from 3 percent in 1900 to 32 percent in 1955, largely because of this new emphasis on serving the whole community by expanding access to higher education.[47]

But Medsker also pointed out the deficiencies of a comprehensive institution that was becoming the primary point of entry to postsecondary education. For one, there seemed to be confusion over the primary mission of the comprehensive but loosely coupled community college. Administrators encouraged terminal education, but two thirds of students nationally enrolled in a transfer-oriented academic curriculum. To make matters worse, only a third of those transfer-oriented students would actually transfer to a 4-year college or university. From the 1930s to the 1950s, various studies put the average national transfer rate for the general student population between 15 to 33 percent, although the average transfer rate of those students who earned an associate's degree was around 56 percent. However, there was a vast discrepancy in the rate of transfers because of the divergent quality of different schools. Some public junior colleges transferred only 10 percent of all students, while transferring 11 percent of those who earned associate's degrees. Other schools transferred as many as 67 percent of the general population and 73 percent of those receiving associate's degrees.[48]

Medsker criticized the general inefficiency of this situation, but he did not know what to make of it because, as he vaguely argued, this situation was "largely the result of circumstances outside the control of the junior college or of the students themselves." Medsker seemed to glimpse the solidification of an institutional structure that was becoming tied to the ideological contradictions of American society. These vague outside circumstances Medsker referred to had something to do with the "cultural and traditional values" of Americans. Many people saw public education as a means for social mobility and increased economic equality, but this notion ran counter to the rational designs of progressive administrators. Medsker also implied that junior college students were too ambitious for their own good. Progressives believed that higher education was a meritocratic prize reserved for the worthy who earned it through individual hard work. Thus, failing students were not the responsibility of either society or educational institutions; failure was because of individual choice or lack of appropriate character. But as more radical social theorists would later argue, this meritocratic belief conflicted with the hierarchical reality of capitalistic American society. Throughout the 20th century, lower classes and ethnic minorities often remained in servile conditions because of lack of economic and social capital, not because they did not try to improve themselves. Thus, Medsker's fatalistic tone represented the uneasiness that many progressive educational leaders felt toward democracy. Just how many Americans *should* have access to higher education?[49]

If junior college administrators were truly interested in expanding access to higher education then they could have invested sufficient resources in student services and academic counseling to help less-prepared students more fully realize their aspirations and succeed in higher education. Instead, junior college officials took a laissez-faire approach, which Medsker aptly called "survival of the fittest." This institution did not invest much time, money, or energy in actually guiding or mentoring disadvantaged students drawn "heavily from the lower half of the socioeconomic distribution." Because this growing institution did not seem concerned with preparing disadvantaged students, Medsker questioned whether junior colleges should become the new foundation for American higher education. Before New Left critics uttered such a claim, Medsker suggested that junior colleges seemed to be structuring the failure of many academically unprepared and economically disadvantaged students, although he was no social democrat and he was not altogether upset about this situation. Adopting a common progressive myth, Medsker believed in a Jeffersonian aristocracy of talent whereby only the capable should rise from the muck of the lower classes. The rest deserved to stay where destiny had placed them.[50]

Medsker was not the first to make such a stark judgment, nor would he be the last. Structuring the failure of unprepared students quickly became one of the central goals of this institution. Not everyone at midcentury saw the newly conceived community college in lofty, democratic, and egalitarian terms. From the start, University of California officials were supportive of the emerging community college system because of its value as a screening service to divert many postsecondary students from the selective and resource-limited universities. By 1937 there were 17,941 first-year students enrolled in California junior colleges compared with only 7,564 first-year students at the University of California. The University of California, Berkeley, sociologist Burton R. Clark famously argued in 1960 that while community colleges encouraged the aspirations of the multitude, this institution really served the function of what he called *cooling out* or sidetracking those "unpromising students" who lacked the social and economic capital to succeed. The community college transformed aspiring students who wanted to transfer (but lacked the skills, money, or initiative to do so) into terminal students who would achieve an alternative occupational credential for low- to midskilled jobs.[51]

Clark's case study of San José Junior College became one of the most important and influential reports on the community college at midcentury.

Clark specifically focused on the organizational structure of the junior college to document an empirical case study of an "educationally unknown" institution. While the 1950s demonstrated a trend toward the multipurpose, comprehensive community college, Clark was skeptical. His choice of subject was clearly the junior college, an institution with a collegiate focus and a struggling vocational education function. While San José Junior College was a managed institution beholden to public school, state, and university officials, the organizational character of this particular institution was largely shaped by the community and the student body because of open-door policies.[52]

In fact there was a clear conflict between the public school officials who wanted to develop vocational programming as the central mission of the school and the students who wanted an academic focus to facilitate transfer to a 4-year university. Because the students kept enrolling in academic transfer classes, "the stated purpose of the district went relatively unimplemented." However, Clark made it clear that the "overwhelming majority" of students who entered a junior college were "latent terminals" who were academically unprepared and had "unrealistic" goals. These students were funneled into failure because they did not have the ability to succeed at higher education. Thus, the junior college seemed to hold the primary function of filtering out or cooling out overly ambitious college-bound students who enrolled in the open-door college with very little academic potential and no future prospects.[53]

Clark acknowledged the pervasive must-go-to-college orientation of American students fed by American public policies based on democratic ideals and equal opportunity. However, Clark argued that the reality of a tiered system of higher education forced most of these students into a "structured failure." The junior college seemed to be designed to cool out overly ambitious students under the guise of equal access because it did not actually facilitate more equitable access to higher education. T. R. McConnell, chairman of the Center for the Study of Higher Education at the University of California, Berkeley, argued in his foreword to Clark's study, "In the long run the reputation of the [junior] college will probably depend on its success in preparing a relatively small proportion of its students for senior college work." This was likely the primary perception of most university researchers, state officials, and junior college administrators throughout the 1950s and 1960s.[54]

Clyde E. Blocker, Robert H. Plummer, and Richard C. Richardson Jr. published a capstone study of the American community college in 1965 in which they documented the growing centrality of the 2-year college in American higher education during the 1950s and early 1960s. The 2-year college was becoming a giant sponge for the growing number of the uneducated, "functionally illiterate" hordes of American students seeking entrance to institutions of higher education. While 2-year colleges were being asked to service all students who wanted access to higher education, the authors did not think these institutions could do much of anything for the lowest 20 percent of Americans, "as measured by intellectual ability and academic achievement." And because of its close ties to the local community, the 2-year college was susceptible to a "wide range of functions," depending on local interest groups and community needs. Blocker, Plummer, and Richardson argued, "The two-year college is probably more diverse in defined functions, programs, clientele, and philosophical bases than any other educational institution in existence." It was a community-based organization "of and for the people it serves," but this responsiveness caused some difficulties, such as an overall lack of clear purpose and an inability to demonstratively succeed at any one of its multiple missions.[55]

Not only did this institution have muddled missions, there was also a bewildering array of 2-year colleges with many different institutional forms that suggested an uncontrollable organizational anarchy.[56] There were private junior colleges, public comprehensive community colleges, technical institutes, and extension centers of state universities. This formal diversity made it difficult, if not impossible, to discuss this polymorphous institution as a single entity. During the 1960s the 2-year college was still "young and relatively untried." Thus, the exact parameters of its future were still uncertain. There was wide debate over educational programming, staffing, and financing. Blocker, Plummer, and Richardson argued that a priority list had to be developed by local colleges and communities to objectify a clear institutional mission. But funding was clearly an urgent issue because the average expenditure for each 2-year college student was "much too low" to meet the complex programmatic needs of these institutions. The authors argued that the 2-year college held "great promise." However, they also warned that in order to become a stable and legitimate institution, the 2-year college would have to leave behind "extravagant claims" and find an effective function that fits the needs of a local community without succumbing to "expediency and opportunism."[57]

But many community college leaders found this sober and restrained warning distasteful, especially during the heady optimism of the 1960s. Following the charismatic cheerleading of Jesse Bogue, Edmund J. Gleazer Jr.

became another idealistic booster of the expansive multimission of this institution. Gleazer was executive director of the AAJC in the 1960s. His most famous tract was *This Is the Community College*, written in 1968 to popularize what he considered to be the pinnacle of American meritocracy: the open-door comprehensive community college. This polymorphous institution was rapidly expanding and beginning to capture the public's attention in the late 1950s and 1960s. The development of community colleges had become a highly local phenomenon driven by grassroots organizers, expanded state financial support, and national educational policy. Access to higher education was beginning to be seen as "more than a privilege; it is a citizen's right." Expanded educational opportunity was also seen by many policy makers as a sensible investment in local and state economies. At the end of the 1950s about 20 percent of college students started higher education in a community college. That number grew to almost 33 percent by the late 1960s. In 1967 over 900 community colleges enrolled about 1.7 million students, and 650 of these institutions were publicly supported community colleges with over 1.5 million students.[58]

But through the 1950s these institutions sprouted haphazardly, because in most states there had been little central planning of locations, missions, or curriculum. By the 1960s many new policy initiatives in several states were beginning to centralize planning of state systems of higher education. California and Florida were early trendsetters. Not only were community colleges trying to solidify their new-found identity as comprehensive institutions of higher education, but state boards, university officials, and accrediting agencies were also trying to create minimum standards as a condition for receiving expanded state funds.[59]

The junior college had slowly evolved into a "comprehensive institution" with a diverse curriculum designed to meet the complex needs of a whole community, thereby taking the new name of community college. Gleazer argued that the primary mission of the newly revised community college was the democratization of higher education. Community colleges were based on an open-door policy to extend educational opportunity to a broad range of people with "different aptitudes, interests, achievements, and ages." As a responsive, community-oriented institution, the community college had the ambiguous role of meeting the "innumerable needs" that no other educational agency could possibly meet. Community colleges offered perhaps the most diverse curriculum any American educational institution had ever offered: an academic curriculum to prepare students for transfer to 4-year institutions, remedial education to reteach subjects and skills taught in high school, occupational education, continuing education, and a broad range of community services. Gleazer characterized community colleges as highly complex, creative, and locally responsive institutions: "They seem limited only by the creativity of leadership, the objectives of the institution, interest in the community, the means available, and provisions made by other institutions and organizations." However, by the end of the 1960s more sober analysts concluded that the ebullient rhetoric of community college leaders, like Bogue and Gleazer, presently "outstrip[ed] the scope of local programs" and mystified the specific contours of an "emerging" institution.[60]

To get past the missionary rhetoric of many community college promoters, the Carnegie Commission on Higher Education conducted an empirically based policy study to review the expansion of the community college through the 1960s (reinforcing the newly minted name of this revised institution). And with a close eye on the restructuring of higher education in California, this policy report also made many recommendations for the continued expansion of the community college across the nation. By the 1960s most states had developed public community college systems. The Carnegie report argued that the public comprehensive community college should be connected to the local community and completely funded by federal, state, and local governments. The authors of this report wanted the open-door college to be "available, within commuting distance, to all persons throughout their lives." The commission charted the rise of enrollments from 600,000 in 1960 to almost 2 million by 1969, and suggested that this trend would continue to rise for at least the next decade. While the report urged a comprehensive mission incorporating "academic, occupational, and general education," the reality was that only about 33 percent of community college students would actually transfer to a 4-year college or university. Thus, despite the lofty rhetoric, the open-door college seemed to have one practical mission: cooling out students and preparing them for terminal occupational programs in the semiskilled labor market.[61]

The report also noted that nonwhite minority students (except for Japanese and Chinese Americans) were still underrepresented in public community colleges. However, the commission devoted only two sentences and one table in the appendix to the topic of race and access to higher education, so the subject was obviously not yet an urgent priority. Besides, the commission recommended restricting access to this institution, so there would be no room for new underserved populations. The report wanted open-door colleges to accept only high school graduates and "otherwise qualified individuals." This was not a policy that would have helped increase minority access to higher education because Latino Americans, African Americans, and Native Americans all had low rates of high school completion during the 1960s. Thus the commission's focus on rational and efficient institutional policy implicitly seemed to justify the inequitable and racist status quo of American society. Higher education had historically been restricted to middle-class and upper-class whites.[62] While the community college increased educational opportunity to many otherwise unqualified students, it was managed and restricted, ultimately structuring the failure of thousands of less-prepared students through lack of planning and survival of the fittest policies.

Community Colleges, Segregation, and Equality, 1960s–1980s

Very little historical work has been done on the issues of racism, segregation, and educational inequality in the community college. This lack of scholarship is partly because very little, if any, educational demographic data broken down by race were collected by American educational institutions prior to 1963.[63] Based on an analysis of the U.S. census, Hurley H. Doddy argued that from 1940 to 1960 the total population of college graduates rose from 5 to 8 percent while the number of nonwhite college graduates rose from 1 to 3 percent. The enrollment percentage of nonwhite students based on total population was less than half the rate of white students in every region of the country except the West where 6.7 percent of nonwhites enrolled in college compared to 7.9 percent for whites. However, only 8.4 percent of nonwhites in the West achieved 1 to 3 years of college, compared to 13 percent of whites, and only 5.4 percent of nonwhites in the West attained 4 or more years of college, compared to 9.8 percent of whites.[64]

Kenneth Meier argued that from the 1930s to the early 1960s, "[the] poor and minorities were rarely an object of research or even much curiosity on the part of the American Association of Junior Colleges and most local leaders."[65] During the late 19th and early 20th centuries northern educational philanthropists and southern educational reformers were in many ways white supremacists who insisted on a second-class education for blacks to restrict them to subordinate roles in the southern economy.[66] In 1939 Horace Mann Bond, a black historian and social scientist, argued the South was dominated by a "planting aristocracy" that had used the public schools "to maintain both the structure of social classes and that of racial caste" to protect their economic and social interests. Bond noted that "the masses of white people in Southern States have, slowly and grudgingly, fought toward the achievement of systems of universal education for white children," but blacks were left largely outside the push for reform.[67]

In Koos's treatise on the junior college movement no mention was made of race or segregation. However, in Koos's text on secondary schools published 2 years later, he did include some mention of race, which can be used to get a sense of how much access nonwhite Americans were able to gain to higher education. Of 740 pages of text, Koos devoted less than one page to "secondary-school facilities for negroes". He noted that only a "very small proportion of the negro population of high-school age" was enrolled in secondary institutions. In a chart at the beginning of the book, Koos noted that only 4.3 percent of the "native-born negro" school-age population in the United States was enrolled in public high schools. This was less than half the rate for "native-born white" students (9.5 percent) and also less than the average rate for all "foreign-born" ethnic groups (4.9 percent).[68]

Negro junior colleges did receive some attention in the 1930s. Walter Crosby Eells included the equivalent of one page on Negro junior colleges in his textbook *The Junior College* (one page out of more than 800). It seems that most of the Negro junior colleges in the United States were not even known to the AAJC, although Eells said that representatives from 16 of these Negro schools purportedly attended the annual meaning in 1929. Eells stated that the AAJC directory listed 14 Negro junior colleges, but he claimed personal knowledge of at least 33 segregated Negro institutions. This lack of knowledge on Negro junior colleges was because of an institutionalized neglect of these segregated schools. Eells admitted that the junior college community had "a lack of definite information regarding [its] present existence and status." Part of this lack could no doubt be traced to the racial animosity harbored by many white junior college leaders. A lack of information on junior colleges may have also been in part because of the nonaccredited status of most Negro institutions of higher education until the late 1920s and 1930s. Black schools were often excluded from the mainstream accreditation and funding processes of state education systems; thus, they often operated without any oversight from state educational officials and national educational organizations.[69]

The Journal of Negro Education, inaugurated in 1932, devoted several pages of each issue to updates on the accreditation of Negro schools. It wanted to publicize "the degree of progress which Negro colleges are making in improving their status as institutions for higher education." This journal was also the only scholarly or professional source that persistently attempted to keep track of Negro junior colleges, which were mostly invisible to the white junior college movement because segregated southern schools constituted a separate system of schooling that was of no concern to most white educators. Most of the known Negro junior colleges were created in the mid-1920s. A majority of these schools were in Texas and most were private institutions. Three of the 17 segregated southern states in the 1930s had white-only junior colleges and no Negro junior colleges. One state, Delaware, had no junior colleges at all. In the other 13 southern states, 27 Negro junior colleges enrolled about 3,164 students, while 491 junior colleges for whites enrolled 119,147 students. Segregated Negro junior colleges constituted 5.21 percent of all junior colleges in the South and enrolled 2.58 percent of all junior college students, but African Americans were 24.5 percent of the total southern population.[70]

Interestingly the attitudes of some of the black scholars writing for *The Journal of Negro Education* displayed the same sort of progressive elitism as white junior college leaders. Nick Aaron Ford said that Negro junior colleges were important institutions that would clear out the clutter of unprepared students from black 4-year colleges. Junior colleges would serve primarily "students from backward communities" who needed "stricter supervision" to help mold "individual development and conduct." With these less-promising students out of the way, black 4-year colleges could "devote their time, energy and talent to the select few who will become the race leaders of tomorrow."[71] The Truman Commission called for an end to discrimination in higher education in 1947. Less than a decade later the Supreme Court ruling in *Brown v. Board of Education* in 1954 outlawed segregation in public schools. Then in 1956 *Florida ex rel. Hawkins v. Board of Control* effectively outlawed segregation in higher education. But despite new policy initiatives and judicial reform, both de facto and de jure segregation remained in effect in much of the country until the late 1960s and early 1970s. The 17 southern states that had de jure segregation until the 1950s did not quickly end these legal statutes, and even when they did, de facto segregation was left in place.[72] In 1949 there were 50 segregated private higher education institutions nationally for black students. Twenty-two of these institutions were black public and private community colleges mostly in the South, serving roughly 6,447 students. In a 1962 study of southern and bordering states' private and public community colleges, only 19 out of 245 schools (8 percent) specifically served blacks, all of them public and most of them in Florida (13). The remaining six institutions were in three other states. This left 13 of 17 southern states (76.5 percent) without a black-serving community college. And those few institutions that did serve African Americans offered a distinctly unequal curriculum. As far as the sparse records indicate, only five formerly segregated junior colleges had integrated by 1960.[73]

The only state to receive some scholarly attention on the issue of segregation in junior colleges was Florida. Eight segregated junior colleges in this state were open to African Americans in the early 1960s. According to Carroll L. Miller, they all offered "limited terminal programs which tend to perpetuate job placements in low level positions and which offer no opportunities for Negro youth." By the 1967–68 school year, most community colleges in the state had been integrated, but the largest Florida community colleges were at least 92 percent white, with three colleges over 96 percent white. In the late 1960s Florida's population was 78 percent white with about 15.3 to 17 percent black and about 5 percent Latino. Florida should be considered an extreme example of segregation in community colleges because this state had legally segregated public schools, including its system of higher education, until 1960. It is interesting to note the ambivalence of junior college leaders and scholars to the issue of racial segregation and educational inequality. Medsker's 1960 review of junior colleges in various states never once mentions the issue of race. In his section on the Florida community colleges it did not even occur to him to mention that this public junior college system was completely segregated and, therefore, by definition was not actually designed to "serve the entire state."[74]

In 1966 Arthur M. Cohen documented the integration of Miami-Dade Junior College, which began as a single administrative unit overseeing two racially segregated campuses in September 1960. The Northwest Center campus was connected to a segregated black high school and enrolled 185 black students. Three miles away the Central Center campus was connected to a segregated white high school and it enrolled 1,200 white students. Slowly, as designated by the gradual desegregation plan drafted by community college and state officials, black students and faculty were integrated into the Central Center campus. By 1962 the black Northwest Center campus was closed, and the Central campus became Miami-Dade Junior College. This newly integrated community college was about 92.5 percent white in 1962 and grew astronomically to 21,661 students by the 1967–68 school year. But despite Cohen's claim for the "success of phased integration," the integrated Central campus actually became less diverse 1 year after integration. The white student body grew from 92.5 percent to 93.9 percent of the total student population. Thus, African Americans became an increasingly marginalized minority presence in a predominantly white and probably hostile educational environment.[75]

While Florida may have been a successful example of peaceful integration, it still demonstrated the lack of access to institutions of higher education for nonwhite minorities, even to the supposedly open-door community college. Even though nonwhite minorities had won access to white institutions of higher education, there were still many segregated community colleges. When integration happened, enrollment of ethnic minority students in white colleges rarely reached parity with the racial demographics of the regional communities. In the 1967–68 school year all across the nation, large community colleges with 3,000 or more students were all highly segregated by race. Jefferson State Junior College in Birmingham, Alabama, was 95.5 percent white in a state that was almost 30 percent black. Of the seven large community colleges in Texas at the time, five were over 90 percent white (two of which were over 97 percent white), while only two large junior colleges enrolled significant numbers of black and Latino students: El Centro College in Dallas, the second largest community college in Texas, had an 18.2 percent minority student population, while San Antonio College, the largest college with 12,717 students, enrolled 53.5 percent minority students. Two of the three largest community colleges in Illinois were over 93 percent white in a state that was between 83 percent to 89 percent white. Five out of the seven largest community colleges in Michigan were over 93.4 percent white, and one college in Highland Park, the black ghetto just north of Detroit, enrolled 45.7 percent black students. Between 1960 and 1970 Michigan was nearly 89 percent white, about 10 percent black, and about 1 percent Latino.[76]

As Leland L. Medsker and Dale Tillery acknowledged, by the late 1960s it was "clear that neither higher education generally nor any segment specifically is providing equal opportunity for minority students." But of all segments of higher education, the open-door junior college was "the least restrictive in reference to minority enrollments."[77] But simply gaining access to desegregated predominantly white institutions of higher education by the 1960s did not mean that nonwhite students experienced a welcoming, non-discriminatory environment. Black students in particular faced social segregation, exclusion, and racial hatred on many integrated college campuses throughout the country. Mark A. Chesler and James Crowfoot argued that this racial hatred on college campuses lasted well into the 1980s. They also reported that the issue of racial exclusion and hatred within integrated schools continually went unnoticed and undocumented by most scholars because of the "sheer invisibility of racism to white people." Chesler and Crowfoot went so far as to say that the institutional racism at the organizational level actually enabled and sanctioned white racism on most college campuses. Even through the 1990s the legacy of segregation and white racism continued to be a factor on college campuses. Sylvia Hurtado and her colleagues argued that

> the historical vestiges of segregated schools and colleges continue to affect the climate for racial/ethnic diversity on college campuses. . . . Because they are embedded in the culture of a historically segregated environment, many campuses sustain long-standing, often unrecognized, benefits for particular student groups.[78]

Nonwhite American and immigrant students also argued that the general education curriculum in most institutions of higher education bore a marked white and Western bias, which some students found "irrelevant, if not outright racist."[79]

By the 1980s and 1990s, it was still not clear that nonwhite minorities were making up lost ground in terms of taking full advantage of more open systems of higher education and earning more proportional amounts of postsecondary degrees. Between 1976 and 1994, college enrollment rates improved and attainment of baccalaureate degrees increased for African Americans, but not by much in comparison with the total college student population. Increases in college attendance and degree attainment were mostly because of black females, while the rates of black males were relatively stagnant.[80]

In 1987 Richard C. Richardson Jr. and Louis W. Bender argued that "no one believes that more than two centuries of segregation and discrimination will be erased in one generation by improved access to baccalaureate education." Richardson and Bender conducted two studies to investigate higher education policies targeting minority students in higher education, specifically in terms of measuring the progress of minorities in attaining postsecondary degrees.[81] They found that hierarchically structured systems of education, in combination with segregated residential communities and disproportionately funded local school districts, systematically perpetuate inequality and place urban minorities at a disadvantage in postsecondary degree attainment. Many urban community college districts were distributed to promote de facto segregation patterns, and there was no adequate pipeline from many urban high schools to postsecondary degree attainment. Because a majority of urban high schools students were not adequately prepared for college, community colleges were the "primary access point" for minority students in urban America. And even then, anywhere from 60 percent to 95 percent of urban community college students needed some form of remedial education.

Also, a culture distinctive to urban community colleges impeded the preparation of minority students in terms of academic achievement and successful transfer to baccalaureate-granting institutions. Community colleges were cheap, local, and often very supportive of students, but they also offered lower standards, a watered-down curriculum, and little opportunity to teach students self-direction and self-discipline. In short, many community colleges made a compromise. They lessened academic rigor and lowered standards to become custodial institutions that offered a kind of social welfare to help improve minority education at a lower level. But Richardson and Bender's assessment was not ultimately unkind to this institution. They argued that community colleges were doing the best they could under difficult and constrained circumstances:

> When one looks below the surface of test scores, economic uncertainty, and previous educational performance, one finds human beings who are striving to realize the American dream in the face of many barriers. Many will not achieve that dream, but some will. Moreover, it is the dream that is important, not the success ratio. The community college for many of these students truly represents America's last frontier.[82]

Whither To? Reaching a Plateau of Orthodoxy, 1970s–1980s

By the end of the 1970s most junior colleges had become reinstitutionalized as comprehensive community colleges with multiple educational missions serving a diverse array of community needs. This transformation included converting many former vocational and technical colleges into comprehensive community colleges. Nationally the community college had become institutionalized as an important part of state systems of higher education, and its established organizational and ideological structure perpetuated a stickiness that makes it resistant to change. By the 1970s the community college found a stabilized yet contradictory identity. It was being governed by self-reinforcing institutional norms and myths that had solidified through the last several decades of organizational consolidation and increased legitimacy.[83] While individual agents do have some power to perpetuate and modify existing institutions, no single individual or group is ever in complete control of an institution, in part because of larger environmental influences and constraints. Thus, social change is always contested, partial, and incomplete.[84] While the community college did manage to secure an institutional identity, it was riddled with controversy and subject to endless criticism and debate; however, the basic institutional structure seemed impervious to change.

The 1970s was a decade of trials and tribulations for the community college. Enrollment slowed across the board, and institutions of higher education became direct competitors for reduced pools of college students. To make themselves more attractive to less-qualified and more vocationally oriented students, administrators at many 4-year colleges and universities expanded their curricula to include more occupational and remedial programs, which put them in direct competition with community colleges for vocationally oriented students. During the 1970s the institutional efficiency of community colleges also became more of an issue and made them look less attractive than slightly more expensive public universities. Community colleges lost over 50 percent of their students to attrition between the first and second years, and only about one third of all incoming first-year students completed an associate's degree or transferred to a 4-year institution.[85]

In response to growing competition and a tarnished image, the community college turned to increase its educational efficiency. It also expanded into new markets by promoting itself as an institution that could meet the specific needs of the local community and provide any services local customers might want. But in the expansive search for new educational markets, community colleges began to run up against several obstacles. For one, state financial resources became constricted by the late 1970s because of national and international economic crises, the Organization of Petroleum Exporting Countries oil embargo, and stagflation, and for the next several decades state governments invested less and less in higher education. From 1985 to 1996 there was an 18.2 percent decline in state funding of public higher education in the United States. Despite calls for increased federal and state funding from influential policy analysts such as the members of the Carnegie Commission on Higher Education, federal and state policy makers became much more tightfisted with public money and began to restrict funding to only those programs with a clear economic justification and social value. Another obstacle was the sustained, if not growing, institutional confusion over the schools' complex comprehensive mission. Community colleges began taking on the chaotic characteristics of a shopping mall. However, when times were tough, it was rarely clear which programs deserved priority funding, as institutional units more frequently battled over scarce resources. The comprehensiveness of community colleges led to another obstacle: Some faculty members resisted change when community colleges veered too far from traditional core missions in search of new educational markets.[86] As Dale Tillery and William L. Deegan argued, a widespread reevaluation of community college priorities occurred in this transition period, which boiled down to "who should be educated and who should pay for such education?"[87]

By the early 1970s a sort of community college orthodoxy emerged. A new institutional identity rose from the ambiguous nature of the older junior college. In 1971 847 public junior colleges enrolled more than 2.1 million students, and 244 independent junior colleges enrolled more than 131,000 students. Community colleges had just been through their most intense period of growth between 1960 and 1970, and by the early 1970s they were enrolling more than a third of all first-time students each year. The importance of this uniquely American institution was becoming more readily acknowledged by higher education officials and policy makers. The comprehensive community college was becoming an indispensible part of state systems of higher education. James W. Thornton Jr. argued that all institutions of higher education were ambiguous; therefore, there would never be a definitive, "unambiguous, and fully accepted statement of the purposes of American higher education." Yet Thornton acknowledged the great strides made by the community junior college, which was his own unique transitional term for this institution. He argued that the community college was "progressing steadily toward a definition." By the 1970s several accepted functions of the comprehensive community college congealed into an orthodox institutional identity. These orthodox functions, which became a litany of sorts for community college leaders, scholars, and education professionals for the next quarter century, included general education, community service and education for adults, counseling and guidance of students, technical and vocational education, academic transfer education, and the new function of helping advance disadvantaged students in basic skills and opportunities. By the 1970s many community college leaders and education professionals embraced the idea that true democratization of higher education meant "the elimination of barriers based on class, poverty, race, or culture." Institutions of higher education would make an effort to meet the diverse needs of previously disadvantaged students, and this became a new ideal. The comprehensive community college would be at the forefront of this effort.[88]

But the energy and enthusiasm of the 1950s and 1960s, which coalesced around a clear if complex institutional mission, began to recede as the 1970s wore on. By 1981 K. Patricia Cross argued that community colleges had reached a plateau. Since the late 1970s, she said, "the sense of common purpose in community colleges has receded, and new ideals have not yet emerged." Cross used data from a nationwide survey of 18 community colleges to discuss the disparity between present and future institutional priorities. Multiple participants (faculty, administrators, trustees, students, and community members) were asked to prioritize different institutional goals in terms of what was currently important and what should be important. A broad consensus on the accessibility of community colleges formed in terms of open access, the importance of the general education curriculum, and the importance of the vocational/technical curriculum. Students and community members agreed that the personal development of students and the counseling and advising services should be better. Faculty and administrators also agreed that developmental/remedial preparation and creating a collegial community atmosphere should be better. Cross argued that the idealism and social change of the 1960s was gone. Now community colleges were in a "phase of maturity" as they worked toward "pragmatic, conventional goals." It was unclear what new goals might emerge or take priority, but Cross argued in a later article that community colleges could not pursue all facets of a comprehensive mission equally, let alone with excellence. Trying to hold on to the comprehensive mission was a gamble, which mostly likely would lead to "mediocrity across the board." Cross seemed to hearken back a generation to older calls for restricting the boundless optimism of this beleaguered institution.[89]

Anne-Marie McCartan also acknowledged the fading optimism of the 1960s. She pointed out how the 1980s were giving rise to "a heightened intensity and concern about the future directions of the community college." McCartan tried to diagnose the major causes of the decade's malaise, which she though was widely felt. She pointed to the demographic shifts and new student populations. New ranks of nonwhite minority and lower-class students had brought about unprecedented diversity in college classrooms. The curriculum was also changing. More students were going into remedial classes and occupational programs, and fewer students were transferring. Many education professionals felt the state was extending more influence over community college operations, although there was not much evidence to substantiate this phenomenon. State 4-year colleges were starting to compete with community colleges over traditional-age students and vocational programming. As McCartan saw it, the debate over community college missions was focused on the dysfunctional nature of comprehensiveness. Many critics of the status quo argued for a single function to bring more coherence and prestige to the institution. Some wanted to focus on a lifelong learning mission centered on community development, and others wanted to reconceptualize the community college as an institution of higher learning dispensing an academically oriented general education. While McCartan was able to sketch out the parameters of this debate, she was not sure what terrain this debate would play itself out on. Nor was she sure who would ultimately decide the new direction community colleges would take, although she did hint to the fact that state legislatures and state boards of higher education were taking the lead because of tightening revenues and reduced enrollments. This prediction would prove to be prophetic.[90]

Adding insult to injury, several high-profile economic analyses of community college financing were conducted in the early 1980s. The news was not good. Brookings Institution researchers David W. Breneman and Susan C. Nelson published the most influential report in 1981. They argued that the 1980s would be a decade of "declining enrollments," "excess capacity," and "intense" competition for all institutions of higher education. State governments were trying to gauge public finance, demand more justifications for limited resources, distribute financial obligations among various levels of government, and eliminate some social programs and services. Thus, in such a competitive environment, the institutional missions and purposes of community colleges needed to be examined in terms of efficiency and outcomes. Breneman and Nelson argued that the outcomes of community colleges were debatable, and based on their analysis of longitudinal data, they concluded that most students, especially more able high school graduates, were better off choosing a 4-year college or university to obtain a baccalaureate degree. Under the most optimistic financial conditions, the authors argued that the community colleges should increase vocational-technical programs, remedial education, and noncredit community service activities while holding the transfer function steady.[91]

A by-product of the struggle for funding and resources in the 1970s and 1980s was the increased turn to a more flexible, part-time faculty workforce. Part-time faculty in community colleges went from 38 percent in 1966 to between 50 and 60 percent in 1980. By 1998 part-timers constituted close to 64 percent of all community college faculty. By the late 1990s the "silent explosion" of part-time faculty became acknowledged as yet another institutional problem. Many scholars, administrators, and education professionals worried that part-time faculty members were being exploited through lower wages, fewer benefits, and no job security. Full-time faculty were also worried because traditional faculty functions, such as student counseling, staff meetings, and organizational governance, were falling solely on their shoulders. There was also concern that part-time faculty would dilute the quality of community college education because the so-called alienated freeway flyers taught about 30 to 40 percent of all full-time equivalent contact hours. The issue of an exploited class of part-time faculty and its effects on the quality of education remains marginalized to this day, as the economic necessity of contingent labor has become a more immediate concern regarding institutional efficiency.[92]

Organizationally, community colleges were also becoming more bureaucratic and centrally coordinated, especially by state lawmakers and boards of education. In 1960s and early 1970s, many community colleges were still developing, and there was a widespread sense of local possibilities. Many faculty and administrators were caught up in the idealized policies of opening access to higher education, helping disadvantaged minorities, and servicing the needs of the community. Often, "broad social support and respect" were shown for such optimistic missions. But increasingly, community colleges became structured bureaucracies near the bottom of hierarchical state systems of higher education. As funding diminished and became more centrally dependent upon state governments, community college administrators became caught between the demands of the state, the concerns of the faculty, the needs of the students, and the stark realities of an ill-defined and underfunded comprehensive mission. In an environment of reduced enrollments, full-time equivalent student ratios began to dominate institutional priorities. All institutions of higher education were becoming more driven by marketplace considerations. As Richardson, Fisk, and Okun explained, "The philosophic commitment of the sixties to provide opportunity through *open doors* [italics in original] had been transformed into the legal and economic imperatives of the eighties to meet affirmative action guidelines and to ensure institutional survival." As community colleges began to function more like businesses, the collegial culture began to change. Full-time faculty became overburdened by the demands of teaching difficult students and increasing bureaucratic requirements, such as revising traditional curricula to meet new institutional assessment standards. Competing units in the bureaucratized community college wrestled over funding and prestige, which often fragmented collegial relationships and curricular coherence. Often the comprehensive community college became paralyzed by divisive organizational politics. As one faculty member explained, "The community college is becoming a petrified system. . . . It does terrible things to a teacher to be battling against an unresponsive system." To deal with the increased work load, many faculty reduced teaching to *instrumental bitting,* in short, easily swallowed nibbles of information. Students were becoming "consumers of prepackaged learning." The educational vitality of the community college curricula ossified into bureaucratic social service organization.[93]

To revitalize the institution, several voices in the 1970s and 1980s called for a renewed emphasis on the community service mission of the *community-oriented college.*[94] In 1980 Edmund J. Gleazer Jr. tried to further articulate this vision by arguing for a new emphasis on community involvement and lifelong learning. Gleazer argued that the community college as an institution seemed trapped in its traditional roles: acting as the collegiate transfer facilitator and providing remedial programs and occupational training. According to Gleazer, community colleges had not done a good job of organizing together in their states to directly affect public perceptions and state policy, nor had they done a good enough job of collecting data to prove their institutional worth in the new cost-sensitive environment of besieged budgets. Gleazer optimistically wanted to expand the mission of the community college still further. He wanted this institution to become the nexus of a community learning system. Community colleges would become a centralized community institution that would facilitate connections between individuals, community agencies, and public institutions. The community college helped foster lifelong learning of the entire community.[95] Gleazer's expansive vision was revisited and institutionalized in a 1988 report published by the AAJC, *Building Communities: A Vision for a New Century.*[96]

However, the parameters of community responsiveness and lifelong learning were overly idealized and very ambiguous. In the ensuing debate over the new directions of the community college most participants argued for more practical pursuits. Some critics of the status quo argued against new missions, albeit remaining sensitive to the community service mission. Many pushed for a more occupational emphasis because this seemed economically and educationally advantageous to the middle position of community colleges in state systems of higher education. Darrel A. Clowes and Bernard H. Levin argued that career education was the "only viable core function" of the community college in the 1980s and 1990s because the traditionally academic-oriented transfer function had been "diminished," and because most community college students had more "immediate goals" than a bachelor's degree. In a return to the early evangelism of the junior college leaders, some thought a new emphasis on career education would help increase student enrollments, would help the community college compete with nonselective 4-year colleges, and would become a vehicle to "reestablish the transfer function in modified form" by focusing on a new vocational-technical transfer pipeline. Clowes and Levin argued that other missions, such as community service and remediation, could be refashioned as support functions for career education. But they did not explain what would happen to the traditional academically oriented general education curriculum, nor did they explain the larger ramifications of a career-oriented community college in the hierarchically structured state systems of higher education. Wouldn't such an emphasis trim this comprehensive institution down to nothing more than an occupational training center for low-wage workers? While career education might have been a viable mission, Clowes and Levin did not make clear whose interests would be served by such an institutional focus.[97]

By the 1980s vocational education was becoming more of a central mission for many community colleges. Many scholars, faculty, and students thought this emphasis was creating some problems. From the 1960s to the 1980s, vocational enrollments were increasing much faster than liberal arts enrollments, although the academic function of community colleges was still considered their primary mission. However, many longitudinal research studies in the 1980s seemed to indicate that transfer rates were decreasing; thus, some critics argued that the liberal arts transfer curriculum was in trouble. Part of the problem was the inability of community colleges to take the problem of academically underprepared students seriously and design effective systems of remedial education. Because of the momentum of the civil rights movement in the 1960s and 1970s, community colleges accepted more and more racially discriminated, economically disadvantaged, and academically underserved populations who had received a poor-quality secondary education. Many of these students were not academically prepared for college, and this created a catch-22 for community college faculty: Keep college-level standards and fail a lot of students, or lower academic standards to meet the subpar skills of new student populations.[98]

Dennis McGrath and Martin B. Spear argued that this complex and unfair situation created "role ambiguity" for faculty. It also led to "a progressive, if silent, academic drift—away from rigor, toward negotiated anemic practices." The liberal arts curriculum was becoming a "scaled-down" and "weak version" of college-level academics, and this was demoralizing students and setting them up for failure. By the late 1980s and early 1990s, the academic crisis of the community college became clear. If this institution was going to seriously entertain the notion of offering a liberal arts curriculum, then faculty needed to rebuild the intellectual culture and the collegiate community of the community college. Faculty would also have to develop more rigorous and coherent academic practices to promote access and excellence. But it was unclear if relatively uneducated and academically inexperienced community college faculty had the intellectual capacity or wherewithal to initiate such practices.[99]

But there was also an ethical imperative at the center of the comprehensive community college that many people began to lose sight of during the 1980s. George B. Vaughan argued that minority participation in higher education has been an important policy issue since the Supreme Court's *Brown v. Board of Education* decision in 1954. During the civil rights movement from the 1950s to the 1970s, the issue of minority participation in higher education was regarded as an ethical concern connected to the national values of democracy, freedom, and equality. However, by the 1970s and 1980s the national higher education policy discourse shifted from the ethical issue of minority access to the economic issue of competitiveness in global markets. The previous concern for minority access to higher education was not lost, but it became reframed in terms of economics and human capital formation. The national economy needed the full participation of the American workforce, including minorities, to foster workforce development and economic growth. What had been lost in this new narrative, however, was the ethical imperative of increasing minority access to higher education for the sake of individual students' personal growth, the well-being of local communities, and the national ethical imperative of increasing sociopolitical equality and democracy. Two-year public community colleges were the major point of entry to higher education for most nonwhite minorities and lower-class students. In 1991 community colleges enrolled about 43 percent of all African American students in higher education, 55 percent of all Hispanics, 41 percent of all Asians, and 57 percent of all Native Americans. Public community colleges had become responsible for almost half the nation's minority college students, and this trend was increasing. The community college had become the gateway to opportunity for previously disadvantaged populations; therefore, many thought it had a particular ethical responsibility to help these students climb up the inequitable social ladder of success. But if community colleges became just training centers servicing the larger stratified economy, then what would happen to the precarious predicament of these underprivileged students?[100]

By the end of the 1980s community colleges had conflicting sets of expectations that seemed impossible to reconcile. They had been asked, on the one hand, to meet the individual needs of educationally underserved and disadvantaged students. On the other hand, they had also been asked to train skilled workers for national economic development. Plus, they were asked to accomplish both of these missions while serving the larger community, and on a shoestring budget with a mostly contingent workforce. This conflict in goals led to a mismatch between three competing interests: what was best for the community college as an educational institution, what was best for the national economy, and what was best for individual students.

From the 1930s many community college leaders have tried to emphasize the mission of regional and national economic development, which tends to lead students away from baccalaureate attainment and toward shorter-term vocational and technical certificate programs. That is why students have been resisting this mission for most of the 20th century. However, by the 1970s and 1980s, this vocational emphasis seemed to become the primary emphasis of the community college. But in emphasizing the needs of the economy and focusing on economic efficiency, community college leaders and state policy makers failed to understand the essential role of community colleges in serving educational and economically disadvantaged students. According to George B. Vaughan, the community college has taken on one of the most difficult tasks in higher education: to educate students with special needs, many of whom are first-generation college students, come from the lower socioeconomic groups, and score in the bottom 50 percent on standardized tests. Can community colleges offer these students a quality education with minimum funding?

Vaughan argued that the higher education policy community needed to return to the central question of "what is ethically right" and to reevaluate the purposes of community colleges within the American system of higher education. The seeds of this reevaluation had already been sown in the conflicted policy discourse on community college, but the sociopolitical and economic environment of the 1980s and 1990s was becoming less hospitable to the ethical imperatives of democracy and equality.[101]

2

INSTITUTIONAL AMBIGUITY
Continued Struggles of the Contradictory College

In the wake of the civil rights movement in America, many radical thinkers sought to critically analyze the rhetoric and policy of early junior college leaders to ascertain the true mission of this institution in light of America's professed ideals of democracy and equality. A band of New Left critics exposed the hypocrisy of junior college leaders and pointed out the many educational failures of a beleaguered, second-rate institution of higher education. The community college was once assumed to be the people's college, but critics pointed out that this institution rarely served the interests of the people. It especially did not serve nonwhite minorities and the poor who more often than not earned second-class educations in underfunded and underresourced urban institutions. The New Left critics of the 1970s and 1980s exposed the underside of the community college and opened up a new critical discourse that focused on the failures of this newly legitimated institution, and thereby put the community college and its leaders on the defensive. In the wake of this critical development, community college leaders, scholars, and the policy community have tried to understand the predicament of the community college in more empirical detail to reengineer a renewed vision of the open-door community college for the 21st century. Consensus over a revised orthodoxy for the community college has not yet been reached. Criticisms still abound. The prospects of the community college and its mission remain clouded by contention and doubt. To be sure, this institution has earned a permanent place in state systems of higher education and regional labor markets, but whether this institution serves the ends of democratic opportunity, social efficiency, or capitalist accommodation (or some measure of all three) is still widely debated and will continue to be debated for the foreseeable future.

A Critique of Orthodoxy: The New Left Evaluates
Community Colleges, 1970s–1980s

Many political critics and social scientists were animated by the civil rights and countercultural movements of the 1960s. An ethos of romanticism, critical bravado, and utopianism pervaded not only popular social movements, but also scholarly circles—especially those of historians and social scientists. The New Left became the political moniker of a diverse group of neoprogressive and quasi-Marxist political activists who were antagonistic toward the sociopolitical status quo and who were seeking to foment social change however possible.[1] Many participants in the New Left during the 1960s used the New Left ideological frame of reference during the 1970s to critique education and schooling in the United States, often pointing out how education was nothing more than the social reproduction of an inequitable, class-based society.[2]

Burton R. Clark's cooling-out thesis was famously extended by leftist critics many times over during the 1970s and 1980s. The basic argument, as Fred L. Pincus explained, was that community colleges "did more to reproduce class and race inequality than to provide meaningful avenues of upward mobility." Community colleges were the lowest track in a hierarchically arranged system of higher education, and lower-class students were structurally herded into subpar institutions of not-so-higher education. New Left critics also pointed to the capitalist environment surrounding community colleges, which structured an inequitable and competitive labor market that forced lower-class students into vocational programs and poorly paid jobs. Critics have argued that community colleges should challenge inequitable capitalist relations in several ways. They wanted this institution to empower lower-class students by teaching a broad set of technical skills and laying a critical foundation in the liberal arts, as well as establish relationships with unions and politically progressive community groups to promote democratic participation and social equality. In many ways the New Left critique expanded the democratic-oriented rhetoric of Bouge and Gleazer because it focused more on the underprivileged classes that had been excluded from American society and educational institutions.[3]

L. Steven Zwerling wrote one of the first extended New Left monographs criticizing the community college in 1976. He argued that the "people's colleges do not serve the people" because they were embedded in an inequitable class structure, and they had the "hidden social function" of reproducing a hierarchical social order. He also argued that community colleges were second-best institutions of higher education that systematically denied working-class students a quality education while they also lowered student aspirations through a cooling-out process that encouraged students to take their place in the "lower ranks of the industrial and commercial hierarchy." Zwerling also made more deterministic arguments, somewhat in contradiction to earlier claims, by stating that all schools in the United States were "instruments of social and political control" that consciously socialize students into a particular class. He also argued that high rates of student attrition at community colleges were "one of the two-year colleges' primary social functions." Zwerling wanted his book to expose the "deceitful, manipulated reality" of the community college that was "rigged" in many ways against lower-class students. He thought that community college students could be taught the truth about their situation, which might empower them to demand community colleges be reformed. Ultimately Zwerling wanted to foment change in the community college so that it could be remade as a more progressive institution and, thereby, help to "provoke a reformation of society."[4]

Howard B. London conducted the first ethnographic study of the culture of community colleges in the mid-1970s. His account delivered a veiled yet trenchant critique of community college students and faculty as half-conscious and limited agents. In the constraining environment of the community college, students and faculty structured self-defeating rituals of defensive resistance: absenteeism, limited effort, and cheating on the part of students, lowered academic standards and demoralized resignation on the part of faculty. Through subtle hostility and resignation, students and faculty "ensur[ed] the very defeat they wished to avoid." As one student described it:

> In a way it's puzzling, because we're here to get a better job, to make something of ourselves, but we put down the school and stay away from it. This teacher gives you a lot of reading and writing to do and immediately you're pissed off. . . . It's biting the hand that can feed you. You'd think people would try harder, but they don't and that's bad for them, for me, for anybody.

London's study revealed antagonistic relationships that defined the interactions of students and faculty and thereby limited any possibility of true education from taking place. As one student explained, "I think it's because people have a need to pull other[s] down to their level. Working-class people are notorious for this. . . . the students may resent the teachers because the teachers represent education and intellect."

London critiqued Clark's cooling-out thesis as superficial and "distorted" because Clark did not actually observe firsthand how the students internalized their scholastic failure. Quoting German sociologist Max Weber, London argued that the process was much more an "inarticulate half-consciousness" on the part of students and faculty. Both parties were trapped in a struggle over identity, aspirations, and social class, and both parties were constrained and defeated by the institutional parameters of the community college. London took his conception of educational struggle from Willard Waller's classic 1932 study *The Sociology of Teaching*. In this famous work Waller argued that American schools were "despotic political structures" where students were "subordinated" to "autocratic" authority figures, such as teachers and administrators. Waller argued that schooling was in a constant state of "perilous equilibrium" wherein "conflict groups" played out their roles of authority and resistance to authority in an uneasy yet ritualized politics of "ever-fickle equilibrium." London used Waller's conceptual insight to expose the conflicted terrain inside community colleges, which undercut and defeated the lofty rhetoric surrounding this institution.[5]

In 1985 Lois Weis reiterated what had become the standard complaint of New Left critics of the community college: These colleges were institutions of social reproduction in a racist and sexist society. But community colleges were not completely determined by the oppressive social structure of U.S. society, as they also sought to embody a democratic ethos that offered increased opportunities for social mobility. Weis's contribution to the critical literature on community colleges was to differentiate the experiences of working-class African Americans who occupied a "caste" distinct from the travails of working-class whites. Weis's ethnographic study of the African American cultural experience of community colleges explored how racialized and class-bound students could "embrace and reject schooling at one and the same time." Weis also pointed out that while community colleges might help individuals escape the chains of underclass life, "the group can never follow," thus, "the college cannot possibly work for blacks as a collectivity." Therefore, Weis looked beyond the myth of an enlightened faculty, and she argued for a modest program of teaching students and faculty about their position in a racialized and classed society.[6]

Fred L. Pincus took community colleges to task for their growing emphasis on vocational education. He saw the vocationalization of community colleges as part of an institutionalized tracking system that was being erected to divert community college students to lower-status occupations in an inequitably stratified and class-bound society. He also criticized institutional collusion with corporations in the form of customized contract training. This training included community colleges offering tailored employee training to local businesses. Pincus did not believe the notion that everybody benefits when community colleges serve local industries, and he argued that not all parties necessarily gained from contract training. Corporations were able to get cost-effective training services, and community colleges were able to bring in new sources of revenue and enrollments, but the benefits to students and to the society at large were more ambiguous. Contract training represented a larger "drift toward narrow vocationalism at the expense of critical thinking and broad-based knowledge," which gave students employable skills in the short term but put them at a disadvantage in the long term by reducing the chance of further economic mobility through higher levels of degree attainment. Pincus argued that institutions of higher education should have broader goals than simply putting students to work with "just enough technical skills and 'positive' attitudes so that the corporation can operate at a profit." For Pincus, contract training represented the abdication of educational ideals and the renunciation of liberal curricular principles. Community colleges were already not helping many students attain bachelor's degrees. About 15 to 25 percent of community college students transferred to a 4-year school, but overall only 10 to 15 percent of these students would earn bachelor's degrees. Pincus argued that the new trend toward increased contract training would only further reduce the chances of students' push for upward economic mobility.[7]

The most acclaimed and sophisticated work of New Left criticism came in 1989. Steven Brint and Jerome Karabel wrote *The Diverted Dream: Community Colleges and the Promise of Educational Opportunity in America, 1900–1985*. In this book they argued that the educational system in the United States had always been "hierarchically differentiated" because it was "closely linked" to the capitalist labor market and to the inequitable class structure of American society. But they also stressed the fact that the American educational system was a relatively open and democratic structure, especially in the 20th century. Most Americans viewed education in America as a ladder of opportunity for upward economic mobility. Thus the institution of community colleges was defined paradoxically in relation to the broader contradictions of American society. The community college embodied an egalitarian promise, but at the same time it also reflected the constraints of the capitalist economic system in which it was embedded. The United States was an optimistic society that generated more ambition than it could structurally satisfy, which created a need for elaborate and often hidden tracking systems to channel students into occupationally appropriate avenues, largely based on their socioeconomic origins.

From its beginnings the community college had the contradictory function of opening higher education to larger numbers of students from all socioeconomic backgrounds, while supporting a highly stratified economic and educational system that created a need to select and sort students. This cooling-out function, or *the diversion effect*, caused ever-increasing numbers of lower-socioeconomic-status students in higher education to be diverted into more modest positions at the lower end of the labor market. Burton Clark once admitted that "for large numbers failure is inevitable and *structured* [italics in original]." Brint and Karabel argued that not only do community colleges help "transmit inequalities" through their sorting function, but they also "contribute to the legitimization of these inequalities." This institution helps legitimize inequality by uncritically parroting meritocratic rhetoric that often blames the victim for failing to succeed in a structurally rigged class system. Brint and Karabel forcefully argued,

> The very real contribution that the community college has made to the expansion of opportunities for some individuals does not, however, mean that its *aggregate* [italics in original] effect has been a democratizing one. On the contrary, the two-year institution has accentuated rather than reduced existing patterns of social inequality.[8]

Brint and Karabel focused specifically on the increased vocationalization of the community college as it developed over the course of the 20th century, which often disproportionately affected the poor, the working class, immigrants, and ethnic/racialized minorities. The secondary school curriculum became more vocationally oriented in the early 20th century, and early junior college leaders sought to carve out a distinct educational niche for their institution by providing postsecondary occupational certification for regional labor markets. However, it is unclear if early vocational programs were able to place their students into skilled work because of the lack of any type of evidence to prove such a claim. Many scholars have pointed out that the majority of junior college students during the first half of the 20th century resisted terminal programs and sought instead an undergraduate academic curriculum that would allow them to transfer to a 4-year university. Part of this resistance was because the majority of students who enrolled in junior colleges were high school graduates who wanted to earn a bachelor's degree, while the more occupationally inclined either dropped out of high school early to get a job or waited until earning their high school diploma to enter the workforce. Yet the point of Brint and Karabel and others remains substantial. Junior college leaders in conjunction with community business leaders did actively try to manipulate student aspirations by engineering more and more terminal programs. They also encouraged this route more passively by neglecting a pedagogically appropriate curriculum and adequate student support services geared toward less academically prepared students who tended to either drop out or would settle for a terminal occupational certificate. During the 1970s, up to 75 percent of low-achieving students dropped out during their 1st year in urban community colleges. Critics also pointed out that it was not an accident that the lowest-achieving students in secondary and postsecondary schools have historically been, and continue to be, the economically disadvantaged, ethnic/racialized minorities, immigrants, the disabled, and dislocated low-skilled workers.[9]

At the beginning of the 1990s, several mainstream academics justified the basic outline of the New Left critique of community colleges. In their comprehensive review of the literature on how college affects students, Ernest T. Pascarella and Patrick T. Terenzini argued, "There is reasonably strong evidence in support of Clark's argument that community colleges can also function to 'cool out' students' educational aspirations." David F. Labaree concurred. He stated that over the course of the 20th century, the community college had developed a safe, "narrowly defined vocational" niche at the "bottom rung of the status hierarchy in higher education." Community colleges were denied the ability to grant the coveted credential of social mobility, the bachelor's degree, and thus this institution was damned to a "permanently junior status," acting more the role of an "agent of social reproduction rather than a pathway to opportunity." In his analysis, Labaree argued that a close reading of history seemed to support the views of New Left critics such as Brint, Karabel, Pincus, and Zwerling. According to Labaree, the community college was caught in a bind between conflicting democratic and capitalist goals, and "in spite of 'false promises' to provide equal opportunity, the primary function of this institution is to promote the reproduction of social inequality."[10]

Revised but Confused Orthodoxy: The Contradictory Community College's New Missions, 1990s–2000s

From the 1970s into the 21st century the debate over the purposes of the American community college became more diverse and more heated, largely because of the charges of New Left critics. Traditionalist defenders of the community college had a strong reaction. They argued that this institution kept the door open to deserving 2-year graduates so they could transfer to 4-year universities, while offering other less-talented students a route to occupational training and some measure of economic rewards. In the middle of this debate, and at the front lines of the battle for efficiency and equity, marginalized and undertrained community college education professionals have struggled over the last century to find a professional identity. They are caught in the midst of the uncertainty surrounding shifting community college missions. Compounding the confusion further, the parameters of the debate began to perceptively shift by the 1990s as the community college noticeably began to change in response to a postindustrial, globalized U.S. economy. The debate over the diverse mission and coherence of the community college continues unresolved into the 21st century. In fact, the ambiguity of and the conflict over the diverse community college mission seems to have itself become institutionalized, subtly enshrining the institution with a new moniker: the contradictory college.[11]

In the 1990s Arthur M. Cohen and Florence B. Brawer, authors of the most widely read textbook on community colleges, defended this institution against its critics. Cohen and Brawer argued that New Left critics were blinded by ideology. They said these critics were overly focused on the "American social-class system" and "the fanciful dream of class leveling." Cohen and Brawer argued that hierarchical class systems were inevitable, and that educational institutions cannot "break down class distinctions." Thus, they implied, such critics miss the real work that community colleges do in providing equal access to what Cohen and Brawer assumed to be a meritocratic higher educational system. Cohen and Brawer wanted a narrower research focus that would closely appraise the complex work community colleges actually did in the effort to serve a diverse array of individuals who had nowhere else to turn. As Arthur Cohen famously argued, "For most of the community college students, *the choice is not between the community college and a senior residential institution; it is between the local college and nothing* [italics added]." But as one historian of the community college has argued, defenders of the community college status quo have always rationalized the good intentions of the institution by "pointing to the degree of access" it provides students, while ignoring the larger structural constraints that work at counterpurposes to those of the institution and that limit the ability of individuals to gain a measure of educational, social, or economic success. W. Norton Grubb and Marvin Lazerson have argued that community colleges are *both* "egalitarian institutions extending schooling upward for greater numbers of students" as well as "inegalitarian institutions keeping the masses away from the university."[12]

In 1994 Kevin J. Dougherty reexamined the critical debate over the origins, functions, and purposes of the community college to try to resolve scholarly disagreement by focusing on the actual work that community colleges did and the larger social, political, and economic constraints that affected the institution. Dougherty critiqued the three dominant critical schools of thought: functionalist, Marxist, and institutionalist. Functionalist scholars advocated the community college as a democratic educational initiative focused on increased opportunity, meeting the needs of society, and protecting the academic quality of universities. Instrumentalist Marxists have criticized the community college as a capitalist tool that reproduces social and economic inequalities. Institutionalists have also criticized the community college, but instead of focusing on the capitalistic structure of society these scholars focused on the institutional dynamics of the system of higher education and how community colleges serve as a diversion to preserve the academic integrity of universities. Dougherty did not disagree with any of these theories, but he argued that each was limited and flawed in some respects; thus, each offered only a partial explanation of the origins and purposes of the community college.[13]

Dougherty said the community college has been and continues to be a hybrid institution full of contradictory purposes. The community college was constrained by its sociopolitical environment but also exercised some relative autonomy in terms of institutional missions and practice. Dougherty demonstrated that community colleges, while responsive to a wide variety of external influences, were only loosely coupled with social and economic pressures because educational administrators and state officials direct this institution according to their own interests, such as gaining votes, increasing their prestige, or engineering social and educational efficiency. Thus, the performance of community colleges has been only loosely linked to the cultural, political, and economic structure of society, that is, there has been no deliberate conspiracy to keep students from succeeding in higher education and attaining bachelor's degrees. However, Dougherty did make clear that community colleges, as institutions of higher education, were not very good at their job of demonstrating positive student outcomes, especially in helping students earn bachelor's degrees through transferring to 4-year colleges and universities. According to Dougherty, community colleges were not structurally determined institutions designed to cool out students, they were just

inefficient, nonencouraging, antiacademic, low-performing, and overly vocationalized institutions with contradictory goals. This stark judgment moved
community college discourse worlds away from the heady optimism of the
mid-20th century.[14]

The organizational and pedagogical inefficiency of community colleges
was further documented by several scholars in the 1990s. Joanne Cooper and
Ken Kempner demonstrated how fragile and dysfunctional the organizational cultures of community colleges could be, especially with transient
leadership at the top. Cooper and Kempner painted a portrait of bullying
senior faculty, out-of-date curricula, and factional power struggles between
newer and older faculty and between faculty and administrators. In more
than a few community colleges, faculty and administrators were a primary
part of the problem of poor student academic achievement. W. Norton
Grubb and associates conducted a nationwide study specifically focused on
the conditions of teaching in community colleges. Until the late 1990s
almost no empirical investigation of teaching in what was assumed to be a
teaching institution was conducted, let alone empirically based evaluations
of teaching effectiveness. Grubb argued that while teaching was the central
organizational purpose of community colleges, it was often "an isolated and
idiosyncratic activity" that was largely ignored by the institutional culture.
Community colleges, according to Grubb, "have failed to assume much
institutional responsibility for the quality of instruction," and therefore good
teaching in community colleges was "essentially random." In effect community colleges had institutionalized mediocre teaching. Community college
administrators needed to redesign institutional commitments to teaching,
including funding priorities, to create the conditions for more collaborative
and student-centered pedagogies in a reimagined teacher's college, otherwise
the community college's commitment to open access would be reduced to
empty rhetoric.[15]

Of course Grubb's judgment of mediocre teaching was nothing new to
insightful community college instructors. Robert M. Persig reminisced about
his experience as an instructor in a teacher's college in the 1950s:

> At a teaching college you teach and you teach and you teach with no time
> for research, no time for contemplation, no time of participation in outside
> affairs. Just teach and teach and teach until your mind grows dull and your
> creativity vanishes and you become an automaton saying the same dull
> things over and over to endless waves of innocent students who cannot
> understand why you are so dull, lose respect, and fan this disrespect into

the community. The reason you teach and you teach and you teach is that this is a very clever way of running a college on the cheap while giving the false appearance of genuine education.[16]

But missing from Grubb's critique on teaching, and from most critical exposés on community colleges, was a hard look at the community college student. As any community college faculty member can tell you, many students are simply not up to the task of higher education, and these students can frustrate even the best educational intentions and methods. A significant percentage of students in every class refuse to do much at all to better themselves: They regularly miss more than 10 percent of required seat time, they don't read course textbooks, they don't complete homework, they don't participate in class, and they don't ask instructors for help, all the while expecting their lackluster performance will earn them a passing grade by the end of the term. Many faculty, as critics have amply demonstrated, simply lower their standards out of despair, pity, or fear of student evaluations. Students who would fail under the most basic higher education standards are routinely allowed to pass watered-down courses in the community college. Some faculty try to keep some semblance of standards, and they do their best to inspire the unmotivated, but in the end these faculty more often than not are forced to lower the hammer on upward of 50 to 75 percent of students in any given college-level class. One anonymous adjunct faculty described this precarious predicament in *The Atlantic*:

> For I, who teach these low-level, must-pass, no-multiple-choice-test classes, am the one who ultimately delivers the news to those unfit for college: that they lack the most-basic skills and have no sense of the volume of work required; that they are in some cases barely literate; that they are so bereft of schemata, so dispossessed of contexts in which to place newly acquired knowledge, that every bit of information simply raises more questions. They are not ready for high school, some of them, much less for college.
>   I am the man who has to lower the hammer.

The perpetual challenge of the community college instructor is trying to deliver some semblance of higher education to a student population whose members can barely read, refuse to do homework, and do not understand the value of learning. It is an almost impossible task under the best of circumstances.[17]

But there is also substantial evidence that community colleges, independent of student characteristics, reduce the ability of students to earn a baccalaureate degree by about 15 to 20 percent. According to data gathered in the

1990s, community college students who were able to attain a baccalaureate degree were more than twice as likely as 4-year students to take more than 6 years to degree. But there was positive news: Students who were able to successfully transfer to a 4-year institution seemed to be at no disadvantage and were just as likely as 4-year students to graduate, aspire to graduate school, and attend graduate school. However, successful transfer students were more likely to be young, white, male; academically prepared in high school; continuously enrolled; to have high degree expectations; and to come from families in high socioeconomic brackets. These "traditional" students represented 56 percent of successful transfers who obtained a bachelor's degree in the 1990s, but very few community college students in the United States have many of these characteristics. There was also evidence that community colleges did cool out and lower the educational aspirations of students when compared to students in 4-year institutions. However, when community college students were compared to students with no postsecondary education, it seemed that community colleges did in fact have a positive warming effect, which raised the educational aspirations of students with no previous postsecondary futures.[18]

Other voices in the 1990s were much less critical of the community college. Some focused less on the academic shortcomings of this institution and more on its idealistic goal of being open to the needs of the community. Marlene Griffith and Ann Connor reiterated Gleazer's call for a more community-oriented college. Griffith and Connor claimed, "The public comprehensive community college is committed to serving *all* segments of its community [italics added]." These defenders of the community college were worried that the open door was beginning to close. They saw the comprehensive missions of the community college as competing with each other. They saw new restrictions on enrollment through tests and tuition increases. And they saw a diminishing of the educational opportunities available to the community. Griffith and Connor wanted a renewed commitment to the community college as a teacher's college focused on the learning and diverse needs of its unique students. They wanted a renewed commitment to the community college as an institution responsive to the "economic and social realities of their communities." Above all Griffith and Connor wanted community colleges to strive after "lofty and idealistic" missions, such as upholding the tradition of democracy's college, while also keeping flexible and in tune with the real needs of the local community. But the central claims of Griffith and Connor sink beneath their idealistic rhetoric as a testament to the ebullient optimism and naive myths of traditional community college boosterism that has been constant since the mid-20th century.[19]

John E. Roueche, Lynn Sullivan Taber, and Suanne D. Roueche also argued for a more community-oriented college. Roueche et al. interviewed the CEOs of 14 community colleges across the United States and Canada to survey how specific colleges were trying to become more responsive to local, regional, national, and even international communities.[20] Taber argued that while the idea of a community-based college has been widely discussed, there had been no "consistent vocabulary," nor had there been any empirical reports on specific community outreach programs or successful practices. Taber also explained how many community colleges in the 1980s and 1990s were balancing the trade-offs of trying to find funding for community outreach programs and trying to cut back on resources without losing community support. There were no easy answers as the community-oriented college tried to be all things to all people, but Roueche et al. did put forth a plan whereby community colleges could strike a balance between multiple partnerships. They reframed the community college mission in terms of multiple, overlapping fields of development: economic development, community development, people development, organizational development, and resource development. And they stressed that in an environment of reduced state resources, solidifying multiple, mutual relationships within the community could help foster a foundation for renewed legitimacy and collaborative funding.[21] But other scholars, such as John S. Levin and John D. Dennison, warned that community colleges might be more concerned with institutional legitimacy and political stability, thereby using a community orientation to become "less for the community" and more for the "social organizations in the community."[22] Levin and Dennison noted that the new social functions of the community college were less concerned with community needs than with institutional survival.

Part of the inherent contradiction of the community college has been the fact that this institution has never known organizational stability because of its high degree of community and labor market responsiveness. According to John S. Levin, the community college continually revises its "ever-expanding" mission in an attempt to "be all things to all people." Economic and political developments in the 1980s and 1990s pushed many community colleges away from comprehensiveness and back toward the terminal vocational emphasis of the early junior college leaders. A new era of constrained resources, combined with legislative calls for economic development and institutional accountability, helped move the community college to reduce its long emphasis on liberal arts education and community services to develop a new vocationalism, which supposedly would integrate the various goals of regional economic development, workforce training, and semiprofessional education. Thomas R. Bailey and Irina E. Averianova argued that the comprehensive mission of the community college had been downgraded as career education and the "entrepreneurial college" became the "only viable core function for most community colleges."[23]

But John S. Levin went further. He argued that the community college acquired yet another new institutional mission, even though many administrators and faculty were not yet fully conscious of this change. Despite the transfer mission's remaining a primary emphasis for most community colleges throughout the 20th century,[24] the constant management and change of institutional purposes by community college leaders, the business community, and state officials have remained intense. Over the last couple of decades community colleges in the United States and Canada, with the support of government and corporate policies, have taken a more corporate and businesslike approach to education. Community colleges have become focused more on money and less on educational objectives. As a result these institutions have shifted the curricular focus toward competitive, workplace skills (learning for the sole purpose of earning) to meet what business leaders and eager-to-please administrators considered to be workforce needs. John S. Levin and D. Franklin Ayers, among others, have demonstrated how many community colleges have "altered their role from a social to an economic agency," and have evolved into a new vocational institution: the *nouveau* college.[25]

Community college administrators have increasingly adopted an ideological stance of neoliberal corporatism over the past couple of decades, which has directed them to focus on efficiency, productivity, marketplace needs, and economic ends, making educational institutions homogenized and education programs commodified and vocationalized. Education has been reduced to occupational training and marketable skills. John Levin argued that by the end of the 20th century community colleges had become different institutions with an altered identity and mission. The educational endeavor of community colleges has become primarily a capitalistic enterprise. "A globally competitive environment, economic in nature and capitalistic in ideology" has "opened the doors to more business-oriented practices and a corporate style of management." Levin concluded, "The former mission of community colleges, while vibrant in rhetoric, was becoming obsolete."[26]

One specific indicator of the re-visioning of community colleges in terms of economic development was the growth in contract training as an important resource-generating community college function. Contract training developed as a priority during the 1990s as many business enterprises incorporated new technology into the marketplace and demanded an increasing level of skills from employees. By the early 1990s over 90 percent of community colleges in the United States were offering contract training. The increase in this particular workforce development activity was driven partly by a growing need for alternative sources of funding and increased student enrollments, partly by a desire to raise the responsiveness of colleges to community needs, partly because of attempts to strengthen local prestige and political support for community colleges, and partly by new demands from government agents, community college associations, and businesses for state-sponsored human capital development. The long-term impact of increased contract training remains unclear, but community colleges have been able to raise revenues and student enrollments while gaining more support from the community, businesses, and the state. Contract training, however, may have some unintended consequences: There seems to be a growing divide between credit and noncredit courses, which makes it difficult for students to continue their education and apply contract training courses toward degree programs. Additionally, a general eroding of institutional commitment to the traditional curriculum seems to be occurring, as new monies are increasingly being used to invest in resource-generating programs rather than buttress established but resource-starved areas such as liberal arts.[27]

Global responsiveness and the new vocationalism have been perhaps the most dramatic new trends among community colleges, but they have not been the only new institutional missions developed during the 1990s.[28] In the two decades following the dramatic events of the late 1960s, several socio-political grassroots mobilizations for minority civil rights, immigration reform, and cultural diversity coalesced by the mid-1980s into a broad social and academic movement for political pluralism, equal rights for all people, and multiculturalism. This movement sparked a wide debate over national identity in the late 1980s and throughout the 1990s, which many came to call a "cultural war."[29] In 1993 James Valadez argued that many community college students, especially nonwhite minorities, first-generation students, and immigrants, lacked the "cultural capital" to succeed in institutions of higher education in the United States. Valadez explained that there were many unstated "linguistic codes" and "cultural competencies" that helped facilitate student success in college. Many students also brought cultural resources and competencies that were not always "recognized or valued by the institution," and these cultural resources became a liability that impeded students from succeeding in the institution. Valadez argued that the accepted and taken-for-granted institutional functions often acted as barriers to many students who needed "a system of emotional as well as academic support," not only to help them succeed in the institution but also to help mediate and overcome the educational failures they experienced from previous schooling.[30]

In the 1990s many scholars employed the theory and politics of multiculturalism to investigate current educational practices and the future possibilities of community colleges. Multiculturalists argued that this institution had come to serve a very diverse student population, thus, it must not only respect but also celebrate the cultural differences of its students and the local community. Community colleges needed to engage students holistically in a learning process that empowers students to become "full participants in both education and social life." This included a broader view of vocational education that would combine technical training and an education in democracy that could be used to help workers barter for better wages and working conditions. Some critical multiculturalists carried this project further by arguing that community colleges should also teach students to criticize the inequitable power relations and social hierarchies that control knowledge production, cultural transmission, and social identities. This critical pedagogy, developing political and social insights by writers of the New Left, sought to teach students to develop a critical consciousness to raise self-esteem, encourage motivation, and ultimately empower students to take charge of their own future.[31]

Perhaps the most exciting trend, but very frightening to many traditionalists, has been the move toward making community colleges baccalaureate-degree-granting institutions. This movement could potentially redefine the whole identity of the institution. Discussions of community colleges' granting bachelor's degrees began in the 1980s, but only a few states had actually developed these degree programs by the 1990s. The rhetoric surrounding this new programming articulated a move not to change the previous missions of the open-door comprehensive community college but to add an additional mission that had the potential to alleviate some of the continued inequality in community college students' ability to successfully transfer to 4-year institutions to earn a bachelor's degree. Theoretically, with baccalaureate degree programs on the community college campus, many of the roadblocks to transferring would be removed because students could stay at a local low-cost institution near supportive networks of family, friends, and employers. This would naturally increase the chances of many students who would otherwise never attain a bachelor's degree. Some have also framed this new mission in neoliberal rhetoric, arguing that better-educated local workforces can meet the specific needs of regional labor markets.

Some critics, however, have warned that developing baccalaureate degree programs might overshadow the established missions of the comprehensive community college and threaten open-door policies. These critics have pointed to a few former community colleges that used baccalaureate degree programs as a vehicle to transform into 4-year state colleges. But this debate is still young and has more questions than answers at this point. As of 2000 only 57 community colleges in the United States had developed these degree programs, prompting the Carnegie Foundation for the Advancement of Teaching to brand these institutions as baccalaureate/associate's colleges. Offering bachelor's degrees at community colleges will potentially increase community college students' access to these degrees; however, these degrees have been so far offered primarily in vocational/technical fields such as nursing, which is a high-demand field with currency in local labor markets. Extending the baccalaureate to arts and sciences would take a restructuring of the faculty and curricular apparatus to hire more highly trained PhDs to create 4-year academic programs. This would most likely create a greater rift between remedial and college-level faculty and programs. And awarding liberal arts bachelor's degrees could potentially flood local markets with devalued credentials from already stigmatized second-class institutions at the bottom rung of the higher education hierarchy. Holding a community college bachelor's degree might turn out to be nothing more than a second-class credential, much like the associate's degree, which would invariably be downgraded in the public's eye to a third-rate credential or worse.[32]

By the late 1990s and early 21st century, it became increasingly clear that community colleges had comprehensive missions, multiple organizational ideologies, divisive organizational cultures, and an extremely diverse student population. The 21st-century community college is not an easy institution to define, let alone govern. Over the past decade many scholars have argued that community colleges needed to embrace organizational multiplicity. In coming to terms with the conflicting nature of such a comprehensive institutional structure, scholars have fruitfully applied the insights of postmodernism. Many have conceptualized the community college as a cultural text with a multiplicity of interpretations. Kathleen Shaw has not only researched the complex and fluid multiple identities of community college students, but she has also studied political and organizational ideologies, in particular organizational cultures and their effects on specific academic programs. In one study, Shaw investigated remedial education programs as an "ideological battleground," whereby larger political debates over the nature and purpose of higher education interacted with district-level policy and organizational cultures. She explored how larger political ideologies and district policies have been mediated by the local organizational culture and were either reinforced or resisted through formal and informal educational practices. In another study, Shaw and Howard B. London argued, "Ideology and culture are seldom monolithic. It is far more likely for an institution to have internal factions that emphasize or contest different aspects of its culture."[33] Thus, community college policy, institutional missions, and educational programming should be seen as pluralistic and divisive political processes in which different parties struggle over the definition and control of organizational identities, purposes, and practices. Community college administrators are not really leaders who plan and initiate change, rather they are mediators (often with their own interests) caught between warring factions, trying to negotiate institutional policy and disciplinary practice.[34]

In taking stock of the conflicted diversity of the community college in the 21st century, Thomas Bailey and Vanessa Smith Morest were able to briefly summarize the predicament of this contradictory public institution of higher education:

> Community colleges face an especially difficult task. They enroll those students who have the most daunting educational, economic, and social barriers to their education, yet they have the fewest resources per student to serve those students . . . . At the same time, as public institutions, they are asked to carry out a variety of different functions, some of which conflict with their access and equity missions.

Smith Morest argued that the public community college was so overloaded with diverse missions that "it is impossible to do any of them well." While Bailey and Smith Morest noted the rise in vocational enrollments and the increase of contract training and continuing education programs, Smith Morest argued that community colleges were still committed to traditional academic and vocational programs.[35]

Increasingly, however, these traditional programs have taken on new hybrid forms. One example is vocational-transfer programs in traditional vocational areas that used to result in terminal certificates or an associate's degree, such as nursing or electrical engineering. Now these programs are geared toward creating pathways to baccalaureate attainment at 4-year institutions. But Smith Morest noted that a serious conflict may be arising between credit programs, academic and vocational, and noncredit programs, mainly vocational. This potential conflict, she explained, could create "a new schism" between credit and noncredit programming by segregating working adult students into noncredit training programs. Many scholars, including Bailey, Bragg, Smith Morest, Grubb, and Lazerson, have all argued that community colleges need to somehow find ways to integrate their diverse institutional missions into a coherent vision for education. But to do this successfully, community colleges would need broad financial support from state policy makers who would need to create a comprehensive policy to promote educational equity and give community colleges the resources to create a coherent, comprehensive mission that can fully meet the plethora of state and local needs. While money is not a sufficient cause of institutional integration and efficiency, it is a necessary component.[36]

But state support has been steadily waning over the past several decades, and it has dramatically decreased because of the Great Recession of 2007–2009. Amid recent calls for increased institutional efficiency of community colleges, many believe the older rhetoric of democracy and educational opportunity may be eroding. The tuition costs of community colleges have increased considerably over the past 20 years while state government funding of higher education has decreased. Thus, students bear much more of the financial burden to finance their education. In 2001 the average cost of tuition and fees for a full-time community college student was $1,705 per year, plus books, transportation, living expenses, and the opportunity costs of forgone wages, which can make a community college education prohibitively expensive to many low-income students. The financial burden is even greater for low-income students who need remedial education because it takes these students more time to obtain a certificate or degree. About 42 percent of first-year students need at least one remedial education course, and 60 percent of students in remedial courses are African American and Latino/Latina students. A recent study of Los Angeles community college students found that students who needed the most remediation spent up to 5 years in the community college, and those who successfully transferred to a 4-year institution spent up to 3 more years earning their bachelor's degree.[37]

So those students with the most need have to pay the greatest personal cost. For underprivileged students, the cost in time, tuition, and foregone earnings is greater than it is for the more academically prepared and socio-economically privileged. Lower-class students have also lately been penalized with less financial aid, meaning they have to take on more student loans, which will take a significant and often crippling percentage of their future income. Also, the evidence continues to show that upper-middle-class community college students are much more likely to successfully transfer to 4-year institutions. Because of a growing influx of middle-, upper-middle-, and upper-class students to community colleges because of the lack of space at overcrowded universities, this trend could have the potential to displace current resources that support lower-class and at-risk students. [38]

However, in the face of fiscal constraints, state policy makers have lately ignored issues of decreased opportunity and educational inequality. Instead, a national discourse of institutional effectiveness has swept the nation. Alicia C. Dowd has argued for a broad coalition of community college professionals, activists, and academic researchers to resist the totalizing logic of this new effectiveness discourse to engage in a political dialogue. Dowd argues the effectiveness discourse can oversimplify the complexity and diversity of the community college, and it can also displace larger sociopolitical issues. Dowd argues that previous policies focused on the democratization of higher education and increased educational access should not be displaced by new institutional efficiency concerns. While institutional efficiency measures can strengthen pedagogical practice, Dowd wants policy makers to also align the community college with the larger issues of "reducing social and economic inequality and strengthening democratic processes."[39]

But beyond the more idealistic claims for equal access to higher education and the strengthening of democracy, many practical issues are still unresolved. The whole notion of increased efficiency becomes a problem because this particular institution may have a serious design flaw. What happens to the majority of community college students who never transfer to a 4-year institution and obtain a bachelor's degree? Is the terminal, vocational mission of the community college of any benefit to those students who will only graduate with an associate's degree or vocational certificate, or does the 21st-century community college remain a holding pen for the masses of "young idle youth" who cannot find adequate employment in the constricted labor market, and who are being subtly encouraged in the open-door college to take whatever jobs might be readily available? Does the community college actually help students gain well-paid employment, or are community college credentials merely devalued commodities in a discriminatory labor market?

Are There Economic Returns to Community College Credentials? An Economic Assessment, 1990–2010

Wrapped in the broader debate over the competing missions of the community college is the assumption that any amount of certified education increases an individual's social mobility and economic welfare. But does a community college credential actually produce solid economic returns for students? At the core of recent calls for institutional assessments of the community college is the unquestioned assumption that community colleges adequately serve the majority of students who do not transfer to 4-year institutions and earn bachelor's degrees. But what if community colleges, as Brint and Karabel argued two decades ago, structure the failure of even successful community college students because of the degraded value of subbaccalaureate degrees in a highly inequitable and discriminatory labor market?[40]

Reviewing 20 years of research from the 1970s and 1980s, Ernest T. Pascarella and Patrick T. Terenzini revealed that not much was known about this issue. In the 1980s W. Norton Grubb noted that based on the available research, subbaccalaureate vocational programs "do not confer on students the labor market advantage that is their principle reason for being," although "there is some evidence of successful programs." He also noted that secondary-level vocational programs are "uniformly negative" in their effects, while the outcomes of community colleges, based on the very limited available evidence, are decidedly mixed. Grubb also pointed out that vocational guidance in secondary and postsecondary schooling is also "not particularly effective" in helping students train for and make the transition into midskilled jobs because vocational guidance involves the impossible feat of "occupational forecasting." Grubb's conclusion: Vocational programs are highly overrated, are ideologically motivated, have few positive effects, and they are "successful only under special circumstances." Despite the lack of efficiency or success, vocational education programs and vocationalism has gained enormous influence because of the institutional and political power of its defenders.[41]

By the 1990s Pascarella and Terenzini reported an increase in research on the economic returns to subbaccalaureate education. Several important research papers and literature reviews in the mid-1990s were more optimistic than Grubb but certainly revealed decidedly mixed results for economic returns to subbaccalaureate education. Kevin J. Dougherty reviewed the limited research on subbaccalaureate degrees and credentials and found the evidence troubling. He argued that the evidence on whether a community college education delivers increased earnings compared to a high school diploma was "quite mixed," and at best subbaccalaureate education gave graduates a "very slight edge." But in some studies there was contrary evidence that community college students actually did worse economically than workers with only a high school diploma. Whitaker and Pascarella found that subbaccalaureate education led to a "significantly lower occupational status" and lower earnings than a bachelor's degree, and these authors recommended community colleges only as a stepping-stone to a 4-year baccalaureate-granting institution. Stern et al. found some evidence of increased earnings for those with an associate's degree, but the earnings seemed to decline over the course of a worker's lifetime, and the value of the associate's degree might be more of a reflection of personal characteristics than the degree itself since associate's degree earners tended to come from "more educated or affluent families than those who completed high school only." Overall the results were "divergent," and Stern et al. warned that one could not make any generalizations about the monetary effects of subbaccalaureate education. But based on the evidence, and controlling for personal characteristics, Stern et al. estimated the value of an associate's degree was between $1,000 and $2,000 a year more than a high school diploma for people between the ages of 24 and 32, and that the earnings differential was greatest for women with a vocational degree while almost nil for males.[42]

Grubb conducted the first comprehensive scholarly attempt to find solid evidence on the midskilled or subbaccalaureate labor market to evaluate the claims about education's economic returns, especially for midskilled workers who in the early 1990s constituted the majority of the workforce, 60 percent of all employed workers. Grubb researched specific occupations in four midskilled labor markets at the local level. He found that the subbaccalaureate labor market is mostly a "local phenomenon" with the parameters of the market determined by the vagaries of the business cycle. A subbaccalaureate worker is not very mobile in job searching, most likely tied to a specific locality, and any vocational credentials earned will have their highest currency in the local labor market where the community college or technical school is known.[43]

A few important characteristics of the subbaccalaureate labor market affect student transitions from school to work, one being the large number of small businesses and firms in this market. These firms hire few workers and offer smaller salaries and less opportunity for advancement than larger firms. These small firms are not well informed about educated labor supplies; they are not often tied to or communicate with local educational institutions;

and they usually have informal hiring practices; which makes it difficult to prepare students for interviews or specific job related skills. Smaller firms also tend to be more dependent on flexible and multiskilled employees because short-handed firms often blur occupational boundaries to get the job done cheaply and with fewer resources. Another characteristic of the midskilled labor market is the highly cyclical nature of market demand. This creates unstable employment opportunities, which in turn increases informal hiring policies, which then makes it difficult for job seekers and administrators of vocational programs to determine exactly what local employers want and when they want it. Because of the inefficiency of the subbaccalaureate market, it is very difficult for educational institutions to know, let alone teach, the skills employers want. And further, Grubb pointed out that because of the blurring of occupational boundaries and the flexible nature of smaller firms, "most of the competencies required by employers in the sub-baccalaureate labor market *cannot* readily be taught in schools and colleges."[44]

Based on the available evidence, Grubb was very clear in pointing out that community colleges can "*under the right conditions* [italics in original] provide students with substantial benefits." But under suboptimal conditions community colleges "may benefit not at all." Specifically Grubb pointed out that the benefits of a community college are maximized if students can enroll in economically viable occupations and find related employment in the local labor market, but this is rarely the case because community colleges tend to be isolated islands disconnected from other educational institutions and the labor market.[45]

Grubb also investigated the value of short-term job training programs often offered by community colleges through federal and state contracts, although they are also offered by a host of other ad hoc institutions supported by government contracts. Since the 1960s short-term job training programs have increased in size and purpose. Grubb sought to evaluate the outcomes of these programs to determine if they were successes or failures in their goals of employment gains, increased annual earnings, and reduction of welfare payments. Overall Grubb found these programs lead to "small but statistically significant increases in employment and earnings and (for welfare recipients) small decreases in welfare payments." Grubb pointed out that "the social benefits usually (but not always) outweigh the costs" (meaning that programs make financial sense in terms of cost-benefit analysis). However, he argued that the personal benefit to individuals is "quite small from a practical standpoint," and any gains are not only "insufficient to move individuals out of poverty or off welfare," but gains also disappear over time. Grubb argued that the modest and trivial gains of job training are not impressive and, further, populations of enrollees such as youths and welfare recipients see negative results, calling into question the overall effectiveness of job training programs for everyone. Grubb also criticized these programs as "too short, too focused on immediate employment rather than on the enhancement of skills, unaware of pedagogical issues, and independent of related efforts." Grubb argued that short-term job training disconnected from mainstream educational institutions and programs seem to be "push[ing] individuals into the labor force without increasing their skills substantially," which can hurt individuals in the long run in access to future education or in finding good careers with the possibility of advancement. He argued that more "*sustained* [italics in original] interventions are necessary to improve the life chances of low-income individuals."[46] Here was Grubb's conclusion:

> The results from nearly thirty years of evaluating job training programs are remarkably consistent—surprisingly so, given the variation in the programs supported and the differences in the methods used to evaluate them. Many job training programs lead to increased earnings, and the benefits to society generally outweigh the costs. However, the increases in earnings, moderate by almost any standards, are insufficient to lift those enrolled in such programs out of poverty. Welfare-to-work programs also increase employment and reduce the amount of welfare payments received, but they rarely allow individuals to leave welfare. Furthermore, any benefits probably fade after four or five years: job training programs do not seem to put many individuals on career trajectories with continued earnings increases, as formal schooling does.[47]

Grubb's recommendation was not to abandon second-chance job training programs but to better coordinate and integrate these programs with mainstream educational institutions, like community colleges, that offer degree programs. Thus, short-term job training programs could be used as a vehicle to attract a significant source of government funds and as the first stage in a coordinated pipeline to longer-term educational goals. However, this idealized educational pipeline rarely becomes reality for most students in these types of programs.[48]

A couple of publications from 1998 to 2001 reached some positive conclusions about the economic returns of subbaccalaureate education in the form of associate's degrees and community college vocational certificates. A collection of studies by Sanchez and Laanan and another study by Grubb revealed some evidence of significant returns for the associate's degree and the vocational certificate. But several studies in the anthology by Sanchez and Laanan seemed to overstate these returns by not properly filtering out several key variables, such as the personal characteristics of students (which can skew actual worth of the credential) and using students' last year in college as the baseline for income comparisons (which can skew actual earnings data because many students are not working full-time while in college). Also, the positive earnings data presented by Sanchez and Laanan seem to be highly dependent on different regional and state economies, which makes national generalizations on earnings potential for subbaccalaureate credentials a problem, but this issue is not adequately discussed.[49]

In the late 1990s Michael B. Paulsen reviewed the literature on the returns of investment in subbaccalaureate credentials, and he found the student populations of subbaccalaureate institutions, largely community colleges and 2-year technical institutes, skewed the labor market value of this type of education and make estimates very "problematic." According to Paulsen, the average community college student who has never attended a 4-year institution and who doesn't even earn a degree sees earnings of about 9 percent to 13 percent greater than a high school graduate with similar background characteristics and no college. One year of community college credit, independent of earning a degree, can lead to an average in increased earnings between 5 percent and 8 percent, and 2 years of credit can lead to 10 percent to 16 percent increased earnings. The effect of a subbaccalaureate education, either a credential or an associate's degree, can lead to earnings increases between 15 percent and 27 percent. The average earning potential is greatest for women and low-income students, but there is evidence to suggest that the average earnings increases for subbaccalaureate credentials may be greatly affected by the significant earning potentials from an associate's degree in nursing.[50]

Other recent analyses of subbaccalaureate credentials are less optimistic than Paulsen's. Kienzl echoed Grubb's conclusions and found that "the economic benefits to a sub-baccalaureate education are unclear or ambiguous" and that a bachelor's degree "remains the most economically beneficial" educational credential. Economic data further corroborate these general, more pessimistic, findings. From 1973 to 2005 in constant 2005 U.S. dollars the real hourly wage for an average worker with only a high school education has decreased from $14.39 to $14.14 an hour, while the real hourly wage for an average worker with some college but less than a bachelor's degree increased slightly (less than 0.1 percent) from $15.50 to $15.89 an hour. Mishel, Bernstein, and Allegretto argued that the policy of educating low-skilled workers and making them midskilled workers "does not make sense" because "we have too many middle-skilled workers already." Further, they said,

> Given that the wages of entry-level college workers and those of all college graduates have declined or been flat over this business cycle, a strategy of vastly increasing the number of college graduates seems certain to drive down the wages of current and future college graduates. The possibility of increased off-shoring of white-collar work may make such a strategy even more untenable in the future.

Altogether, the economic outlook for the current and future value of subbaccalaureate credentials appears bleak.[51]

In spite of a rhetoric of optimism, the consensus of many scholars on the positive outcomes of vocational education appears to be bleak. Student preparation for and placement in careers have been lauded by all as a noble idea, but there is little evidence over the past century that American schools, especially subbaccalaureate institutions, are particularly successful with these tasks.[52] Indeed, few community colleges have clear and well-developed connections to the labor market, nor do they have a formal understanding of what skills students need, how these skills are measured, and how they should be promoted to future employers.[53] As a result, many subbaccalaureate vocational curricula and short-term job training programs, such as welfare-to-work initiatives, have shown little success in increasing students' employment or earnings. Some scholars have even argued that short-term job training programs can be harmful to certain types of students, decreasing their earnings or welfare support.[54] In sum, little evidence exists to show how well occupational programs prepare students for employment and place them in careers, primarily because few community colleges are able to reliably track students' job placements or advancements. Furthermore, colleges do not yet have a good way of assessing whether vocational programs are teaching students the skills employers want, let alone the lifetime learning skills students need to navigate a rapidly changing American economy.[55]

The subbaccalaureate labor market poses several challenges to developing vocational education and career pathway programs. Employers in this market are frequently small businesses that hire few workers and offer lower salaries and fewer opportunities for advancement than larger organizations.

Furthermore, these small businesses are often not well informed about the supply of educated labor; few are in continuous communication with local community colleges or other educational institutions, and they usually have informal hiring practices, which makes it difficult to prepare students for interviews or specific job-hunting skills. Smaller businesses also tend to be more dependent on flexible and multiskilled employees who can cross occupational boundaries to accomplish a job cheaply and with fewer resources. As such, many "of the competencies required by employers in the sub-baccalaureate labor market cannot readily be taught in schools and colleges."[56]

In addition, the subbaccalaureate labor market is dependent upon the highly cyclical nature of demand. This creates unstable employment opportunities, which in turn increases informal hiring policies, which then makes it difficult for job seekers and vocational programs to determine exactly what local employers want and when they want it. These features of the subbaccalaureate labor market make it difficult for community colleges to determine—let alone teach—the skills employers want and need.[57]

Available data are mixed on how well students make the transition into well-paying jobs in the subbaccalaureate labor market. The benefits of vocational education can be maximized if students can enroll in economically viable occupations related to their credentialing, but even then the benefits of vocational credentials are mediated by socioeconomic status, race, gender, and even academic markers such as grades and test scores. And the economic benefits of a vocational degree or certificate decrease the more disconnected community colleges are from regional labor markets and job placement agencies. Overall, the benefits of some college or an associate's degree continue to be unpromising in the United States and may further decrease in value as the number of bachelor's degree holders continues to increase and as the effects of the Great Recession of 2007–2009 run their course.[58]

By the end of 2009 national unemployment rates already exceeded 10 percent, although this number hides recurrent racial disparities, as 16 percent of African Americans were out of work (with over 18% of black men unemployed). The total number of unemployed and underemployed Americans was around 17.5 percent. These numbers also mask the many state and regional variations in the U.S. labor market. By August 2009 California had already exceeded 12 percent unemployment, with certain regions in the state exceeding 15 percent. The labor market reflects long-term inequalities in American society and there are still deeply entrenched differential employment rates according to race, gender, and age. Earnings differentials were noted in the U.S. Census report "Income, Poverty, and Health Insurance

Coverage in the United States: 2008," but few news organizations bothered to pass much of this information to the American public. One variation that did receive treatment was age. The national unemployment rate for teenagers reached 25.5 percent in September 2009, the highest rate it had ever been since collection of this data began in 1948. Inflation-adjusted median household income in 2008 had fallen around 3.6 percent, reducing middle-class households to income levels not seen since 1997, and these income levels are expected to drop further by 2010. Latinos saw the greatest reduction in income at 5.6 percent (to $37,913), then Asians at 4.4 percent (to $65,637), African Americans at 2.8 percent (to $34,218), and whites only lost 2.6 percent (to $55,530). Clearly widespread inequality in incomes remains a problem, with the average African American family earning 38 percent less than the average white family. An additional 2.6 million people also fell into poverty in 2008, with Latinos (23.2 percent in poverty) and African Americans (24.7 percent) still disproportionately impoverished. Most likely these numbers will only get worse in 2010 before they get better.[59]

With the massive economic downturn of the past 2 years, even college graduates have been affected. The hiring of new graduates with a bachelor's degree or higher is expected to fall by 22 percent in 2009. Even students with law degrees from top universities are finding it difficult to find jobs because top law firms are cutting new positions by about 50 percent. With jobs so scarce for new graduates, a new avenue of inequality has come to light. College graduates from wealthy families have begun to pay thousands of dollars to buy their way into unpaid internships via private placement firms.[60]

Human capital in the United States has been greatly devalued because of the growing economic inequality of the past 30 years and the current recessionary period. In these tough economic times, community college credentials and certificates may become almost worthless commodities as the economy has greatly contracted. However, thousands of new students and laid-off workers are seeking refuge in this institution. But budgets of community colleges are being slashed, faculty and staff laid off, new hires frozen, and course offerings trimmed. Miami Dade Community College, to take but one example, has lost 18 percent of its funding from 2006 to 2009, about 11 percent just in 2009, and administrators expect about 30,000 students will not be able to enroll in the classes they need or will be turned away completely because enrollment capacities will be exceeded. The paradoxical predicament of the community college has never been greater than now and its future never more uncertain.[61]

President Obama has pledged $12 billion over the next decade to increase community college graduation rates in order to meet the needs of the midskilled labor market, but questions remain.[62] Will this money really be allocated by an overextended federal government dealing with a lingering recession, an astronomical federal deficit, and major health care reform? How will this money be allocated? And with the cutbacks of the last few years, do community colleges have the capacity and resources to meet the growing numbers of students they are expected to serve? And when the president pledges to increase the number of Americans with college degrees, does this generalized pledge simply mean more community college associate's degrees and certificates in a labor market flooded with underemployed and underpaid Americans with bachelor's and advanced degrees?

The uncertainty clouding the American economy has again revealed the contradictions at the heart of the community college and its place in American society. There are no easy answers to any of these questions, and the time has come to admit this hard fundamental truth. If this institution is going to live up to its promise as a gateway to opportunity then its missions will need to be *clarified* through some sort of national consensus of policy makers and practitioners, *unified* through local and regional organizational planning, and *resourced* through increased federal and state fiscal commitments. However, the institutionalized stickiness of the comprehensive and contradictory community college has made it extremely resistant to change.[63] Educational reformers, policy makers, and even administrators often appear as no more than ceremonial figures presiding over a loosely coupled educational institution that seems locked into an incoherent future.[64] Still, faith in the "politics of agency"[65] may yet work wonders, as educators and administrators act on the conviction that the community college can be refashioned into a more equitable and efficient institution of higher education. Modern humanity is defined by such faith: that we can better rationalize and organize social institutions to achieve our ideals. Thus, in the words of a preeminent political philosopher, "We can only do what we can: but that we must do, against difficulties."[66]

3

OVERBURDENED AND UNDERFUNDED

The California Community College

D uring the early 20th century many of the first junior colleges in the United States emerged in the state of California. By 1960 California had the first fully articulated state system of higher education in the nation, and the newly christened community college served as the foundation of this system. In 2006 California had over 109 community colleges and more than 2.5 million students enrolled in the largest community college system in the world. California also pioneered evaluation of institutions of higher education, and it was the first state to implement a statewide accountability system for community colleges. The current national debate over the performance of the community college also surfaced in California before most other states. California has long been a trendsetter in higher education across the nation and the world.

Community colleges in California are being criticized today for many reasons but mostly for poor student achievement. Because students are not succeeding, the community college is being blamed for failing to meet the competitive needs of state and national economies, as well as the personal needs of students. These accusations are beginning to be made in many other states as well. To understand the validity of these criticisms, it would be instructive to study the historical evolution of community colleges in the state of California to better understand the issues this institution has faced as it evolved into its present form. But it is also important to understand how this institution was historically embedded, and thus constrained, within three larger social structures: a hierarchically tiered system of higher education, a racially segregated society, and a fiscally strained state. California has always been a bellwether of national trends in higher education, so examining the history of the community college in California can be instructive for the nation at large.

While some historical work has been carried out on K–12 public schools and higher education in California,[1] no extended study has been conducted of California community colleges.[2] In fact, few historical studies of any state community college system or individual community college are available. While California community colleges have been given the most attention in the limited historical work available, the work to date has focused mostly on the first half of the 20th century. It has not touched on the issue of social and educational segregation in the state, nor has it explored the extended battle for state funding and the rising movement for institutional evaluation. This chapter fills in the gaps by addressing these important issues.

The main argument of this chapter is threefold. First, California community colleges have historically been managed institutions beholden to the interests of university officials, state legislators, and public school administrators who used them as a filtering-out mechanism.[3] Second, Californian society, labor markets, and public schools have been highly segregated for most of the state's history. Charles M. Wollenberg has argued that "California's long history of school segregation and exclusion has been virtually ignored by educators and historians, let alone politicians and the general public," but California is not the only northern or western state to ignore its past of segregation and racial prejudice.[4] Community colleges in California were institutionalized and embedded in an economically and racially stratified society. For most of the 20th century the community college's primary goal was to send lower-achieving and lower-class high school graduates into the unskilled or midskilled labor market. Finally, community colleges have never been given adequate financial resources to accomplish their myriad missions as set forth in the Master Plan and its successive revisions. But this financially constrained institution has been at the forefront of calls for institutional efficiency in higher education. The California community college was designed as an inefficient and underfunded filtering mechanism for a hierarchically tiered system of higher education. This faulty design was copied across the nation. But if the community college in California and the nation at large is to overcome this legacy, then policy makers and education professionals must engage in a full reckoning of the past, creating the necessary conditions for a re-visioned institutional future. It is possible to reconstitute the community college as a more equitable and efficient institution. However, the history of the California community college is more of a cautionary tale rather than a blueprint for reform, so hopefully other states can avoid the same fate.

Origins of the California Junior College

William Rainey Harper, the first president and central organizing force of the University of Chicago, not only had a hand in creating the first junior college in Illinois, Joliet Junior College, but he also played some part in establishing junior colleges in California. It seems that he shared his ideas on the reorganization of higher education with his colleagues David Starr Jordan, president of Stanford College; Benjamin Ide Wheeler, president of the University of California, Berkeley; and Alexis Lange, professor and dean of the School of Education at Berkeley. Jordan and Lange were very excited about Harper's ideas, including the one for a junior college and a more selective university, but Lange in particular would be referred to as the father of the California junior college movement. At the turn of the 20th century, high schools in California had been offering a college preparatory curriculum accredited by officials from the University of California. The ideas and influence of Jordan and Wheeler were primarily transferred through Professor Lange who worked with California State Senator Anthony Caminetti on Senate Bill 528 in 1907. This piece of legislation formally allowed California high schools not just to prepare students for college but also to offer a junior college curriculum that was the equivalent of first- and second-year undergraduate courses at the University of California.[5]

Between 1907 and 1921 the first community college system in the United States was formed in California with a total of 18 junior colleges, articulation agreements with the major state universities, and a secure source of funding from the state legislature based on average daily attendance. In 1910 Fresno was the first city in California to officially open a six-year high school with an annexed junior college, offering courses in an undergraduate transfer curriculum and a vocationally oriented curriculum under "Agriculture, Manual, and Domestic Arts, and other technical work." Over the next 10 years 17 more junior colleges sprang up: Santa Barbara and Hollywood in 1911, Los Angeles in 1912, Fullerton and Bakersfield in 1913, and by 1920 there were colleges in Azusa, Gilroy, Modesto, Riverside, Rocklin, Sacramento, Salina, San Diego, San José, Santa Ana, Santa Maria, and Santa Rosa.

In 1910 college officials began to award the junior college certificate, which would later become known as the associate of arts degree. This credential allowed any high school student automatic admission to the University of California as a junior. An early bill was proposed in 1909 to set aside state funds for annexed junior colleges, but it was vetoed by the governor. In 1917 the state legislature passed the Ballard Act, the first bill in the country to officially set aside state and county funds for public junior colleges. In 1921 the legislature passed the Junior College Act to create a permanent Junior College Fund to further support these fledgling institutions, annually allotting $2,000 to each junior college district and $1,600 to each individual junior college, plus $90 for each unit of average daily attendance during the school year. On top of these state funds, junior colleges could obtain additional financial support from junior college district taxes, high school taxes, and fees for nonresident students.[6]

California was the first state in the nation to offer government support to junior colleges, and it is perhaps this financial and political support, in conjunction with active university leadership, that provided such fertile ground for the development of America's first community college system. But, of course, one must keep in mind that California already had an established state system of higher education, the University of California, which was unprecedented in its autonomy and support from the state because of a provision in the revised state constitution of 1879. By 1905 the University of California had already set up matriculation agreements with several normal schools and private colleges. By 1919 California had the first multicampus university system in the United States with the incorporation of the Los Angeles Teachers College, which became the University of California, Los Angeles. And by 1920 all the public State Normal Schools had been rechristened by the state board of education as State Teachers Colleges, which later became the California State University system. The growing number of junior colleges only added to what was by 1920 the most comprehensive and coherent system of public higher education in the United States. For the first half of the 20th century California maintained the largest college attendance rate in the nation, although the lower tiers of the system absorbed most of this growth. By 1930 the junior colleges became the primary point of entry for all first-year students to higher education in California. By 1940 there were 49 public and 15 private junior colleges in California with 72,198 students enrolled in public institutions and 1,480 in private institutions.[7]

But it is important to remember that junior colleges had an ambiguous institutional identity until the 1930s and 1940s. Until this point, most junior colleges were physically housed on high school campuses. Chafee Junior College in Riverside County was an exception, as its administrators were able to secure separate facilities early in the 1920s. Some junior colleges operated in shared facilities on state college campuses, but junior college and senior college student populations were largely kept separate. The institutional flux of San Diego Junior College is a perfect example of the ambiguous identity of these early schools. San Diego Junior College was formed in 1920 and it operated out of San Diego High School. In the mid-1930s the junior college moved from the high school to share space at San Diego State College; however, the junior college classes and instructors were still financed by the city public school system. In 1937 adult education junior college courses were organized by the Department of Adult Education of the city public schools, which operated as a distinct administrative unit. In 1938 a separate campus was created for the junior college vocational programs and adult education, but academic programs were still housed on the state college campus. It took several more years before the academic programs were brought over to this new facility and San Diego Junior College became a fully equipped and autonomous educational organization.[8]

Wheeler and Lange saw community colleges as a way to expand access to postsecondary education in California, especially to outlying areas of the state that were far away from the university centers at Palo Alto, Berkeley, and, later, Los Angeles. But the junior college was also a way to keep universities selective and specifically focused on research and advanced disciplinary training. University of California President Robert Gordon Sproul believed that the university should only serve "the important groups in the commonwealth."[9] At the same time, junior colleges could be a vehicle to direct and divert some students toward the semiskilled labor needs of the state and local economies. These university leaders envisioned a state system of education in which vocational training would be offered in high schools and the new junior colleges, while advanced professional training would be reserved for the university. By the 1930s, junior colleges across the state began to supplement predominantly academic curricula with terminal technical and vocational programs. This vision of the junior college was embraced not only by presidents and professors from the University of California and Stanford University but also by junior college administrators across the state. California had the largest collection of junior colleges of any state in America until the 1930s. California junior college leaders also established themselves early as the heart and soul of the national junior college movement, proving to be the junior college's most vocal supporters.[10]

Alexis Lange and his colleague Robert J. Leonard, professor of vocational education at the University of California, Berkeley, along with Edwin R. Snyder, the first California commissioner of vocational education, lobbied the State Board of Education to expand vocational education in public high schools and the new junior colleges. Jordan believed the university was only for "exceptional students."[11] Lange was also quite clear about who should and should not attain a university education. He argued in 1918 that the junior colleges should "turn many away from the university into vocations."[12] At a meeting of the California Teachers Association in 1916 Lange claimed, "The mass of high school graduates cannot, will not, should not become University students." They should instead attend junior colleges and earn a terminal certificate in "general or specifically vocational" education.[13] In 1936 Robert Gordon Sproul, president of the University of California, explained that the university was only for those students who were "capable of carrying on university work" and that the remainder of the aspiring, yet "incapable," California population would be "den[ied] admission." Sproul justified this arrangement by arguing that state educational officials had a duty to "send their students forth into life, each securely established on his proper level."[14]

By the 1930s junior college leaders in California had become focused on vocational programming, partly out of ideological reasons to formulate socially efficient school systems, and partly out of practical reasons, as the majority of junior college students in the state did not seem to be transferring. William W. Ferrier reported in 1937 that "approximately three fourths of the pupils have not gone after graduation to institutions of higher learning." Ferrier also argued that junior college students were "as a rule not particularly interested in the more abstract phases of the regular academic program."[15] In 1938 Merton E. Hill conducted a statewide survey of California junior colleges and argued, "As nearly eighty per cent of the junior college students will probably not go on to college, it is evident that the institutions are performing very creditably their assigned functions."[16] Despite such low transfer rates, the majority of junior college students entered this institution with the goal of obtaining a university degree, which created an often competing focus between students and administrators: Students sought out the academic transfer curriculum, yet university and junior college leaders promoted the vocational curriculum.[17]

While the junior college seemed to offer democratic equality and meritocratic opportunity to new generations of high school graduates, it also structured a socially efficient and hierarchically tiered system of higher education that would constrain the social mobility of lower-class, nonwhite, and immigrant students. Thus, the junior college in California was placed at the bottom of the hierarchy. Junior college leaders wanted to use this institution to allow expanded access to postsecondary education, while also structurally limit that education to terminal-vocational pursuits. However, students taking progressive social-democratic rhetoric seriously wanted to exploit the junior college as a vehicle for social mobility and access to a baccalaureate degree. It seems clear that the democratic rhetoric of many progressive educational leaders in California was often deflated by their elitist and hierarchically structured vision for public schooling.[18]

Massification of Higher Education and Postwar Planning

Between 1920 and 1960, California established new junior colleges at the rate of almost two a year. Growth in junior college student enrollments started to drastically increase in the 1930s and continued to grow over the next three decades. In 1937 there were 62 junior colleges in California, 41 public and 21 private, and total enrollments exceeded 37,500 students. In 1947 enrollments in junior colleges were up to more than 61,400 students. By 1965 there were 65 public junior college districts, 77 junior colleges, and more than half a million students. Junior college enrollments outpaced that of state teachers colleges and the University of California. Between 1935 and 1947 public and private junior colleges were enrolling between 33 percent and 38 percent of all postsecondary students in California, more than any other higher education sector. From 1948 to 1959, junior college enrollments grew 80 percent, while the University of California saw little growth at all. Yet skyrocketing enrollment at junior colleges was part of the plan for higher education in the state. William W. Ferrier reported in 1937,

> There is a rapidly growing sentiment throughout the country that the changed and changing economic and social conditions will call for the retention of all our young people in school to a later age than heretofore, and the signs are that the junior college, especially the public junior college, will be held to be largely the place for that added training.

Student enrollments dramatically exploded in the postwar period because of the influx of returning veterans, the GI Bill that pulled them out of the labor market and into postsecondary institutions, and the economic growth and prosperity of the 1950s. By 1955 California junior colleges were enrolling about 72 percent of all the first- and second-year undergraduates in the state who were attending public institutions.[19]

Part of this increased enrollment in junior colleges at midcentury was because of the transformation of adult education in the state. Traditionally public schools supervised adult education programs, often organized as night classes. These programs focused on parent education, academic courses, vocational education, and Americanization programs to teach English and citizenship. In the 1950s the California junior colleges began to encroach on adult education in the community, partly because of the expanded funding possibilities of categorical per-pupil state funds set aside for adult education programs. Junior colleges began to develop adult education divisions to serve the defined adult populations, which kept adult students and traditional students in separate curricula. This created some administrative confusion as adult education programs were duplicated in junior colleges and public K–12 schools.

In the 1950s the State Advisory Committee on Adult Education tried to coordinate adult education programs. This body published a guiding principles policy framework in 1961, but the issue was never fully resolved because of the decreasing traditional student population enrolling in junior colleges. By the 1960s the term *adult* was used "primarily for record-keeping purposes." The State Board of Education and the state legislature wanted to reduce spending on categorically defined adult education programs, which were largely noncredit community services, while trying not to penalize older students in college credit programs. An adult was defined as any student over 21 years of age enrolled in fewer than 10 units, and the state funded these students at a lower rate than traditional college students, but a growing population of adult students were enrolled full-time in academic classes.

By the 1970s almost all community college students were defined as adult students, which was simply "a person nineteen years or older not concurrently enrolled in high school." Thus, the differential funding division in community colleges became credit or noncredit courses, not age. In the 1970s many community colleges assumed sole jurisdiction over adult education programs, but some communities' public schools continued offering adult education programs as well. However, the adult education terrain become increasingly complicated with the proliferation of nonprofit and for-profit adult basic education programs. These adult programs expanded during the mid-1970s and 1980s because of increased federal funding that was often linked to economic development policies.[20]

Until the 1960s junior colleges had been designed to serve high school students and traditional college students and became the primary point of entry for most traditional-age college students entering postsecondary education in the state. To understand why the junior college became a more central feature of the emerging higher education system in California, it is important to understand the control state legislative authorities had over educational budgets, and the control state university leaders had over institutional legitimacy and standards. The not-so-hidden hand of these groups was present throughout the formative stages of the junior college in California.

As far back as 1921 the legislature called for the "scattering of the students in their earlier years" to junior colleges and normal schools to save money for the more important work being done in the "high-grade university." In 1931 the state legislature gave the governor the power to hire an educational research foundation to study postsecondary education in the state and make recommendations for a plan to efficiently organize a statewide system of postsecondary institutions. The Carnegie Foundation for the Advancement of Teaching formed a commission of seven members led by Henry Suzzalo. The Suzzalo Report was presented to the state legislature in 1933, marking one of the first attempts by an American state to rationally organize a tiered system of higher education.[21] This report argued that junior colleges should assume the base of the emerging system of higher education, training students for semiprofessional and vocational work, while the highly selective University of California would be the crowning apex of the system. Legislative and professional oversight over the junior college had always been geared toward the priorities of the university, and this arrangement would later be consecrated in one of the most important higher education policy documents of the 20th century. The policy structure designed in the 1930s and consecrated in the 1960s came to be known around the world as the California model, which was later emulated around the country.[22]

A movement in national educational policy circles during the postwar period sought to link academic achievement to national economic development and promote national security and U.S. power in the face of international competition with the USSR during the Cold War. In the face of external economic geopolitical competition, consolidation of national resources and cultural values became very important. There was a great effort to solidify national values and develop human capital through state systems of education, especially higher education. These goals became a policy priority, as noted in such influential reports as the Truman Commission's *Democracy and Higher Education* (1947), James B. Conant's *Education in a Divided World* (1948) and *Education and Liberty* (1953), Eisenhower's Committee on Education Beyond the High School reports (1956, 1957), the National Education Association's *Higher Education in a Decade of Decision* (1957), and Hyman Rickover's *Education and Freedom* (1959). In this atmosphere California legislators, policy makers, and university officials planned for the expansion of the state system of higher education under the twin banners of meritocracy and national economic development, all the while assuming these two principles were synonymous.[23]

The Suzzalo Report led to further initiatives that attempted to create a coherent and coordinated higher education policy for California. *A Report of a Survey of the Needs of California in Higher Education* was compiled in 1947 by the Committee on the Conduct of the Study of Higher Education in California. This committee had been appointed by the governor and approved by the state legislature in Assembly Bill 2273. This report became known as the Strayer Report, after the chair of the committee, George D. Strayer, professor emeritus at Teachers College at Columbia University. The report identified the future higher education needs of the California population and offered a plan to unify the five public sectors of postsecondary education in the state into one coordinated system: adult education programs, junior colleges, teachers colleges, state colleges, and the University of California. *Coordination* became a political buzzword for University of California officials and state legislators who were concerned about the growing competition between these sectors for public money.[24]

The Strayer Report acknowledged the lowly status of junior colleges in the state and how some Californians viewed them as inferior to state colleges and the University of California. The report largely agreed with this view and stated that the junior college was essentially "a secondary school with special functions to perform." The report also criticized junior college faculty as a status-hungry group that aspired to be college professors and who wanted to see the junior college set apart from secondary schools as an institution of higher education. The Strayer Report cautiously warned that junior college faculty should not be so ambitious. Committees investigated the conditions of two of the larger junior colleges in the state and concluded that to become actual institutions of higher education, junior colleges would have "to be provided not only with additional apparatus, library facilities, and equipment, but with more capable faculty members." According to the report, to equip junior colleges to conduct actual college-level work above the nominally equivalent first 2 undergraduate years would be an overwhelming financial burden on the state. Thus, the report recommended that junior colleges should keep their first- and second-year undergraduate transfer programs but urged state policy makers to emphasize the "unique function" of the junior college, which was to "provide semi-professional and vocational education."[25]

The Suzzalo and Strayer reports envisioned the junior college as a lesser postsecondary institution that was to be structurally limited by a narrow set of institutional goals and reduced state funding. The Strayer Report forecasted that junior colleges should enroll about 37 percent of all postsecondary students in the state and remain the largest sector of the higher education system. However, while junior colleges were expected to enroll the largest percentage of students, the report also recommended they receive the lowest funding per student: $83.48 per student less than that of the state college sector and $388.47 per student less than that of the University of California. From the start, junior colleges in California were *third class institutions* of higher education merely supporting the advanced work being done by *real* colleges and universities in the state.[26]

And as semi-higher institutions junior colleges were managerially treated like K–12 schools. For the better part of a century, the California junior college was institutionally measured and evaluated by state and university officials. In 1938 Merton E. Hill published the first comprehensive statewide institutional evaluation of junior colleges, *The Functioning of the California Public Junior College*, sponsored and published by the University of California, Berkeley. Sproul argued in the foreword that the "pioneer era of the junior college" was ending and a new era of scientific management with controlled experiments and facts was being inaugurated. Thus, university officials in conjunction with junior college presidents would use this new knowledge to rationally determine the appropriate "methods of differentiating abilities," so that postsecondary institutions could be efficiently managed to meet "the needs of the student and of society."[27]

Hill documented, analyzed, and evaluated the California junior college, which he called a semi-higher institution. The majority of Hill's report is descriptive, as it focused on the individual curriculum, missions, and organization of the 42 public junior colleges in the state. But Hill also provided some statewide data on junior college enrollments, grade point averages, transfer rates, and some data that can be used to estimate persistence rates. In the fall of 1937 roughly 16 percent of the high school population in California was going on to higher education. Eleven percent of high school students enrolled in junior colleges. The 42 state junior colleges enrolled more first-time students (17,941) than the University of California (4,304) and the seven state colleges (3,260) combined. While there were 17,941 first-time students, there were only 9,302 sophomores, which meant that an estimated 48 percent (8,611) of California junior college students either transferred or dropped out during their 1st year of college. This number is roughly consistent with a national study in 1937 of over 15,500 students in 25 universities in which more than 50 percent of the students dropped out or transferred between entering the university and finishing the sophomore year.[28]

But the evidence indicates that from 1935 to 1937 only about 1,864 students on average transferred to one of the two campuses of the University of California. These two campuses were the primary 4-year institutions where a student could earn a bachelor's degree during the 1930s, although there were also seven public state colleges (converted from normal schools) and two highly regarded private universities, University of Southern California and Stanford University. If the 48 percent attrition rate held roughly constant from 1935 to 1937, this would mean that at least 22 percent or more of this population was successfully transferring to 4-year colleges and universities, which is consistent with data presented by Walter Crosby Eells who computed a transfer rate between 20 and 25 percent. But when the number of transfer students is divided by the total student population for 1937, only about 7 percent or slightly more of all first- and second-year students transferred during these years.[29]

It is clear from Hill's data that transfer students to the University of California had been steadily increasing from 1919 (64 total transfers) to 1937 (1,996 total transfers). But if you consider that the state went from 18 junior colleges in 1920 with total student enrollment about 1,500, to 42 junior colleges in 1937 with total student enrollments near 29,000, then the total yearly transfer rate probably never exceeded 10 percent of all students. Hill, however, put the total transfer number at about 20 percent a year, which can be deduced from a statement in his report that "nearly eighty percent of the junior college students will probably not go on to college." This percentage is roughly equivalent to the high school graduation rates between 1910 and 1930, which hovered between 13 to 15 percent. But once junior college students successfully transferred, they still had trouble completing the requirements for a bachelor's degree. According to Hill, from 1921 to 1935, only 63 percent of junior college transfer students at the University of California earned a bachelor's degree. If these university persistence rates were constant for other 4-year colleges and universities in the state, this would mean that less than 13 percent of all California junior college students were able to earn a bachelor's degree from 1921 to 1935.[30]

Another important empirical report on the California junior college was written by Burton R. Clark during the 1950s. He conducted the first in-depth institutional assessment of an individual junior college—San José Junior College. His relatively small monograph would define junior college policy for over a decade, with ramifications up to the present day, even though his study was limited to a single junior college. Clark was specifically concerned with evaluating the organizational structure of this institution to see if it was managed efficiently and to see if it was producing an adequate level of education that would benefit the students and the state. He was disappointed with what he found. Overall this junior college was operating inefficiently because of a conflict between administrators and students over the purpose of this junior college. Students wanted an academic education that would help them transfer to a 4-year college or university, while the school administrators wanted the institution to focus on terminal vocational programs that would give San José Junior College a unique and rationalized function in the San José metropolitan area. Despite the efforts of administrators and faculty to divert students to vocational programs, the academic transfer curriculum enrolled close to 60 percent of all students in 1953, and this increased to 75 percent by 1956. However, Clark pointed out that the majority of these students were reaching beyond their actual abilities.[31]

Student attrition was severe each year, and most of the students enrolled in the academic transfer curriculum would never transfer or graduate with an associate's degree. From 1953 to 1957 over 30 percent of students on average left the school between fall and spring semesters, while an average of 55 percent of students left between spring semester and the following fall. Out of about 3,700 students who were enrolled in fall of 1953, just over 16 percent were able to earn an associate's degree in 4 years with about 5 percent of students earning associate's degrees each year. About 22 percent of all junior college students in California transferred to 4-year institutions. Clark found that about 25 percent of all enrolled students from San José Junior College were able to transfer, and they typically transferred after enrolling for 2.3 semesters. This particular institution lost on average about 85 percent of its students each year, but only about 25 percent of these departures were transfer students and/or graduates with an associate's degree. This meant that about 50 to 60 percent of students each year from 1953 to 1957 were noncompleters. They either dropped out, or perhaps they dropped out and later returned. This led Clark to argue that the majority of junior college students, regardless of their aspirations for transferring and earning a bachelor's degree, were actually "latent terminal" students who, in reaching beyond their actual means, were "student[s] who ha[ve] assigned [themselves] to failure." Thus, Clark famously concluded, "The public junior college tends to be a classification and distribution center from which large numbers of students leave education after a relatively short stay. . . . The student who filters out of education while in the junior college appears to be very much what such a college is about."[32]

The push to enact a unified system of higher education led to more policy reports over the next decade. The two most important were *A Re-Study of the Needs of California in Higher Education* (1955) and *A Study of the Need for Additional Centers of Public Higher Education in California* (1957). These reports basically echoed the core sentiments of the Strayer Report. In 1959 representatives from various public and private institutions of higher education in California were brought together to form a master plan for higher education to rationalize the expansion of the state system in the face of "the forthcoming flood of applicants." Clark Kerr, the new president of the University of California, wanted to build on the early policy consensus formed with the postwar planning commission, the 1944 Strayer Report, and the 1955 McConnell Report, all of which had envisioned an important and expanding role for junior colleges as the cornerstone of a newly rationalized and hierarchical system of higher education.[33]

Essentially, the Master Plan Survey Committee, led by Arthur G. Coons, wanted to formalize the recommendations of the earlier reports by creating a higher education planning process to create a single governing body that would efficiently guide the development of the state system of higher education. The result was the 1960 Master Plan for Higher Education in California. This *plan* institutionalized a three-tiered system of higher education with differentiated missions (University of California, California State Colleges, and California Community Colleges), a coordinating council to govern the system, new governing autonomy for the California State Colleges (later renamed California State University), and clear policies for admissions and institutional expansion. The master plan further restricted admission to the University of California branch (from the top 15 percent to the top 12.5 percent of high school graduates) and the California State Colleges branch (from the top 40 percent to the top 33.3 percent of high school graduates). The foundation of the new state system of higher education became the Community College, which would provide open access to all California high school graduates and siphon off a planned 50,000 students eligible to attend the University of California and California State Colleges over the next 15 years. As Clark Kerr paradoxically reasoned in 1978, the master plan promoted "mass and universal access" to higher education, while allowing "the elite sector to become more elite." Kerr explained, "The vast expansion of the community colleges" was designed to be "the first line of defense for the University of California as an institution of international academic renown." By 1966 there were 66 junior college districts with 76 public junior colleges serving about 460,000 students.[34]

Thus, the master plan seemed to support the junior college more as a cooling-out institution rather than one designed to increase access to higher education. In 1960 Burton R. Clark argued that while junior colleges encouraged the aspirations of the multitude, this institution really served the function of cooling out or sidetracking those unpromising students who lacked the social and economic capital to succeed, and transformed aspiring students who wanted to transfer (but lacked the skills, money, or initiative to do so) into terminal students who achieved an alternative occupational credential at the community college. Clark made it clear that the overwhelming majority of students who enter a junior college were "latent terminals" academically unprepared and had unrealistic goals. These students were "funneled" away from successfully finishing an academic transfer curriculum because they did not have the ability to succeed at higher education. Thus, the junior college seemed to have the primary function of filtering out or cooling out overly ambitious college-bound students who have little academic potential. California postsecondary planners seemed to take Clark's conclusions to heart.[35]

In his retrospective policy tract, *Crisis in California Higher Education*, Arthur G. Coons explained the policy community's consensus, which seemed to echo Clark's basic conclusions about the junior college. Coons had been chairman of the California Master Plan Survey Committee from 1959 to 1960, and from 1965 to 1968 he was president of the Coordinating Council for Higher Education in California, the central government agency coordinating the state's higher education system. Coons was quite clear that the master plan called for the diversion of lower-division undergraduates to the junior colleges, "principally freshmen who otherwise might enroll in the State Colleges or the University of California." In 1968 Coons stated that junior colleges were responsible for "80 percent of all lower division students enrolled in the state." Coons was very aware that this meant diverting students, many of whom would have been qualified to enroll in a 4-year college or university, to an institution that was still marked by "the aura of secondary education." To meet the heavy burden placed on this institution, junior colleges were "steadily being cast in collegiate terms," albeit not completely. Coons explained, "Junior college leaders tell me there is still a long way to go to develop adequate external awareness, or the tradition of collegiate life." However, he claimed, "Many of these junior colleges are doing a good job." California junior colleges turned community colleges were doing the best they could in their effort to educate the redirected majority of first- and second-year students in the state. But these institutions were still constricted by inadequate financial support, untrained teachers, and a lack of student services to meet the needs of many underprepared students. Thus, community colleges assumed a lesser-quality curriculum that came closer to secondary education rather than preparing students for higher education.[36]

Segregated Education in California and the Junior College

Junior colleges in California were supposed to be open institutions of higher education for all high school graduates who could benefit from some college-level education. However, it is not clear just how open these institutions were or when they become open to *all* students regardless or sex, race, income, or ability. Nationally, there were some academic requirements on junior colleges from the start. In 1928 Frederick L. Whitney wrote an article on standards and accreditation for junior colleges, and he argued that most junior colleges had clear entrance requirements, which usually meant completion of a good portion of the high school curriculum, although some states had age restrictions or required an exam. Some states had more lenient requirements and permitted specially admitted students.[37] Private junior colleges seemed to have had the most open enrollment policies, probably because they were more dependent upon student tuition. However, some private junior colleges, like the one at the University of Chicago, began to segregate students based on sex. There were also entire sex-segregated institutions, all male or all female. In 1930 there were five male-only private junior colleges in California and two female-only private junior colleges.[38] The California State constitution of 1879 mandated that "no person shall be debarred admission to any of the collegiate departments of the University on account of sex." The University of California was a trendsetter in the nation in coeducation, and most likely all public junior colleges in the state eventually followed suit, but there are no data to verify this.[39]

While some institutions were segregated by gender, it is unclear if California junior colleges were overtly segregated by race. Even if it was not official policy, until the 1960s most states in the United States actively segregated nonwhite students in educational institutions or classrooms from K–12 to higher education.[40] During the late 19th and early 20th centuries northern educational philanthropists and southern educational reformers were in many ways white supremacists who insisted on a second-class education for blacks to restrict them to subordinate roles in local economies. Little is known of segregated junior colleges because early junior college leaders and the AAJC did not keep track of most of these institutions.[41] While the California junior college was open to all high school students in the state regardless of sex, a history of segregation in the state raises questions about how open these institutions were to nonwhite minorities.

The California state constitution officially outlawed slavery in 1849, but laws still prohibited nonwhites from voting, holding office, testifying in court against whites, and forbade mixed marriages and returning fugitive slaves to other states. California's first school laws did not explicitly mention race, probably because few ethnic minorities were in the state during the mid-19th century (mostly Chinese men). But as school systems developed, it was assumed all nonwhites would attend segregated schools. State school laws were amended in 1855 and 1863 to distribute funding primarily to white schools and to prohibit "Negroes, Mongolians and Indians" from attending white public schools. The school laws of 1866 and 1872 sanctioned segregated schooling for nonwhite children, but some communities did not even bother to support nonwhite schools; thus, many nonwhite children were effectively barred from an education. Other communities had small populations of school-age children, and integrated schools became sanctioned by necessity or by choice. However, there was widespread racism among the white population, and according to Roy W. Cloud, even white educators who supported integrated schooling still "for the most part, held to the theory of the inferiority of the colored peoples." The first legal challenge to segregated schooling in California was initiated by African Americans in *Ward v. Flood* in 1874. The California Supreme Court upheld the right of every child, regardless of race, to an education, but it also justified the principle of separate schools in accordance with the Fourteenth Amendment and California law—22 years before the U.S. Supreme Court would make the separate but equal ruling in *Plessy v. Ferguson* (1896).[42]

Challenges to segregation at the local level were much more successful but never complete. In 1875 the school board of San Francisco, the largest city in California with the largest nonwhite minority population, decided to end school segregation but only for black children. San Francisco's ruling marked a statewide turning point that eventually led to an amendment of the state constitution in 1880. According to the amendment, "Schools must be open for the admission of all children," except for "children of filthy or vicious habits, or children suffering from contagious or infectious diseases."[43] But the California Supreme Court still left the option of separate schools that were used to legally segregate Asian, Mexican, and Native American children until the early 20th century.[44] School officials often used citizenship as a means to exclude Asians, Mexicans, and Native Americans because these foreigners were not yet Americanized, a cultural euphemism for an assimilated citizen. But the Americanization process, when it was genuinely offered, meant giving up ethnic cultures, values, and languages to embrace a white supremacist, Anglo-protestant Americanism.[45] Clearly the education available in the late 19th and early 20th century was mostly open to white, middle- to upper-class, native-born children. In 1911 native-born children of native-born fathers (most likely all white) composed only about 42 percent of the children in California public K–8 schools but made up 60 percent of California high school students and 69 percent of California university students.[46]

There were many white supremacist and nativist reactions to the successive waves of immigrants to America, especially Chinese contract workers and later Japanese immigrants. The Chinese Exclusion Act of 1882 passed by Congress was the first restriction on immigration in the United States, and it was extended in 1892, 1902, and indefinitely in 1904. Combined with the Contract Labor Law of 1885, these two acts made Chinese immigration illegal for any purpose. In 1924 the National Origins Act, also called the Johnson-Reed Immigration Act, was signed into law and totally excluded Asian immigrants. This act ensured that America would remain a nation of whites who were of predominantly northwestern European heritage until 1965 when the Hart-Celler Act removed racial quotas.[47]

California led the nation in anti-Asian agitation from the early 20th century until World War II, and many white supremacists in California saw the Japanese in particular as a racially inferior enemy of the United States. Historian Kevin Starr argued that California in the early 20th century conducted its own private war against the Japanese: "The worst possible kind of war, born of fierce racial hatred, uncompromising and annihilating in intent." There was a "fierce and persistent racism of California," and many nativist whites believed that Asians, especially Japanese, represented a Yellow Peril, an encroaching race bent on world domination. At an anti-Japanese rally in 1900, San Francisco mayor James Duval Phelan told the crowd, "These Asiatic laborers will undermine our civilization and we will repeat the terrible experience of Rome." In 1905 the *San Francisco Chronicle* called the Japanese in the state "scum" and "human waste material." In 1906 members of the Anti-Japanese League were able to convince the school board of San Francisco to expel "all Chinese, Japanese, and Korean children" from white schools and to force these students to attend a segregated public school that had been serving San Francisco's Chinese students. Of a public school population of about 25,000 students, fewer than 100 Japanese and Korean students were the target of this decree. Most Japanese parents kept their children at home instead of sending them to the segregated school.

The Keep California White! campaign influenced the California legislature to pass a series of anti-Asian and anti-Japanese laws, including the Alien Land Laws of 1913 and 1920, which made it illegal for Asians to own land in the state. The smaller community of Japanese in Los Angeles did not face as much discrimination as Asians in San Francisco because Los Angeles was much more dependent on nonwhite immigrant agricultural workers, and there were no white unions to be threatened by a nonwhite labor force. Despite less-overt hostility, it was always clear where Asians stood in the racialized hierarchy of segregated Los Angeles. In 1920 one member of the Los Angeles Chamber of Commerce made it clear that Asians were only a contingent labor force: "The question can he be assimilated is beside the mark. We do not want to assimilate him." This hatred of the Japanese combined with the looming war with Japan led to the wholesale roundup of over 120,000 Japanese Americans on the western coast of the United States on March 1, 1942, ordered by U.S. Army General John L. DeWitt. He called Japanese Americans' citizenship a mere "scrap of paper" because he knew, as did a lot of other racist Americans, that "a Jap's a Jap. They are a dangerous element, whether loyal or not."[48]

In one of the most significant milestones for equalized education in California, Mexican Americans won the right to equal, nonsegregated schooling in *Mendez v. Westminster* in 1945. The Mendez ruling was upheld by the 9th Circuit Court of Appeal in 1947, and this ruling would lay the foundation for the eventual repeal of the final segregation laws in the state constitution on June 14, 1974. The practice of de facto segregation, often because of restrictive residential covenants and gerrymandered districts, was not explicitly challenged until the mid-1960s and 1970s, but these challenges did not often change residential patterns.[49] De jure and de facto segregation in residential districts has been a fact of life in California for all nonwhite minorities throughout the 20th century, and even some white minorities have felt the sting of segregation in California, such as the Okies who migrated to California looking for work during the Great Depression.[50] Segregated housing in large urban areas where most minority populations resided led to the creation of de facto segregation in public schooling. This created a system of separate and unequal schooling opportunities that kept many minority students from being prepared for or wanting to enter higher education.

The population of Latino, African American, and Asian minorities in California K–12 schools was low until the 1950s because segregation and discrimination in neighborhoods, public school systems, and labor markets didn't give minority students much incentive to finish high school and enroll in higher education. Throughout the 1950s and 1960s national media began to report more and more on the conditions of segregation in California housing, employment, and schooling. The state National Guard wasn't even completely desegregated until December 1959. There were numerous reports of discrimination and segregation in public housing and private residential communities, and it became a well-established fact that nonwhite minorities in California were often forced to live in urban ghettoes.[51]

In 1950 nonwhite minorities constituted only about 12.3 percent to 13.6 percent of California's total population: 4.4 percent African Americans, 6 percent to 7.2 percent Latinos, and about 2 percent combined for Japanese, Chinese, Filipino, and Native Americans.[52] The majority of these minority populations were concentrated in three urban centers: the San Francisco–Oakland Bay area, the Los Angeles area, and San Diego. The largest minority populations were African American and Latino (mostly Mexican and Mexican American), and these populations were concentrated mostly in the San Francisco–Oakland Bay area (African Americans) and the Los Angeles area (Latinos and African Americans). In these major urban areas nonwhite minorities were socially segregated in ethnic ghettos and forced to work in ethnic labor markets or in servile, low-paid positions in the white labor market.[53] But both populations didn't become large and permanently settled until after World War II in the 1940s and 1950s, as the wartime economy drew large migrations of minority workers to these three regions, especially Oakland and the East Bay area.[54]

Jackie Robinson, the first black professional baseball player to integrate the major leagues, grew up as a second-class citizen of Jim Crow California. Robinson described the strict residential and social segregation in Pasadena in the 1930s saying there were segregated movie theaters, segregated public pools, segregated restaurants, and segregated neighborhoods. The public schools and Pasadena Junior College were the only integrated public institutions. Robinson was able to use his superb athletic ability to earn the respect and admiration of whites at the junior college, but he was an exceptional case.

The evidence available seems to suggest that California junior colleges, like other public institutions of higher education in California, were legally open to both sexes and all ethnic groups. However, junior colleges were often built in segregated school districts and disproportionately served the majority race of the local area. And while these institutions would have mirrored the integration policies of most local high schools, they surely fostered norms of social segregation and curricular segregation by race and sex, determined by the larger social segregation of the local population and regional labor markets.[55]

Little has been written on segregation, social exclusion, and access to higher education in California.[56] Until the 1960s it was not really an issue: Simply no significant numbers of minority students were eligible for higher education in the state, so policy makers and higher education researchers generally ignored the situation. When access to postsecondary education became an important political issue in the mid-to-late 1960s, race was often ignored, or when it was mentioned it was lumped with income, region, and language as a marker of disadvantage. In the 1966 report *California Higher Education and the Disadvantaged*, even as the civil rights movement had become a national policy issue, race is completely ignored: "In recent years concern has now focused on higher education as it is noted that individuals may be denied access to a higher education due perhaps to their physical location, their abilities, or their financial capacity to assume in some instances even a minimal cost for a higher education." The report noted that "these and other problems" caused some students to have "a greater 'disadvantage' to overcome" than other students, and this disadvantage was manifested in financial, geographic, motivational, and academic barriers that keep students from gaining access to higher education. Notice that race, racism, and social segregation are not even mentioned as causes of disadvantagedness.[57]

But while public institutions of higher education in California might have been legally open to all races, segregation and racial discrimination still existed on and off campus. In 1921 the University of California, Berkeley, enrolled Chinese, Japanese, Filipino, and Hindu students who constituted about 3 percent of the student body. However, these students suffered from residential segregation in the larger community.[58] While Japanese were able to attend the University of California, Los Angeles, in the 1930s, the landlords next to Los Angeles State College were turning away students based on race until at least 1964.[59] After the *Brown v. Board of Education* ruling in 1954, the University of California, Los Angeles, Student Legislative Council began reviewing sorority and fraternity charters to eliminate racial restrictions on membership. But rather than submit to this oversight and end segregation, 22 sororities left the council in protest. Similar discrimination was taking place in other fraternities and sororities in the state. For instance, most of the fraternities at Santa Barbara College in the 1950s restricted membership to "Christians of the Caucasian race only."[60] And even though nonwhite students could be integrated into California public schools, there was still racial animosity and discrimination between students on campus. One study of public schools in the Los Angeles area published in 1968 explained how students at school often displayed the prejudices of their parents: "The 'nigger' was constantly used by 'Anglo' students and there were general expressions that indicated that Negroes and Mexican-Americans were felt to be intellectually inferior and primitive."[61] While these racist attitudes would have most likely followed students to college, apparently there was no documented study of the racial climate in institutions of higher education in California until the 1980s.[62] Overt racial discrimination was present in private institutions of higher education up until the 1960s. In 1959 the state superior court upheld the right of the Hollywood Professional School in Los Angeles to deny admission to African Americans. The court ruled that "state anti-discrimination statues were never designed for the purpose of regulating what strictly private groups do."[63]

The placement of junior colleges in a segregated landscape did cause some political controversy once African Americans in the state were able to secure enough political capital after the Watts riot to muster a protest. After the riot public pressure demanded an increase in African American access to higher education in the Los Angeles area, which resulted in a plan to build Southwest College between Watts and Inglewood in the black ghetto of south central Los Angeles. However, many area residents and teachers criticized the placement of the school in a "predominantly negro area" because it would be just "one more racially segregated school" and it would do nothing to challenge the established de facto segregation in housing, schooling, and local labor markets, which were at the root of the Watts riots. Some African American groups in the area were also concerned that Southwest College would be designated a trade-technical college, which would divert students into lower-status occupational programs and away from opportunities at an academic curriculum and from access to 4-year universities. These groups were "unalterably opposed" to such arrangements. Amid such controversy, the construction of the college proceeded and another de facto segregated community college campus was created.[64]

But simply gaining access to and graduating from an institution of higher education, even a prestigious one such as the University of California or Stanford, was no guarantee of a better life if the graduate was not white. The example of the Japanese in the 1920s and 1930s is illustrative of this point. The segregated ethnic economy for Japanese in metropolitan Los Angeles and San Francisco was the primary labor market that hired immigrant Japanese and first-generation Japanese Americans. Until the 1940s first-generation Japanese Americans, the Nisei, could find work only in this segregated labor market because whites would not hire them, even those with college degrees. Many Nisei went from college to working as farm laborers or as clerks in stores. Historian David K. Yoo argued that "not only did higher education not pay in terms of employment, but it actually made the realities of life after graduation more painful because of the raised expectations that schooling fostered." One Nisei in the mid-1920s explained his bitter disappointment with the racist and segregated American society:

In going through high school and college, I can't recall how many times I was cast aside just because I am a Japanese. I was barred from parties, dances, swimming pools, etc. for the same reason previously given. Truly America is for Americans and all other races not given its [*sic*] chance. Pretty soon these other races might be rejected from the supposed-to-be land of the free.

Paul Kusuda was a Nisei in Los Angeles attending Los Angeles City College when he and his family were deported to a Japanese concentration camp in 1942. Experiencing wholesale racial discrimination against Japanese people in America, Kusuda began to question his faith in the American Dream: "Time and time again, I have argued that America is not a democracy for white people only. Was I wrong?" As David K. Yoo summarized the Japanese American experience, and one could argue the experience of most nonwhite Americans in California, "hard work, playing by the rules, and investment in education guaranteed nothing."[65]

The first systematic collection of data on ethnicity and access to institutions of higher education in the state was conducted by the California Higher Education Coordinating Council in 1967, but this study was only focused on access to the University of California system. Researchers found that only 3.6 percent of public high school seniors were African American, but only 1.2 percent were eligible to attend the University of California. The same study found that 8.7 percent of seniors were Latino, but only 3.3 percent were eligible for the University of California. In 1968 John Lombardi, assistant superintendent of the Los Angeles district's college division, criticized junior colleges in the state for not doing more to combat segregation and racial discrimination. Lombardi argued that junior colleges had made "no outstanding improvement in the education of minority students," but he said they had reduced the "grosser forms" of racial discrimination on college campuses. But in 1968, according to *Los Angeles Times* reporter Jack McCurdy, junior colleges in urban California areas were still "mostly *de facto* segregated and are growing more so." McCurdy reported that junior college faculty and administrators were still mostly white, and many junior college physical education teachers and coaches were "almost exclusively white" and hostile to African Americans and integration.[66]

In 1970 the Carnegie Commission on Higher Education published data demonstrating that several U.S. states with the largest community college systems were still highly segregated by race. Ironically, the issue of segregation was not directly discussed in this report, and these data were sequestered in an appendix. Analysis of the data gives some concrete focus to the issues of segregation in community colleges across the United States and specifically in California.

California community colleges were highly segregated in the late 1960s. Between 1960 and 1970 the state as a whole was about 76 percent to 80 percent white, 8 percent to 13.7 percent Latino, 5.6 percent to 7 percent black, 2 percent to 2.8 percent Asian and Pacific Islander, and 0.4 percent American Indian with the majority of the nonwhite populations concentrated around Los Angeles, San Francisco Bay area, San Diego, and Sacramento. Of the 32 large California community colleges with over 5,000 students, 21 of those colleges (66 percent) had white student populations over 85 percent with 12 (37.5 percent) having white student populations over 90 percent. Four of these colleges had a black student population above 25 percent; Compton College had a student population that was 48.9 percent black. One college had a Latino population above 25 percent—East Los Angeles with 40.1 percent. Of the 32 large California community colleges, five (16 percent) had minority student populations between 35.1 percent and 52.7 percent: three in the Los Angeles area (Compton College, East Los Angeles College, and Los Angeles City College) and two in the East Bay area (Merritt College in Oakland and Contra Costa College in San Pablo).[67]

It is quite clear that by the early 1970s California was still highly segregated by race because of its history of de jure segregation and de facto residential and labor market segregation. It is also clear that California public schools, community colleges, and state universities were affected by this legacy of racial discrimination, and many community colleges in particular were still highly segregated by race because of their placement in de facto segregated residential areas.

The history of racism and segregation in California makes the highly influential 1970 Carnegie Commission policy document, *The Open-Door Colleges,* very much a problem especially in relation to California's highly segregated educational system during the 1970s. While the Carnegie commission supported "open access to the 'open-door' college for all high school graduates and otherwise qualified individuals," this policy report did not touch the issue of educational segregation, the inability of many minority students in the country to successfully graduate from high school, and the role that community colleges would play in equalizing access to higher education. This policy report was quite clear on the fact that "the proportion of minority-group students in community colleges (except for Japanese- and Chinese-Americans) falls short of their representation in the youthful population." The report does not, however, discuss how community colleges could help overcome this legacy of disproportional representation. *The Open-Door Colleges* points to the California system of higher education and the California master plan of 1960 as a model for the rest of the country in terms of improving access to higher education. But the Carnegie commission did not come to terms with the unequally structured and highly segregated nature of the California educational system that was really not an adequate model for other states to follow in increasing access to higher education or adequately positioning community colleges as a means of social mobility for economically and racially excluded populations.[68]

But even if community colleges offered an open door to students irrespective of race, these institutions were not able to offer anything more than access. A California postsecondary policy report published in 1968 made it clear that community colleges "have the greatest role to play in providing for higher educational opportunities for the disadvantaged" because they are open-door institutions and tuition free. But it also acknowledged that community colleges have "relatively little financial assistance programs available," limited funds for any special programs, and faculty who "have little time beyond the classroom to develop special efforts for disadvantaged students." Thus, community colleges served the disadvantaged in a laissez-faire way by simply being open institutions that would not bar potential students because of academic preparation, race, or age. Obviously this so-called open door institution could do nothing to compensate for the lingering racial hostility and social segregation in the community at large, and further, because postsecondary education was freely available to all students through the community college, it was easy to blame students for their lack of ability or motivation rather than targeting the social environment for structuring the failure of nonwhite students.[69]

The California Postsecondary Education Commission

The California Postsecondary Education Commission (CPEC) was created by the California legislature in 1973 as a planning and coordinating agency, eventually replacing the Coordinating Council for Higher Education. This commission was also responsible for systematically collecting data on higher education in California to be used as a tool to gauge educational equality goals, following the Civil Rights Commission reports on segregation in California, and the widespread acknowledgment of a gap in access to higher education between white and nonwhite minority groups. The CPEC was responsible for developing an "equitable educational system," and progress toward this goal "would be measured in terms of evidence." As one report noted, "Our intention [is] to measure outcomes as well as opportunities." But the data collected by this agency would gradually be used for different ends by the late 1990s: developing institutional assessment measures on the effectiveness of individual community colleges for accreditation standards, formalizing the curriculum, and ranking individual schools. Reports published by the CPEC demonstrate California's brief and ambivalent concern with educational equity. They also reveal how this ethical issue was displaced by the economics of institutional efficiency and the politics of institutional assessment.[70]

During the 1960s the California legislature became more aware of and concerned with the continuing legacy of segregation and racial exclusion as it affected access to higher education. As a response it formed a Joint Legislative Committee on Higher Education in 1967, which remained active only until 1969. The purpose of this committee was to reexamine the state's master plan not only to evaluate various enrollment and budget targets but also to investigate issues of equity in terms of minority access to postsecondary education. A Joint Committee on Higher Education was formed in March 1971, chaired by assemblyman John Vasconcellos, that pushed for more concrete steps to ensure adequate coordination and policy recommendations for the state postsecondary education system.[71]

The result of these efforts was the CPEC, created in large part because of Vasconcellos's work as a permanent follow-up institution to the Coordinating Council for Higher Education in California. This commission was originally composed of 23 members, 12 from the public and 11 from educational institutions, but it was reduced to 15 members in 1979. The commission responded to legislative directives, convened task forces, developed policy, and tracked educational opportunity. One of the main duties of the CPEC was to create successive 5-year plans for postsecondary institutions to monitor the status of the state system of higher education, including minority enrollments and issues of equitable access.

In 1974 Vasconcellos helped pass Assembly Concurrent Resolution (ACR) 151 that requested the public branches of the state system of higher education to submit educational opportunity plans to the CPEC. These plans were to address the predicament of underrepresented students in the state and how the three branches of higher education were seeking to improve "the educational opportunities for ethnic minorities, women, and low-income students." From 1976 to 1978 these reports all basically reached the same conclusions: No branch had fully complied with ACR 151 in developing and following concrete plans to increase underrepresented students, and there had been a net decrease in the number of Latino and black students enrolled in California public institutions of higher education. The University of California was the only branch of the state's higher education system to create an affirmative action plan and submit it to CPEC by the end of 1978, but no programs had yet been implemented.[72]

Despite an emphasis on equity in the founding of this agency, the CPEC had another policy priority from its inception. In conjunction with the coordinating council, CPEC officials investigated the performance of California community colleges in the 1970s. CPEC's role as an institutional evaluator would come to overshadow its original focus on educational equity. The coordinating council and CPEC published four reports from 1973 to 1974 on the community college collectively titled *Through the Open Door*. The Advisory Committee to the Commission Study of Patterns of Enrollment and Performance in California's Community Colleges was formed in 1975 to analyze the material collected by the Coordinating Council for Higher Education and to make policy recommendations. This committee was composed of mostly community college administrators and trustees and representatives from the University of California and California State University, a community college student, and the community college scholar, Leland L. Medsker, who had served on previous junior college advisory and policy committees in California. The final report was prepared by the CPEC. *Through the Open Door: A Study of Patterns of Enrollment and Performance in California's Community Colleges,* published in 1976, was the most comprehensive institutional evaluation of community colleges in the state since the coordinating council's 1965 report.[73]

Through the Open Door explained how enrollments in California community colleges kept exceeding the projections in the master plan. Total enrollments between 1969 and 1974 had grown from 722,480 to 1,137,668, an increase of 57 percent. Further, the student populations were gradually changing to include more diverse populations: "educationally and economically disadvantaged, the physically handicapped, women reentering postsecondary education, senior citizens, workers needing training for re-licensing, and high school students who can profit from college courses." The ethnic diversity of the study body was also changing. However, even though the CPEC wanted to collect student data on ethnicity, it was prevented by law "to insure that discrimination was not practiced against applicants on the basis of their racial and ethnic backgrounds." The report noted that the number of part-time students was outpacing full-time students, and many part-time students attended on an intermittent basis, sometimes taking a semester or two off before reenrolling. By 1974 part-time students made up half of all students taking college credit courses. This drastic change in student composition was having an effect on the functions of the community colleges, as these institutions began to adjust to the diverse needs of these new students. The report argued, "continuing education for part-time, adult students has become the dominant function of the community colleges," and it claimed "no resultant neglect of the occupational, transfer, and general education functions for more traditional students." Thus, the CPEC recommended community colleges should create more programs and services to meet the needs of these new populations because their primary strength was an "ability to respond individually and collectively to State and local needs for new programs and services relatively quickly."[74]

The report also explained that performance evaluations of the community colleges were difficult because of the "complex nature of the new student clienteles and the idiosyncratic nature of their objectives." In fact, the report criticized community colleges for their "inability to quantify and measure their success." The CPEC argued that traditional measures of grades, grade point averages, transfer students, and awarded degrees and certificates were no longer "appropriate." It said new measures should be found, which would capture the objectives of the new student population and more adequately measure how community colleges were helping students reach those objectives. Early performance measures had not been very informative because they were not completely focused on the institution of the community college. For instance, the majority of community college students did not want to attain the associate's degree, so how was this a valid measure of the institution's success? Another example was measuring transfer students. Most of the studies on transfers had focused on how many students successfully transferred to the University of California or a California State College, and also the kinds of grades students earned in these new institutions. However, while two thirds of the community college student population declared intent to transfer, less than one third would. But no study ever focused on community college academic programs or transfer counseling services, nor did any study ever focus on the community college student population and why so many students failed to reach their stated goal. Likewise, it was known that only about 78 awards were earned per 1,000 community college students in college credit courses, but no study had ever investigated the student populations who earned awards, their intended goals, or why they earned a particular degree or certificate.[75]

A better performance marker to gauge the quality of community colleges themselves was student persistence, especially if broken down by particular types of students. However, this performance marker had not often been used in institutional evaluations of the community college, and there was never any attempt to compare the persistence rates of different types of student populations. This particular report stands out as the first to do so, and the data revealed are illuminating.

The CPEC found that 15 percent of full-time first-year students enrolled in college credit courses stayed for only one semester, 44 percent persisted through two semesters or more, and only 8 percent persisted through six semesters or more. Of those students who persisted more than two semesters, only 17 percent earned an associate's degree or certificate. Interestingly, 16 percent of full-time first-year students in college courses enrolled for more than one term, but they did not stay enrolled continuously. The CPEC also found that part-time students had much lower persistence and award attainment rates. Between 46 and 47 percent of part-time students left after one semester, 24 to 25 percent persisted through two semesters or more, and 5 to 6 percent persisted through six semesters or more. Only 3 percent of part-time students earned an award. The CPEC also found that 18-year-old students persisted longer and earned more awards than older students. It also appeared that many students who left after only one semester were enrolled for occupational purposes. Students who left after at least one semester also had significantly lower grade point averages (2.31) than their peers who persisted (2.73), and they were more likely to withdraw from a class or fail a class.[76]

Traditionally, the most legitimate student performance marker for California community colleges was transfer rates to 4-year universities and colleges. It had always been assumed that the primary function of the community college was and continued to be the transferring of students from the junior college to the university. This performance marker was also assumed to be relatively easy to measure. However, that was not to be the case. The first comprehensive statewide study of community college transfer rates was not conducted until 1979 and published in 1980. But it turned out that this early study was plagued by incoherent institutional definitions of a transfer student, which made it exceedingly difficult to measure this marker of student success. It was also almost impossible to establish some subpopulation of potential transfer students that could be measured against actual transfer students to more accurately compare how well the community college was doing in preparing students for the university. Defining an adequate measure of transfer rates for comparative purposes proved impossible during the 1980s, and researchers are still to this day trying to accomplish this difficult task.[77]

The CPEC did its best to come up with basic measures of this effectiveness marker. It kept a sustained focus on transfers by publishing about 30 reports between 1980 and 2005. In a very blunt and generalized analysis of this data, from 1960 to 1985 a slight but significant trend is clear. If the raw numbers of transfers were divided by the total student population, then the transfer rate went from 3.3 percent of all community college students in 1960 to 5.2 percent in 1985. The total community college population also increased from around 400,000 to over 1 million during this time. The rise in transfers outpaced this general enrollment growth and went from 10,977 transfer students in 1960 to 52,043 in 1985. Clearly the transfer process and a refined statewide articulation system were becoming more effective, although reports on the ethnic breakdown of transfer students during the 1980s revealed that white and Asian students accounted for 80 to 83 percent of all transfers, even though they were only 74 to 75 percent of the California community college student population.[78]

In 1984 the CPEC began a statewide reassessment of the system of higher education. In 1984 the state legislature passed SP 1570 that called for the creation of a Commission for the Review of the Master Plan for Higher Education to evaluate the changing education needs of the state and how the system of higher education was meeting those needs. The work of this commission culminated in a revised master plan in 1987. High school graduating classes had been declining some 13 percent since 1974, and projections indicated that high school graduates would decline about another 4 percent by the end of the 1980s. But projections also indicated that between 1990 and 1999, the high school graduating class would increase about 40 percent, and it would be the largest pool of high school graduates in U.S. history. This population would also be more ethnically diverse than any previous student population in U.S. history, and it was expected to enroll in higher education at a higher part-time rate. The public postsecondary student population during the 1990s was expected to increase by over 250,000 students, and the California community colleges would be the primary postsecondary institution to accommodate this growth, taking up over 200,000 of those new students.[79]

The state legislature also passed SP 2064 in 1984, which called for a special reassessment study of the California community colleges as the first priority of the master plan review. In 1986 the CPEC published a report, *The Challenge of Change*, that criticized community colleges and ended with a call for a new master plan. While the CPEC acknowledged that community colleges had been "a gateway to opportunity" for many Californians, simply being an open door was not enough: "Access alone does open the door to higher education, but without success it is a door which too often leads to broken dreams and shattered promises. Too frequently it is forgotten that access without success does not equal opportunity." The CPEC argued that access to higher education "must be meaningful; and to be meaningful, it must be access to a quality system that helps ensure the success of every student who enrolls." While the report did not go into details, it was clearly criticizing the low rates of persistence, completion of degrees and certificates, and low transfer rates of students in the California Community College system. One critic bemoaned, "The state's huge community college system, once a national model for educational opportunity, is a shambles—highly politicized, without a clear mission, and with uncertain and (on some campuses) nonexistence academic standards." What made this poor performance even more galling was the fact that 80 percent of all underrepresented students who entered postsecondary education in the state did so through community colleges. Given California's history of segregation and racial exclusion, it made it seem as if the California community colleges were second-rate institutions designed to further deny opportunity to minority populations just breaking into higher education. What made the situation even worse was the lack of information on various aspects of student academic performance broken down by race and gender on secondary preparation and on postsecondary educational experiences.[80]

To address this situation, the CPEC argued that California community colleges should *not* try to be comprehensive institutions offering everything to everyone, but instead they needed to prioritize and focus on two fundamental missions: high-quality academic instruction to help students obtain associate's degrees or transfer to a 4-year university, and helping vocationally oriented students prepare for an occupation. Remediation in basic skills was important in relation to helping prepare students for academic instruction. Adult education and English as a Second Language were deemed important, but these program areas were placed as adjuncts to basic skills education. All other community-oriented services were still technically authorized, but they were deemed nonessential to the revised mission, and they would no longer be funded by the state. The CPEC also urged the state to further its financial support of community colleges, which had become more dependent upon state funds since the passage of Proposition 13 in 1978. This conservative antitax initiative cut rates on property taxes destined for education. In the wake of Proposition 13, state support jumped to almost 70 percent of the average community college budget, but this support slowly declined because of a depleted state surplus and an economic recession. By 1986 state support was down to 62 percent, and with local taxes frozen, community colleges had to fish for external revenues by charging students fees (6 percent of the budget) and tapping into federal block grants (4 percent of the budget). In essence the CPEC's recommendation was to find "strategies to promote an increase in student access to and success in postsecondary education," and to provide enough state funds to promote more efficiency and equity in the state system of higher education.[81]

However, this goal was not unanimously supported by the entire CPEC. In the *Background Papers* leading to the final report, members of the CPEC acknowledged "tension" between "competitive excellence" and "egalitarianism" in the state policy community; there had been a marked shift "from an emphasis on issues of access/equity to a concern with issues of quality and budgetary constraints." Some members of the CPEC argued,

> Access has been achieved and educational quality is now the goal. In a
> period of limited resources, decisions have to be made, and for many the

option is for quality instead of access. Thus, many believe the issue before California is not increasing access to community colleges, but how to limit access and who will be limited.

Some members of the CPEC argued further that California community colleges were "accommodating too many under-prepared students who are ill-equipped to handle college work." The community college was "struggling to educate problem learners who have many academic deficiencies and limited motivation." Many CPEC members believed that the situation overburdened this institution during a time of tightened budgetary constraints and limited resources. The open door had apparently let too many underprepared and needy students through. It seemed to some on the CPEC that it was time to start closing that door, restricting access, and increasing quality controls.[82]

Despite these misgivings, and some deep suspicions of administrators of California community colleges, the master plan was upheld and renewed by the CPEC for the review of the master plan. The final report of this body was delivered to the governor and the state legislature July 1987. By this time California had the largest postsecondary education system in the United States, although it was still far from being completely unified. There were 9 campuses of the University of California, 19 campuses of the California State University, 106 community colleges, 181 private colleges and universities, and 265 private occupational schools. All together these institutions awarded 50,000 associate's degrees, 86,000 baccalaureate degrees, 28,000 master's degrees, 6,800 professional degrees, and 9,000 doctorates, not to mention thousands of occupational certifications. The state's master plan of 1960 had created a system that operated "in reasonable harmony" over 27 years; however, some developments during that time had put quite a lot of stress on those postsecondary institutions. High schools were not preparing students for college as well as expected. College-bound demographics changed, and students were more ethnically diverse, less academically prepared, and less financially secure. Community colleges had become less academically rigorous, and their transfer function had begun to atrophy. University professors seemed to have forsaken their duty to train undergraduates for the higher-status work of research and of training graduate students. And the private sector grew so large it become almost a fourth segment of the postsecondary system, which was left out of the original master plan.[83]

The CPEC renewed the master plan by presenting four principle goals. The first was promoting unity of all segments of postsecondary education, including the private sector, and also including the secondary sector as well, because the issue of adequate student preparation for college had become a growing concern. The second goal was equity and promoting the unrestricted opportunity of all Californians to access postsecondary education. The third goal was ensuring the quality and excellence of postsecondary education in the state. And the final goal was efficiency and maximizing limited resources to produce the best possible educational product. No mention was made in the finished report of how these goals might conflict with each other, or if push came to shove, which goals would receive priority from the legislature, the governor, or postsecondary governing boards.[84]

But lurking in the background of this report was the knowledge that the postsecondary education system was not working as well as the master plan had designated. The community colleges took most of the blame and were largely singled out for criticism. The final report declared, "The community colleges, with a weak governance system, have been unable to carry out their full responsibilities within the postsecondary education system. The success of the whole system depends on them." The CPEC recommended prioritizing (and limiting) the comprehensive community college mission. The academic function leading to associate's degrees and transferring to 4-year institutions was deemed the primary mission. The secondary mission would be vocational education. Community colleges would have "principal but not exclusive responsibility of vocational education." Any other function would be subordinated to these two institutional missions.[85]

Clearly the issue of improving quality and efficiency had to take priority if the postsecondary system was to operate effectively as the CPEC believed it should. The multipurpose, community-oriented community college had to be redirected to the junior college model so that this institution could reduce the undergraduate burdens of the California State University and the University of California campuses (allowing them to become even more selective). Policy makers believed that if the community college could just get back to its junior college roots then it would become a revitalized undergraduate institution, moving more deserving students toward the baccalaureate degree. This revitalization also meant improving institutional quality. The report recommended that a new agency needed to create formal evaluation mechanisms to gauge the effectiveness of the postsecondary system, but this solution assumed that the major problem facing postsecondary education in the state was *quality*, and not *efficiency*. Or, to put it differently, this report assumed that the educational institutions and the students they served were the main problems to be fixed, instead of looking in another direction—institutional resources and funding.[86]

This report could have asked why the community college and other areas of the postsecondary system had been chronically underfunded by the state legislature, and thus this report might have pointed out that the main problem of the postsecondary system, especially community colleges, was not really the poor *quality* of their programs, although that was an issue, but the *inefficiency* of running institutions on less than adequate resources. For some reason it was assumed that institutions of higher education were in the business of drawing blood from stones, and that any resulting deficiencies were because of defective institutions or defective students. It never seemed to occur to state policy makers that public institutions cannot provide efficient, quality programs without the necessary resources, especially if they are serving high-need populations. It's a classic catch-22. Public institutions are expected to do more with less, and when they cannot, it is the fault of the institutions, not the political system that deprives them of resources and sets them up for failure.[87]

The Master Plan Revised: Declining Budgets and a New System of Accountability

Until the early 1970s California community colleges received the majority of their funds from local districts, around 72 percent of operating budgets and 77 percent of capital outlays during the 1960s. This created very unequal funding and inhibited the expansion of the California Community College system. The 1960 master plan was supposed to increase state support for community colleges to more equitably fund their expanded mission as the primary point of entry for Californian undergraduates. The plan was to incrementally increase state support to 45 percent by 1975. However, once the master plan was adopted state support went from about 30 percent in 1959–60 to 27.25 percent in 1962–63, well below the planned 33 percent that was needed to keep pace with master plan recommendations. Instead of raising state taxes to more equitably fund community colleges, these institutions remained largely reliant on local property taxes. After a decade of lagging state support, the legislature further undercut community colleges. Senate Bill 6 in 1973 mandated a state revenue limit for community colleges that went into effect in 1975. It put a 5 percent cap on funding new enrollments, and while community colleges remained open-enrollment institutions, they were not to be funded for enrollment growth over 5 percent.[88]

As if this was not bad enough, when taxpayers passed Proposition 13 in 1978, it put a cap of 1 percent on all property taxes in the state and made future tax increases much harder to enact. Proposition 13 was a hammer that shattered an already overburdened and underfunded California Community College system. Community colleges lost about $560 million, not adjusted for inflation, in tax revenues for the 1978–79 school year. When Proposition 13 was passed in 1978 the state used a budget surplus to finance about $260 million of this shortfall, but reduced funding by 7 percent and allotted block grant funds that were unrelated to enrollments. The state also took control of all property taxes, which went into the general state budget. Proposition 13 resulted in an enrollment decline of 12.3 percent, the largest single-year enrollment decline to date. In 1979 the legislature passed Assembly Bill 8 as a "permanent" solution to the revenue situation. The state would continue block grants with cost-of-living adjustments. Public schools and community colleges were allotted "marginal," not full-cost, funding for enrollment growth with a fixed-growth limit.[89]

In 1980–81 community college enrollments grew 32,000 beyond the budgeted amount, which resulted in a $50 million budget deficit. By 1981 the state budget surplus was gone, and the legislature needed to make budget reductions across the board. In response the 1983 Assembly Bill 1369 dictated there would be no inflation or growth funding, and $30 million was eliminated from "avocational, recreational, and personal development" programs. This bill further decreased funding by delineating credit and noncredit courses, and differential funding at a lower rate for noncredit courses. The state also required a new statewide classification system to differentiate credit and noncredit courses. In 1983 a nationwide recession caused state funding cuts and Governor George Deukmejian vetoed about $106 million (7.5 percent) from the California Community College (CCC) budget, and he wanted the CCC to make it up by imposing a general student charge of $50 per semester for students taking 6 units or more, and $30 for those taking under 6 units. But because the legislature did not approve a new per-semester fee, the governor vetoed $100 million from the CCC budget and across-the-board program cuts went into effect, which resulted in statewide credit enrollments falling 11 percent. Credit enrollments had fallen from 1,205,585 in 1981 to 981,845 in 1984.[90]

Just as institutions of higher education in California were seeking to address the history of segregation and racial exclusion by increasing minority access, the financial rug was swept out from under the feet of the whole educational system, but especially hard hit were the community colleges. In

1984 Patrick M. Callan, director of the CPEC, wrote a special report on the inadequate funding of the California Community College system. He claimed that the state was "jeopardizing its long-term investment in access and quality in its community colleges" because of lack of adequate funding, and that if new funds were not forthcoming then California community colleges would be "dismantled or their existing vital services curtailed." Because of inflation from 1979 to 1984, California community colleges lost 19 percent of their buying power. Callan argued that between $67 to $135 million was needed to keep colleges on a par with inflation and enrollment growth. Funding for full-time community college students had been 16 percent above the national average in 1980–81 but had dropped to 1 percent below average in 1983–84.[91]

After Robert G. Sproul, Clark Kerr was perhaps the most eminent grand statesman of higher education in the state of California. Kerr had been chancellor of the University of California, Berkeley, for 7 years during the 1950s, and then went on the become president of the University of California for a decade. Kerr also served as chairman of the Carnegie Commission on Higher Education and the Carnegie Council on Policy Studies in Higher Education. Kerr was a driving force in 1959 to create and implement the master plan of 1960, and he had been a tireless supporter of California's higher education system. But in 1993 Clark Kerr saw dark times ahead and he became a prophet of doom for higher education in the state. Kerr published a special report through the CPEC to warn higher education policy makers about "the most severe financial crisis that has ever faced higher education in California." A lingering international recession still gripped the country; federal defense spending had been cut, which drastically hurt one of California's most important economic sectors; unemployment in the state was 9.5 percent (the national rate was 7 percent); and annual economic productivity dropped from the postwar high of 3 percent to below 2 percent since the 1970s. This financial crisis was especially bad news to California's system of higher education because the state was anticipating Tidal Wave 2 by 1997, a large surge of youngsters would be coming to college. From the early 1980s to 1993, the state legislature cut spending on higher education by over 30 percent, the biggest cuts beginning in 1990. Higher education lost some $1.4 billion between 1990 and 1994. Kerr related the sentiments of Tom Hayes, former director of finance for the state of California, who said that the master plan "is broke and can't be fixed" because the budget process is a "battle of knives," and "higher education has no knife." Hayes predicted that in such dark economic times, California higher education would continue to face cutbacks, as other agencies and the government bureaucracy battled over the general budget. Kerr warned that Hayes's prediction did not have to come to pass if only the higher education community of California came together and resolved to find alternative ways to fund the crumbling system.[92]

The same year as Kerr's warning the CPEC reviewed the master plan again and discussed its relevance "in light of 1993 realities." The CPEC affirmed the master plan and the commitment from state legislators to provide adequate support for higher education in California. The CPEC concluded that its greatest challenge in its 20-year history would be trying to get the state legislature to honor the financial commitment it had made in the 1960s.[93] Not 2 months later, the CPEC published another report with a much more somber tone, warning of "California's waning higher education opportunities." The report noted that California was not staying true to its "promise of wide access to higher education" because of the budget crisis of the previous 3 years. At a time when more and more high school graduates were eligible to enroll in the University of California and California State University, state funding for these institutions had dropped and student fees had increased, restricting access and "closing the doors to higher education." The CPEC warned,

> If California cannot find the wherewithal to increase that investment [in higher education], it must develop equitable criteria for reducing enrollment and limiting higher education opportunities. If access must be limited, the state should be guided by an explicit plan rather than by the haphazard consequences of underinvestment. California cannot continue to starve its higher educational institutions of the resources they need to carry out their many missions.[94]

By the late 1990s the reality of tighter budgets for institutions of higher education in California became an ever present reality that would not go away. Although the economic recession had finally passed and the state legislature had increased funding to higher education, a fiscal crisis still loomed, mostly averted by rising student fees. To make up for the budget reductions of the previous decade, maintenance costs and building to accommodate growth had stalled, deferring over $1.2 billion worth of physical plant repairs and needed expansions. Student fees for all three segments also increased. University of California fees more than doubled from $1,624 in 1990 to $3,799 in 1995. California State Universities doubled their fees from $780 to $1,584. And California Community Colleges more than tripled their fees from \$120 in 1990 to \$390 in 1995. Federal and state financial aid in the form of grants did not keep pace with tuition inflation, and students turned more and more to educational loans to pay for school. Between 1990 and 1997 student borrowing jumped from \$1 billion to over \$3.1 billion. By the late 1990s student loans accounted for over 60 percent of all financial assistance to California students. All the while the California postsecondary system was experiencing large increases in student demand because about 450,000 new students were expected to enroll by 2005, mostly in community colleges. The good news was that the state legislature gradually increased spending on higher education between 1995 and 1999. There was a 5.9 percent increase for California State University, 6.6 percent for California Community Colleges, and 7.3 percent for the University of California. Altogether state spending rose from \$4.5 billion in 1995 to almost \$8 billion by 1999, with an additional \$2.5 billion in bonds raised for construction, although these increased funds were barely enough to keep pace with inflation and growth.[95]

The end of the 1990s also saw the reaffirmation of a set of guiding principles for California postsecondary education, although these principles had changed since 1987. The new rhetoric stressed four basic principles: access, affordability, accountability, and cooperation. The budget travails, combined with Tidal Wave II, brought to the fore the issue of access to institutions of higher education not only in academic preparation and physical space but also financial cost. The former principles of quality and efficiency in 1987 were rebranded accountability, which became a catch-all term for increasing the excellence and competitiveness of educational programs while investing less in education (the old game of squeezing blood out of stones). The last principle, simply a renaming of the previous call for unity among the three segments of the postsecondary system, called for coordination and shared sacrifice in meeting new needs while making do with fewer resources.[96]

From the late 1990s through the early 21st century, the CPEC kept the rhetorical priorities of equity, access, and affordability clearly in public view. However, the policy reports released during this period gradually marginalized these principles to bring into focus the new preeminent educational policy of the 21st century: institutional accountability.

In the 1990s the California postsecondary education system inaugurated new data-gathering techniques, information clearinghouses, better articulation agreements between segments, and improvements in educational programming. But these innovations were not created for education ends. Instead, the call for increased accountability was actually a new rhetorical tactic to normalize the explicit prioritizing of certain measures of institutional quality while using this normative rhetoric to implicitly reframe the expectations and responsibilities of the postsecondary education community. The education and social mobility of students per se was no longer the purpose of higher education in California. One could argue it never was.

But in the 21st century, institutions of higher education were narrowly focused on only one arch objective: to be productive, efficient, and cost effective. The postsecondary education community accepted the stark political fact that resources were limited and subject to fluctuation, while student demand was increasing. Thus, community colleges would have to be much more efficient to better meet growing demand while functioning with less than adequate resources. The postsecondary policy community, including the governor, state legislators, the CPEC, postsecondary administrators, and many scholars, all rhetorically normalized the notion of accountability as the defining political and economic priority for higher education in California. It is clear that the policy movement for institutional accountability was never an educational priority; it was always a *political and economic priority* that developed largely as a response to economic crises and constricted financial support from the state. The ends of education in California and the nation as a whole became subsumed in what W. Norton Grubb and Marvin Lazerson termed the Education Gospel. Clearly many people in the postsecondary policy community in California still valued the broader principles of education and equity, but these once foundational and independent values were becoming more and more dependent upon the limited availability of political and economic capital. Community colleges, like all other institutions of education, were now corporate entities in the sole business of economic development, and they would have to maximize returns through efficiency, just as businesses in the private sector.[97]

The presence of accountability measures for the community college in California has been a constant feature since the development of this institution. Largely these measures were used to define and criticize the community college as a higher education halfway house, but nothing was ever really done to improve institutional performance. Accountability measures became more politically important by the 1970s. From the beginning they became tools to measure increasing equity in access to postsecondary education after the civil rights movement. These early accountability measures were rhetorically placed in the service of larger ends, such as equal access and economic development. However, with the rise of a "new standards movement"[98] during the 1980s and the economic recessions of the 1980s and early 1990s, accountability measures became an increasing priority for policy makers and the state legislature for a different reason. The increased importance was not because of any larger social or political goal, even though conservative cultural warriors often espoused lofty principles such as public responsibility. No, by the 1990s there was no longer any larger goal to serve. Institutional accountability was reduced to a simple economic necessity demanded by dire financial straights and foreign economic competition. Educational institutions in America were now largely defined and determined by stark economic realities.

Taking the lead from the Hart-Hughes Act of 1983 that mandated annual performance reports for K–12 schools, California Assembly Bill 1808, passed in 1991, called for the formulation of annual performance reports on California higher education. The purpose of these reports was to provide "demonstrable improvements in student knowledge, capacities, and skills between entrance and graduation." It was also noted that these improvements needed to be made "efficiently," in "time, effort, and money."[99]

The CPEC submitted the first report in 1994, *The Performance of California Higher Education*, and these reports would continue to be delivered through the 2001 school year. The original report had 61 performance indicators, which grew to 75 by 1997 and 80 by 1999. The indicators were grouped into five broad areas: population context, fiscal context, student preparation (secondary), student access (postsecondary), and student outcomes (postsecondary). The first of two issues about these early postsecondary performance reports was the breadth of performance indicators, ranging from general demographic information to secondary statistics and including a large range of postsecondary demographic and outcome measures. The second was the relative absence of community college performance indicators specifically focused on the effectiveness of the institution itself. Most community college performance markers focused on the school's role as a feeder mechanism for universities. Only four performance indicators focused directly on the community college as an institution, and of these only three were actual performance measures: first-time students enrolled, transfer students, associate's degrees, and vocational certificates.[100]

Overall the enrollments of first-time students in California Community Colleges between 1988 and 2000 rose from over 92,000 to a high of almost 105,000 in 1996 before dropping to about 100,000 by 2000. During this time transfer students to California State University and the University of California rose only slightly, with large fluctuations between years that muddle a clear but slight trend upward from the 1980s of about 3,000 more transfers per year by 2000. A more pronounced positive trend was in the awarding of associate's degrees, which grew from over 42,000 in 1990 to over 64,000 in 1999. This same trend is even more dramatic for vocational certificates, which grew from over 16,000 in 1990 to a high of 32,444 in 1998, before dropping to 26,231 in 1999.[101]

A new master plan for education from kindergarten through the sophomore year of college (K–16) was unveiled in 2002. The newly sacred rhetoric of accountability pervaded the document. Creating accountability measures was often described as a means to a high-quality education for students, but this end was overshadowed by a management ethos of bureaucratic rationality: "defining roles and responsibilities," "evaluating outcomes," and "ensuring consequences." The document explicitly conceptualized the essence of accountability in terms of authoritarianism. Accountability means responsibility to authority. Students will be responsible to teachers, teachers responsible to administrators, administrators responsible to legislatures, and legislatures responsible to economic and political bottom lines. But the issue of who should be held accountable for what and to whom is not easily answered because it is a *political* and *moral* question, not a technical question. The moral and political cannot be rationally managed by experts.[102] There is no such thing as objective standards in either creating knowledge or in transmitting knowledge, as the so-called culture wars of the 1990s made abundantly clear. Which students in what schools in whose America and with what resources will be used toward what end?[103] These are messy political questions focused on differing conceptions of the public good. Sociologist Daniel Bell perceptively explained that debates over public good are normative, not technocratic, "where the problem is clearly right versus right, rather than right or wrong; of weighing the claims of group memberships against individual rights; of balancing liberty and equality, equity and efficiency."[104]

The new master plan even admitted this sticky point. The document acknowledged not only that different segments of public higher education have different missions and functions, but it also noted the disagreements over what was to be taught. It plainly stated, "There is no common body of knowledge for which consensus exists about what is expected to be taught to every student," therefore, "there has been no basis for establishing a measure of student achievement." If only this acknowledgment were so forthrightly admitted by all the proponents of institutional accountability. Yet the report's authors pretend as if it never made this concession. It goes on to boldly proclaim that the new California accountability system will have "clear statements" of a "common body of knowledge" that will enable measurable achievement goals that can be captured by standardized tests and institutional report cards. But how can this contradiction be? The whole notion of objective standards and a common body of knowledge is an idealized telos at best, and a mystified fantasy at worst. But there was no acknowledgment of these ends as idealized. Instead, they are simply assumed to be objective realities in a bald statement of faith. Public policy built on such a utopian foundation is bound to fail.[105]

Who decides the contours of the "common body of knowledge"? Who will decide what is standard and what is not? The master plan authors admit, "Not everything that may be important to the successful implementation of this *master plan* and to improving the achievement of every student is easily measured. Nor is everything that can be measured important." But who decides what to measure and why? Who decides what measures outcomes are important or not? Trying to quantify and standardize the complex and messy endeavor of education into measurable learning outcomes is difficult if not dangerous. It is difficult in terms of identifying all the tangible and intangible outcomes of the learning process. It is dangerous in terms of the tendency of administrators, policy makers, and the general public (and perhaps even educators themselves) to narrowly focus on particular measurable outcomes that may be politicized or expedient. In only focusing on easily obtained or politically motivated outcomes, the value of the larger educational process can be lost. For the student, the value of education in its broadest terms is immeasurably more important than any particular and transient learning product. Thus, competent teachers more often focus on educational processes and long-term learning rather than isolated measures of information retention.[106]

And this begs the question: Is institutional accountability really about student learning? Who are educational institutions ultimately accountable to? Any educator would say that ultimate accountability should be to the student whose life is being changed in many ways through the complex ecology of the educational process. But according to the new master plan, ultimate accountability of the institutions is assigned to the taxpayers. However, the meaning of giving ultimate accountability to this fictionalized social entity is ambiguous. One interpretation is that education is merely an economic endeavor in which the best available product should be bought at the meanest price. Or it could be interpreted as some vague notion of social responsibility to the broader public, but then what social, political, or educational ends do all the taxpayers in California supposedly share that postsecondary institutions are supposed to be held accountable for? This begs a further question: Who does California's K–16 accountability system benefit most? Students? Educational institutions? Society? Or the soulless bottom line of legislative budgets? Given the history of the state, it should seem clear that students, educational institutions, and the larger California society have not benefited much from the institutional accountability movement.[107]

But concerns such as these have never been publicly addressed by legislators or the policy community. In fact, legislation continues to be drafted on foundations of faith in the hope that statewide institutional assessment standards will somehow magically cure the difficult problems of the community college. Just after the new master plan was released in 2002, the joint committee responsible for the document consulted with Nancy Shulock, head of the Institution for Higher Education Leadership and Policy at California State University, Sacramento, and Jane Wellman from the Institute for Higher Education Policy in Washington DC. Together, the joint committee, Shulock, and Wellman crafted Senate Bill 1331 that set up four general areas for postsecondary accountability measures (educational opportunity, participation, student success, and public benefit). The bill named the CPEC as the designated agency to implement the new accountability framework. The bill was passed by the legislature in 2004 but vetoed by the governor.[108]

Although this accountability framework for the entire California postsecondary education system was not accepted, another piece of accountability legislation was passed in 2004. California Assembly Bill 1417 required the California Community College system to design an annual evaluation structure to measure district-level performance in meeting statewide educational outcomes. The state required three basic performance outcomes: academic student achievement markers (degrees, certificates, and transfers), vocational achievement markers (workforce development), and noncredit achievement markers in basic skills and English as a Second Language. The California Community College chancellor's office released the first draft of the report in 2007, *Accountability Reporting for the Community Colleges*, which was a draft of the new annual evaluation report. It opens with a general overview of performance markers for the entire state, and the rest of the massive document lists performance markers for each California community college, with reference to similar classified colleges for evaluative comparison.[109]

This new accountability report followed the basic prescriptive formula of all the past reports reviewed in this chapter. It focuses mostly on enrollments, transfers, and awards. The only new, although underdeveloped, accountability information included in this report is a brief survey of the economic returns to a community college credential. In 2005–2006 45.3 percent of California State University and University of California students first attended a California Community College. While the total percentage of CSU and UC students who attended a CCC declined about 1 percent over the past 3 years, the number of CCC attendees has steadily increased numerically every year (93,050 students in 2000–2001 to 110,990 students in 2005–2006). In 2005–2006 55.3 percent of CSU students attended a CCC, compared to only 28.5 percent of UC students. There has been an overall increase of CCC transfers to 4-year institutions from 2000 to 2001 and from 2005 to 2006; however, there was a marked decrease (4,004 students) from 2004 to 2005 and from 2005 to 2006. During this period about 55.7 percent of CCC transfers went to CSU, 14.25 percent went to UC, 16.38 percent went to in-state private institutions, 13.6 percent went to out-of-state institutions, and 83.55 percent of CCC students transferred in state. This report claimed a transfer rate of 40.7 percent in 2005–2006, but the transfer rate is defined as "percentage of first-time students with a minimum of 12 units earned who attempted transfer-level Math or English during enrollment who transferred to a four-year institution within six years." The report also listed the vocational awards by program from 2003 to 2004 and from 2005 to 2006. For this 3-year period there was overall growth in total awards (60,749 to 63,167) and overall growth in degrees and certificates. Finally, the report included an analysis of the income change in three cohorts 3 to 5 years after attaining a degree or certificate. For all three cohorts there was a marked rise in income ranging from $19,365 to $23,723 over 3 to 5 years; however, this is an average with no indication of which degrees or certificates or majors fared better.[110]

The draft of *Accountability Reporting* was the most important accountability report released in California during the early 21st century, but several other performance evaluation reports on the CCC were released in 2007. The CPEC tracked 52,622 community college students over a 5-year period (2001 to 2005) to measure transfer rates and awarded credentials. About 52 percent of CCC students left the institution without transferring or without an award; 22 percent transferred to a California public university (CSU or UC); 17 percent earned a 2-year degree or certificate; and 19 percent were still enrolled in a community college. Of the students who earned a degree or certificate, 20 percent earned more than one degree or certificate, 10 percent transferred, and 7 percent did not transfer. Women made up 57 percent of award earners and 55 percent of transfers. Latinos, African Americans, and male students in general had lower transfer rates and award attainment. The CPEC report noted the "low rates of success," and suggested a few policy points to help increase success and transfer rates.[111]

A report published by the California Community College Collaborative found a marked increase in associate's degrees and vocational certificates in the CCC from 1993 to 2006, which outpaced growth rates for transfer students to 4-year universities. Associate's degrees increased 53 percent, from 51,983 degrees in 1993–94 to 79,467 degrees in 2005–06, while vocational certificates increased 84 percent, from 23,002 certificates in 1993–94 to 42,321 certificates in 2005–06. Altogether the average rate of growth for associate's degrees was 6.7 percent, and vocational certificates grew at 3.9 percent, while the growth rates of transfer students was only 2.2 percent. Many of the sharpest gains in vocational certificates happened in traditionally academic curriculums, such as the biological sciences, physical sciences, foreign languages, and the humanities, where one would not expect to find vocational certificates at all. The report suggested that increased policy focus on accountability markers may have caused the CCC to turn toward shorter-term vocational certificates and associate's degrees as viable and more easily attainable markers of institutional success rather than put limited resources into the more academically demanding transfer curriculum and the student support services necessary to aid students in the process of transferring to a 4-year university.[112]

Besides the *Accountability Reporting* draft, perhaps the most influential accountability reports on the CCC were written in 2007 by Nancy Shulock and Colleen Moore and published through the Institute for Higher Education Leadership and Policy at California State University in Sacramento. These reports represented the most sustained and in-depth analysis of the California community college system since the *Through the Open Door* reports of the mid-1970s. Shulock and Moore were able to document a continuing divide between two groups of students, although they reveal a numerical grouping slightly different from the traditional two-thirds academic and one-third vocational divide. Shulock and Moore divided students into those seeking degrees in academic programs (60 percent) and those not seeking degrees in vocational programs, personal enrichment, and basic skills (40 percent). Those students who were not seeking degrees tended to be mostly over 30 years old (83 percent) and most signed up for less than 12 units (65 percent) and stayed for about 1.5 years (77 percent). But of the 60 percent of students who were degree seekers, 80 percent persisted to the sophomore year, and 50 percent of remained enrolled after 2 years, but only 24 percent completed a certificate, degree, and/or transfer within 6 years of enrolling. Of those 24 percent who earned an identifiable achievement marker, 3 percent earned a vocational certificate, 11 percent earned an associate's degree, and 18 percent transferred to a university. Part of the reason for such low rates of successful completion is the fact that 90 percent of all community college students tested below college level in math and 70 percent below college level in reading and/or writing. But even though the majority of community college students need some type of basic skills course, very few who enroll in these courses will ever make it to a college-level course. Only 25 percent of students enrolling in a basic reading skills class will make it to a transfer-level English class, and only 10 percent of students in basic math skills will make it to a transferable math class.[113]

Shulock and Moore argued that these low success rates point to a systemic failure of the California Community College system. This institution seemed to do little more than "open the door to college." However, Shulock and Moore did not place the blame on a lack of institutional capacity to be effective. Instead, they pointed to the public policies and financial resources that handicap these institutions. They said that California community colleges are not only underfunded but also underresourced to do the tough job they have been assigned. Shulock and Moore pointed out that community college students tend to be "the most expensive to teach given their considerable needs for intensive instructional and support services," but yet community colleges "receive so much less funding than students at four-year institutions." And what funding they do receive is determined either by formula requirements or the political process in which multiple state agencies compete with each other over general state funds. And even when community colleges receive funds, the labyrinth of education codes and other legislation dictates how most of the money can be spent, which severely limits local control over budgets to meet the particular needs of an institution in any given year. Shulock and Moore made it quite clear:

> Community colleges are under-funded for the expansive mission assigned to them. The remedial mission served by the community colleges is not something that can be done on the cheap. More generally, the students increasingly served by community colleges are those who require more, not fewer, institutional resources, because they bring with them such limited understanding of the dimensions of college success.

Ultimately, Shulock and Moore called for a "policy audit" by the state legislature and higher education policy makers to determine how higher education policy in the state can help actualize the accountability rhetoric of student success. Money alone will not ensure higher levels of student success, but without sustained funds no real improvements can be made. Financial resources also need to be matched by more efficient and equitable policy and by leadership—political, administrative, and educational—to work toward the difficult endeavor of helping students succeed.[114]

But what Shulock and Moore fail to address in their push for standardized institutional assessment policies is the very real possibility that an institutional assessment framework will become law *without* the accompanying financial resources that would help make it work. This happened with the various California master plans, and it happened nationally with No Child Left Behind. In fact, Assembly Bill 1417 has already established a statewide community college assessment framework, and this framework will no doubt become more rigidly enforced and more politically important over the next decade. However, given the economic implications of the Great Recession of 2007–2009, it is highly unlikely that adequate resources will be given to the California Community College system in the near future. In fact, because of the sustained state budget crisis of 2008–2009, it is highly likely that thousands if not tens of thousands of community college students will be turned away because of draconian budget cutbacks throughout the higher education system. Given this reality, the whole notion of institutional accountability is a perverse joke. How much more blood can be squeezed from these battered stones?

Conclusion: Accounting and Accountability

Some data suggest that California community colleges have had relatively stable, if not slightly increasing, markers of institutional success over the last century despite huge increases of students, many of whom were historically disadvantaged minorities. Persistence rates from the first- to the second-year seemed to decrease from around 61% (when there were only 100 or more students in junior colleges in 1910–1915) to about 17% in 1918 (1,561 students) to about 45% in 1927 (8,073 students). During the 1950s and early 1960s persistence rates from the first- to the second-year seemed to reach an all-time high of over 65 percent, which gradually dropped to the national average of about 50 percent by the late 1960s and early 1970s. During the last three decades persistence rates have hovered near 50 percent, but Shulock and Moore have evidence that these rates are close to 80 percent for degree-seeking students. Given that more than 2.5 million students are currently enrolled in California community colleges and that many of these students are academically unprepared or at a disadvantage in some way, these numbers are quite positive. More students than ever before in California's history are persisting through at least 1 year of college. However, this trend must to be balanced with the fact that for many community college students this 1st year is composed mainly of remedial classes. Thus, for many students their one year of college is *not really* a year of college. Another positive trend is that more students than ever before are earning certificates, associate's degrees, and transferring to 4-year universities. However, these numbers betray a long-standing history of discrimination in the state and the nation at large. Not only do achievement gaps between ethnic and racialized groups and between economic classes still exist, there are also clear differentials in the economic returns to higher education in the labor market.[115]

Given the astronomical increase in the student population and the huge increase of disadvantaged minorities gaining access to public higher education, the historical achievement trends in California are positive, albeit cautiously so. More and more students are being served by the community college and more and more students are becoming successful in obtaining larger amounts of education and credentials. While these trends are hopeful, a more admonitory tone is certainly warranted overall. Community colleges need to be doing better on a host of educational issues: pedagogical practices, developmental education, and organizational change to name just a few. However, until these institutions receive proper funding and resources, including properly trained full-time faculty, it is not entirely within their institutional capacity to improve on these issues.[116]

Institutional effectiveness markers will not go away. They have become a permanent part of the political landscape, at least for the foreseeable future. Given this reality, it is paramount that scholars and policy makers try to reform the nature of these effectiveness markers while they are still politically malleable. Accountability markers should be reflective of the diverse missions of community colleges, and they should be deliberated on and decided by the relevant stakeholders, not decreed from above by policy makers and legislators. Effectiveness markers should also be qualified because student success is not entirely dependent on the institution, nor are measure markers of success the most important or lasting effects of education. While accountability markers can be a useful tool to help evaluate the performance of institutions, accountability markers should not be allowed to overshadow the complex educational ecology wherein the creative and flexible decision making of teachers must responsively gauge the needs of learners and help students gain knowledge and confidence. Sadly, accountability measures and standardized student learning outcomes often homogenize the learning of diverse groups of students with differing needs and hamstring a teacher's ability to teach and select a curriculum. Community college instructors and students need to have a greater stake in the institutional accountability process.[117]

Accountability measures should also be cautiously handled because of evidence that suggests that individual student characteristics are more important than institutional characteristics as predictors of student success in community colleges, although some evidence also suggests that institutions do have some independent effect on student success outcomes. In the current policy environment, California community colleges as institutions are often solely blamed for the low completion rates of students.[118] This is unfortunate because since the community college's origin in the early 20th century, institutional missions, policy, and funding have rarely, if ever, been under the complete control of community college faculty and administrators. Community colleges only emerged from the yoke of the secondary school system in the late 1940s and 1950s, and they have never been freed from the oversight of legislative and university leaders. Likewise, rarely if ever have the completion rates of community college students been under the complete control of community college faculty and staff, especially the prejudicial treatment of nonwhite minorities in K–12 education and labor markets. While the California Community College system should be held accountable for its role in the state system of education, why do other parts of that system receive less scrutiny and blame? California community colleges must balance multiple and often competing missions (transfer to university, economic development and vocational programming, basic skills, and community education), while serving the majority of undergraduates in the state. How could administrators of any institution hope to manage such a task while being chronically underfunded and underresourced for the last half century?[119]

This perennial question is again being put to the test as the worst economic recession since the early 1980s has hit California and the nation at large. California has been harder hit than most states because of a $42 billion budget deficit gap over fiscal years 2009 and 2010. In 2009 the governor cut 20 percent, about $2.8 billion, from the higher education budget, affecting the University of California and the California State University systems.

Most UC faculty and staff will have to take 11 to 26 mandatory furlough days over the 2009–2010 school year. The UC regents have also voted a 32 percent fee increase for undergraduates ($2,500 a year more). Hundreds of millions will be cut from the California Community College system, about 6 percent of the community college budget, which is fiscally linked with K–12 funding cuts. Many community colleges have shed temporary faculty, put on hold many full-time faculty and counseling positions, stifled cost-of-living increases, increased class sizes, reduced class offerings, and cut about 5 percent of the general operating budget.[120] Cuts to the budgets of the University of California and California State University systems combined with drastic fee increases will further restrict access of qualified students to public 4-year institutions. All the while the raw numbers of eligible students continues to grow. Over 10,000 qualified students were turned away in 2009, and with budget and staffing cuts in community colleges, many thousands of students will be turned away from public higher education in California.[121] To make matters worse, California is projected to hemorrhage budget deficits over $15 billion for at least the next 5 years. Thus, further cuts to social services and education are looming in the near future.[122]

Some analysts believe the current budget cuts will have serious long-term consequences, not only on higher education but on the state as a whole. And there is reason to believe that an anemic recovery could continue to strain state income and lead to further budget cuts over the next decade. Mitchell Landsberg calls the drastic state budget cuts "perhaps the biggest downscaling of government" in California history. Sarah King Head has called this budget downsizing an "apocalypse" that "seems destined to jeopardize the integrity—and future—of higher education in the state." John Aubrey Douglas, a historian of higher education at Stanford University, warned, "It takes a long time to build these institutions, but they can be ripped apart very quickly and then it's really hard for them to recover."[123] Given these stark economic times, by what logic can policy makers demand greater institutional effectiveness? At best one could hope for stagnant rates of institutional success markers, but most likely the performance of the community college in California will get worse before it gets better.

4

THE AMBIGUOUS LEGACY OF THE COMMUNITY COLLEGE

Policy, Administrative, and Educational Implications

P rior to the 20th century, higher education was centered on moral and civic inculcation with a specific focus on training elites for sociopolitical leadership. These traditional purposes were gradually replaced during the 20th century with a new end: training all Americans for work. This trend has been labeled the *vocationalization* of American education. Higher education in the United States is now largely a training apparatus for the nation's capitalist economy. The labor market arbitrates the form and content of mid- to low-skilled occupations and high-skilled professions. Americans view education, particularly postsecondary education and its system of credentials, as an economic ladder of opportunity that will yield financial returns and upward social mobility.

The Reduction of Education to Human Capital

While human capital theory has allowed economists, capitalists, and government officials to enhance the perceived value of human labor, this economic paradigm has created a skewed faith in the education gospel that basically argues that higher levels of education bring higher levels of economic earnings for all workers. This belief is false. While completing a bachelor's degree in the United States has marked economic benefits, these benefits are always averaged sums that mask real inequalities of earnings based on race, class, and gender in what continues to be a socially stratified society. Because human capital theorists cannot adequately perceive or factor in social inequalities, some have called human capital theory not only overly simplistic but also naive.[1] Increased levels of educational attainment in the United States over the past quarter century have also been accompanied by increased levels of economic and social inequality. Nowhere is this issue more concretely demonstrated than in the estimated economic returns of subbaccalaureate education, especially in community colleges, where increased levels of students are enrolling to attain a higher education, but very few of these students ever attain more than a few years of college without any degree completion.

From the mid-19th century until the 21st century, the net national product of the United States has grown on average by 3.4 percent per year. While the development of land, natural resources, and the investment of capital in conjunction with new technologies have all been significant contributing factors in this growth, a major factor behind the economic growth of the United States has been human labor. Economists estimate that between 41 and 49 percent of the growth of the net national product from 1840 to 1990 was because of the development of human labor supplies and laborer skills.[2]

But for much of the 19th century a significant portion of the labor force was enslaved or in a state of debt peonage. Labor markets institutionally discriminated against laborers in forms of wage discrimination based on race, ethnicity, and gender, and also based on race- and gender-segmented occupations. In 1860 black slaves constituted about 21 percent of the labor force, and when they were officially freed, they continued to be economically enslaved by dept peonage in the agricultural economy of the South. In fact, both white and nonwhite agricultural workers in the South were not free because their cash crops were determined by the wealthy merchants in charge of regional markets.[3] Much the same could be said about agricultural and industrial laborers in the North and West.[4] Women were also active yet invisible participants in the labor force for centuries in the hidden market of the home, but this contribution to the net national product has long been neglected by male economists.[5] Despite being overtly discriminatory, labor markets were also regionally segregated, which limited the mobility of laborers to find less-discriminatory markets.[6]

Despite the foundational economic value of labor, laborers were largely (but never completely) neglected by economists and politicians for centuries, as they were often classified as mere commodities to be bought and sold by capitalists in labor markets. When employed, a laborer became another form of raw material to be controlled by managers. However, skilled workers were able to retain some control over their labor and working conditions because of their relative scarcity in some labor markets and the collective power of guilds and craft unions.[7]

But in the United States the full economic value of labor was not realized by economists and politicians until the early to mid-20th century, with the widespread development of three important social institutions: labor unions, secondary and postsecondary public schooling, and formal legal equality. Labor unions espoused a growing body of legal rights for laborers, better working conditions, and some measure of free time to develop nonoccupational pursuits, like education.[8] The development of free public secondary schooling and growing access to postsecondary schooling allowed unskilled and skilled laborers alike to increasingly send their children to school and learn skills that would increase their value as laborers, although the opportunity costs of schooling were still prohibitive to many because of the dependence of families on adolescent labor.[9] And finally, the development of formal legal equality for all American citizens allowed nonwhite and immigrant laborers to more freely unionize, educate themselves and their children, and negotiate their labor in less-discriminatory labor markets—although formal legal equality has not translated into full social or economic equality for many Americans.

In 1960 Theodore W. Schultz, president of the American Economic Association, broke with classical economic theory and repositioned the laborer as the foundational element of modern economies and economic growth. Schultz argued that laborers in the United States were becoming more educated and thus more valuable. He claimed that human skills and knowledge were a "form of capital": human capital. He went on to say, "The productive capacity of human beings is now vastly larger than all other forms of wealth taken together." He tried to separate his theory from classical accounts of laborers as "something akin to property," and he explained that human capital was actually a form of human freedom and choice, helped both by the welfare of the individual and also the economic welfare of society. He argued that racial discrimination interfered with economic development and, thereby, was a nationally self-defeating policy (he did not mention gender discrimination). He even went so far as to claim that "laborers have become capitalist" because their knowledge and skills have quantifiable "economic value," which is greater than nonhuman capital.[10]

By the 1970s the idea of education as a form of human capital investment had taken hold and was fast becoming the reigning theoretical paradigm for justifying the social and economic value of education, especially higher education. In 1976 Kern Alexander explained how the idea of human capital represented an advancement of Western society. Human resources were now understood to be "the true basis for the wealth of nations." But with this new economic celebration of labor came an economically reconceptualized notion of education, which Alexander defined as

> anything which (a) increases production through income in the capacity of the labor force, (b) increases efficiency by reducing unnecessary costs, thereby reserving resources for the enhancement of human productivity . . . and (c) increases the social consciousness of the community so that living conditions are enhanced.

The problem with this new instrumentalist conception of education was that it seemed to reduce a complex human activity to a mere productivity equation whereby increased capacity and efficiency lead to increased production and an enhanced society. Alexander admitted that many educators, not to mention laborers, would find this definition unappealing or insulting. Human beings did not always educate themselves to maximize income. And, lest people forget about the historical institutionalization of labor markets in the United States, Alexander also pointed out that education did not simply translate into increased income, nor were the benefits of human capital equally distributed to all types of laborers in all labor markets. Alexander explained, "The economic value of education is distorted by factors such as intelligence, parent's education, race, sex, urban versus rural, north versus south, health, education quality, and others too numerous to explore." So while the paradigm of human capital did bring increased respect for laborers, it reduced the value of education to a simple economic investment, and it masked the larger social segmentation, segregation, and discrimination that still resided in labor markets.[11]

While some economists have used human capital theory *expansively* to theoretically and empirically explore how increased education and economic development bring increased freedom and sociopolitical development, many economists use this theory rather *narrowly* to empirically explain the correlation between education and increased economic production capacity.[12] David Breneman, like many economists of higher education, routinely refers to the outputs of higher education in terms of individual rates of return, and less frequently, if at all, economists might talk about the social rate of return, but this expansive conception is very hard to quantify. Thus, when it comes to the ultimate value of higher education, invariably scholars, policy makers, and politicians defer to the reigning paradigm of human capital theory and reduce education to an individualistic economic investment, which has now become a scholarly cottage industry.[13]

Many economic studies have been done on the private returns of investment in a baccalaureate degree, and Michael B. Paulsen summarized much of this literature. He demonstrated that the long-term earnings differential between high school–educated workers and college-educated workers (baccalaureate degree holders) has been substantial and has been increasing since the 1980s. Paulsen also reported that the average private rate of return for a baccalaureate degree was somewhere between 9 percent and 15 percent. Grubb and Lazerson estimate the average rate of return in 1980 was 16.5 percent. The average private rates of return, however, vary substantially because of a host of personal factors, such as academic ability, socioeconomic status, family background, quality of schooling, gender, and race/ethnicity. Grubb has also documented that private rates of return vary depending on the professional area of the degree. Degrees from fields such as business, allied health, and technical/engineering have shown strong economic returns, while fields such as agriculture and education have shown marginal economic returns.[14]

Various groups of workers still face discrimination in the labor market as well, which causes "inequalities in the marginal benefits accruing to individuals who invest in higher education." There is also some evidence that what economists assume to be the value of higher education is in fact mostly the skills, abilities, and/or social privileges of talented (and largely white male) individuals. The public and private benefits of schooling reflect the continuing inequality in American society and the labor market: In 2000 the average earnings of a black male with a professional degree was more than $8,000 less than a white male with a bachelor's degree, and a Latina woman with a doctorate degree earned only $3,000 more than a white male with a high school diploma. As this book has already demonstrated, the modest returns for a subbaccalaureate degree calls into question the whole notion of whether obtaining only some college is worth the capital expense and forgone wages.[15]

But more is at stake than uneven rates of human capital formation and inequitable returns from human capital investment. There is something deeply disturbing in reducing human beings to mere economic entities and education to mere economic investment in vocational training. Yet these reductions define the normative rhetoric of most policy makers and many professional academics. The very notion of education has been reinstitutionalized as *vocationalism*. In the 21st century, how does one even make the case for broader human or educational values beyond economic? This profound lack in current policy discourse must be addressed by broad-minded scholars and the public at large before any meaningful educational reforms at any level can take place. By and large Americans have surrendered education to government bureaucrats, businessmen, economists, and academic technocrats. Educational institutions suffer in this country because Americans cannot reconceive the process of education in broader, long-term, humanistic possibilities. Any valid overall assessment of the past and future of the American community college must include a broader understanding and reconception of education. We desperately need a new vision of education in America.

The Legacy of the Community College: A Limited Opportunity

What is the legacy of community colleges? The junior college turned community college was designed to be a socioeconomic institution for sorting students and limited opportunity. It had two major objectives: transfer a select group of prepared undergraduates to the university, guiding them to a professional career, and cool out the majority of junior college students, delaying their entry into the labor market, and redirect them to the mid- to low-skilled labor market. On the one hand, community colleges allowed the universities, such as the University of California, to become more restrictive institutions of higher education. On the other hand, they also offered what appeared to be the democratization of higher education by giving a broad range of students who would have never been able to attend college the opportunity to at least gain some measure of higher education. However, while community colleges offered more students the opportunity for higher education, they also structured the failure of many students by not also providing the necessary support services, financial aid, and trained teachers that would ensure their success (not to mention the needed state programs to address segregated housing and labor markets). Also, the so-called higher education that many community college students get, especially the most academically needy, is often nothing more than a second chance at a secondary education—*not college*. Thus, the community college developed into an underfunded second-class institution at the bottom rung of highly selective and segregated state systems of higher education. It is an institution offering an opportunity to many in need, but if one looks holistically at the history, missions, and performance of community colleges to date, it is not much of an opportunity and not easily obtained by the majority of community college students.

The community college is a structurally limited opportunity that has been used to blame the victims of America's lingering class-based and race-based society for failure. Community college students are offered what appears to be a chance to succeed, but when they fail to obtain success, it appears to be their own fault because of a lack of academic skills or effort. Whatever the cause, the individual was offered an opportunity and he or she could not realize it—case closed. But individualist epistemologies obscure the social and economic capital that is needed to *become* academically competent and *be able* to recognize and realize academic and economic opportunities. Not everyone begins the race of life with equal capacities, and the American people, especially the gifted, socially nurtured, and economically well-placed, have always had difficulty recognizing that many hard-working, competent, and morally upstanding people are born and raised at a disadvantage because they lack the necessary social and economic capital to succeed in a highly discriminating society. Thus, simply offering opportunity to all does not mean that all will succeed because of the inequitable distribution of talent, social capital, and financial resources.

In the case of race, over the past century many nonwhite citizens and immigrants have been actively disenfranchised from opportunities America has to offer because of skin color, culture, or custom. Once state systems of de jure and de facto segregation were challenged and eventually overturned, the community college became the convenient halfway house for increasing numbers of underprepared and undereducated nonwhite minority students in higher education—those generations who had been systematically excluded and discouraged from attaining secondary education until the 1950s and 1960s. Ethnic minority students were able to gain increasing access to higher education by the 1960s, allowing greater numbers to transfer to 4-year universities with access to a bachelor's degree and the possibility of social mobility. But most racialized minorities who entered community colleges up until the early 1980s remained educationally frustrated and economically disenfranchised. It has only been in the last three decades that increased educational and economic opportunities have been acquired by racialized minorities, but they still are disproportionately excluded from the American dream.

A brief look at the evidence at the dawn of the 21st century seems to reinforce the critical objections made by Brint, Karabel, and other New Left critics of the community college. One would assume significant educational progress has been made for racialized minorities in the United States since the 1970s, but there is lack of adequate data to bolster such a claim. And while the educational levels of nonwhite minorities may have increased, the educational levels of whites have also increased; thus, the achievement gap has remained relatively stable since the 1980s, if it isn't actually *increasing*.[16] In the face of structural barriers, many researchers have pointed out that the individual agency of motivated students can mediate the legacy of oppression that has kept various groups of Americans from higher education.[17] But it is also clear that the structural inequalities of the larger society and the state systems of public education still keep a large percentage of ethnic minority students and students of low socioeconomic status from equal educational development, and thereby, equal access to higher education and the social and economic rewards of higher education. The historical achievement and access gaps between white and nonwhite minorities, and more recently between white and Asian students, compared to other nonwhite minorities, have been redefined as an economically structured education debt,which has also been influenced over two centuries of racialized sociopolitical segregation. A legacy of social, economic, and educational inequities has structurally lingered in highly segregated, differentially funded, and differentially resourced primary, secondary, and postsecondary schools.[18]

Majority-minority schools at every level of our educational system are concentrated in poor disadvantaged urban areas that lack many social, economic, and educational resources essential to prepare students for access and success in higher education: equal funding, trained and competent teachers, high-quality curricula, knowledgeable counselors, articulation with postsecondary schools, and social support services to mediate the effects of impoverished environments. Cabrera and La Nasa demonstrated that 71 percent of high school students of the lowest socioeconomic status failed to "obtain the requisite college qualifications" needed to successfully enter higher education. There is ample evidence that most race/ethnicity and class-related differences in academic achievement can be accounted for by academic preparation and achievement in primary and secondary schooling, which means that if all students, regardless or ethnicity/race or social class, were equally educated at the primary and secondary level, there would be near-equal academic achievement and near-equal access to higher education. However, as Samuel Bowles and Herbert Gintis point out, there are still strong correlations between social class and economic earning potential once a graduate leaves school for the labor market.[19]

In reviewing current statistics on higher education in California, it is clear that nonwhite minorities have not yet overcome the legacy of institutionalized racism in California society, and it is debatable if the California community college as it has been institutionalized will be able to do much better to assist these students. The California *Master Plan for Higher Education* of 1960 structured the largest state system of higher education in the United States to accommodate only 33.3 percent of the state's high school graduates while relegating the majority of California youth to an underfunded, underarticulated, and non-bachelor-degree-granting community college system. Even in the most enlightened and expansive higher education system in the United States, the bachelor's degree was structurally limited to 33.3 percent of the population. When one considers the close correlation between school achievement, socioeconomic status, and race, this meant the master plan structured a class-based and racialized hierarchy that has only been partially challenged in the last quarter century through now defunct affirmative action programs. It is unclear if other states are doing any better than California to address historical inequalities.

In a historical study of four centuries of opportunity and exclusion in the United States, Cal Jillson argued,

> Justice requires that we make a conscious national commitment to open opportunity to all Americans, and particularly to those we know to have been systematically disadvantaged at earlier stages in our history. Unfortunately, it is not at all clear that we will do even that.

A look at the history of higher education in the United States and the changing dynamics of student access does reveal some expansion of access and equity in increasing postsecondary education for a broader swath of Americans. However, traditionally underserved populations such as the poor and nonwhite ethnic minorities still struggle to achieve equality of opportunity in American society and its systems of higher education. The community college has been a limited opportunity and a mixed blessing to many, but it has not been enough to overcome a history of class-based and race-based road blocks barring the majority of U.S. citizens from obtaining the American dream.[20]

But the historical analysis of the community college in this book should not be considered a conclusion to predict or delimit the future of this institution. Robert N. Bellah and his colleagues rightly argued that social science should not be seen as an *end*, mindlessly adopted by policy makers for political purposes. Good social science should attempt to define, explain, and judge social phenomena, but it should also become the *means* for public debate:

> The very meaning of "effectiveness" raises value questions—effective for what purposes?—that should lead to moral debate. . . . The vogue of modern policy analysis, which in many instances has taken the place of the reflections of our public philosophers, does not substitute for genuine democratic conversation, for it remains within the esoteric domain of experts, experts who, under the façade of democratic rituals, want to make the real decisions for us. To allow policy analysis to supplant public discussion is, in effect, to abandon the democratic undertaking altogether, and to admit that we have become the administered society.[21]

Hopefully this book reinvigorates the long conversation over the institutionalization of the community college. But more than this, it is hoped this book provokes a democratic debate between legislators, the policy community, community college administrators, faculty, and the citizens serviced by their local institutions. Too often self-proclaimed sages from the academy make their pronouncements and stifle democratic deliberation, as if their hard-earned scientific truths would somehow magically enlighten and change the world. This author believes, in the words of President Barack Obama, that our democracy is a conversation where every citizen has a right and a duty to engage in deliberation about the institutions that mediate and partly determine our daily lives.[22]

This book was written in an effort to explain the history of an important institution so its missions and future possibilities can be more fully debated by the American public. All our lives are shaped, constrained, and made meaningful by a host of social institutions tht we know very little about. Many of these institutions are currently in a state of crisis, and they need to be changed so our society can continue to flourish. Robert N. Bellah and his colleagues argued, "We need to understand how much of our lives is lived in and though institutions, and how better institutions are essential if we are to lead better lives." But Bellah also argued that citizens need to use their understanding to consciously take part in institutions, becoming empowered to change those institutions to help in the daily struggle for survival.[23] Citizens must continue to believe in the "politics of agency."[24] The community college in America has offered a limited opportunity to countless numbers of American citizens and immigrants who would have otherwise had no chance at gaining a higher education. That opportunity should be recognized and celebrated. But the political, social, and economic realities of our unfolding future demand that more be done. This institution, as well as other educational institutions, such as high school and public universities, and of course our society at large, must *all* do more to help achieve and democratize the American dream. While this platitude can be seen as nonsensically idealistic, rhetorical platforms of moral aspiration can help bring focus to debates over institutional mission and policy initiatives. Political myths do have the power to shape normative discourse by helping participants choose between competing visions of the public good.[25] The American dream can be a potent symbol for renewed emphasis on the politics of equality and democracy.

Institutional Reform? Three Principles for Policy Makers

The current national movement for performance-based standards and institutional accountability must be understood in a historical perspective.[26] Education policy has never been a disinterested "scientific-technical enterprise." As Grubb and Lazerson pointed out, "Formal evaluation methods are not necessarily neutral." All policy initiatives and performance measurements should be analyzed and critiqued as mediums of particular political theories advancing partisan interests. While many current community college policy makers focus on important issues, ask important questions, and suggest important policy prescriptions, there is a marked tendency toward shortsightedness and faddist ideas that mirror larger debates over public education in the United States over the course of the last 40 years. The educational policy community needs to take a longer view because the practice of education and the evaluation of educational institutions have long histories.[27] As the current recessionary period in U.S. history has caused economic policy makers and business school faculty to look backward to similar crises in history, so also do many educational policy makers, administrators, and teachers look to the past for greater perspective.[28]

When evaluating educational institutions there is a tendency to emphasize certain student outcomes that are politically fashionable while ignoring others. Deciding the value of student outcomes is a *political decision* privileging certain normative values. Outcomes are often selected without proper consideration of the alternatives. Also, the decision makers usually ignore the educational and ethical implications of different types of outcomes markers. The most ethically profound objectives, such as equity, are the hardest to objectively measure, and therefore, the most likely to be ignored for more observable variables, such as test scores. Also missing is a broader analytic framework to determine how institutional effectiveness measures, such as standardized testing or student learning outcomes, actually affect the lives of students, their learning, and their long-term social and economic development. Often accountability recommendations are based on the crassest form of positivistic reductionism and technocratic faith whereby empirical minutiae is swapped for substantial outcomes of education in its larger sense. And looming ignored below the surface of all reformist policies is the old liberal assumption that all valued ends are compatible. But what if they are not?[29] What if increased efficiency means decreased equality? Or to put it another way, what if increased access to higher education means a relative decrease in institutional efficiency? Does anyone dare ask these types of questions or logically consider their implications?

Studies of the politics of educational reform over the past century seems to reinforce three basic principles.[30] The first is that no one can articulate, let alone measure, all the important parts of a complex human endeavor such as education.[31] This does not mean that the task is impossible, it is just fraught with difficulty. The human endeavor of education is not easy to understand or practice, so it should come as no surprise that it is incredibly difficult to measure its ends. Just as the Nobel laureates Joseph Stiglitz and Amartya Sen and a host of other economists have begun to rethink the validity of the taken-for-granted economic marker of gross domestic product, so also do professional educators and the public at large need to deliberate on the ends of higher education and how they should be more accurately measured.[32] Second, once worthy educational ends are identified, institutional administrators and instructors need to tailor educational assessment to specific learning goals for specific students in specific educational contexts designed to produce specific ends. Chris Anson makes this point very clearly: "The most meaningful assessments provide formative information to those closest to the learners whose abilities are being assessed, in the context of their own curriculum and educational outcomes."[33] Institutional accountability measures should grow out of the practice of teachers and curriculum developers, and not be dictated to them.

Finally, institutional administrators and policy makers need to understand the complexity of educational reform in terms of the *fallibility* of human actions and the *messy* nature of democratic processes. David Tyack and Larry Cuban, two of the most important historians of education in the United States, concluded in a landmark book on school reform: "Better schooling will result in the future—as it has in the past and does now—

chiefly from the steady, reflective efforts of the practitioners who work in schools and from the contributions of the parents and citizens who support (while they criticize) public education."[34] Over the past century, however, administrators, faculty, parents, and citizens at large are rarely allowed to contribute to framing the ends of education.

What are the possible ends of education? What ends are most important? What resources are available? And who should be accountable to whom? The political ideal of democracy in public education still eludes us as a nation because government and professional elites tend to dictate policy without broader debate. But it is more important to learn to recognize that not all ends are realizable or compatible. As Isaiah Berlin remarked, "Not all good things are compatible, still less all the ideals of mankind . . . conflicts of values may be an intrinsic, irremovable element in human life."[35] Sometimes hard compromises need to be made to choose one laudable end over another. Politicians and policy makers rarely acknowledge this bitter truth. All of us want to have our cake and eat it too.

Higher education institutions should be effective at what they do, but education is more of an art than a science, more of an affective experience than an effective enterprise, and its highest goal is the internal transformation of human beings, not the external measurement of particular behavior. Scholars, administrators, and faculty have already identified many practical policy recommendations that can help improve institutional practice and increase measures of student success.[36] A summary of promising practices here is not necessary because most community college administrators already know what needs to be done. The real difficulty is not identifying promising practices. The real difficulty is finding competent leadership to secure the economic resources required to sustain institutional success while also weighing the conflicts between efficiency and equality. To meet this challenge more democratic deliberation should take place over the ethical parameters of what educational effectiveness *should* mean and who should have the power to enact promising practices and on what terms. This deliberation must include community college administrators, faculty, students, and the larger community, not just policy makers. The ultimate effectiveness of any institution of education is enabled or constrained by the social, economic, and political context in which it operates. Policy makers would be better advised to focus on perfecting the *process* of institutional change rather than chasing unattainable measures of perfectibility.[37]

Education professionals must also address the Trojan horse in our midst. The current accountability movement may not really be about the perfection of education. It may not really be about education at all. Aaron Wildavasky, one of the first great scholars of policy analysis, warned in 1979 that the growing accountability movement in education might be the result of economic crises and political posturing. Wildavasky perceptively asked, "Is education being made into, or accepting the role of, the fall guy?" Wildavasky knew the answer of course. Educators had been waving flags since the turn of the 20th century when business-oriented managers began taking over American schools and displacing educational ends for political power and economic efficiency. In 1912 a perceptive New York teacher argued,

> We have yielded to the arrogance of "big business men" and have accepted their criteria of efficiency at their own valuation, without question. We have consented to measure the results of educational efforts in terms of price and product—the terms that prevail in the factory and the department store.

Instead of blindly adopting efficiency metrics from the business world and smashing them down on the complex ecology of educational institutions, educators and administrators at all levels must step up and ask, "Efficiency for whom and for what?" Hopefully this book will help spark a larger debate on the institutional ends of the community college. We must continually ask, "Who will coordinate whom toward what ends?"[38]

In this imperfect world of muted vision, corrupted motives, and constrained action we must rely on the flawed tools of human rationality and an irrational sense of hope to choose the best possible course for the future. As a wise man once profoundly declared,

> There is no escape: we must decide as we decide; moral risk cannot, at times, be avoided. All we can ask for is that none of the relevant factors be ignored, that the purposes we seek to realize should be seen as elements in a total form of life, which can be enhanced or damaged by decisions.[39]

NOTES

Notes to Preface

1. Steven Brint and Jerome Karabel, *The Diverted Dream: Community Colleges and the Promise of Educational Opportunity in America, 1900–1985* (Oxford, UK, 1989); Christopher J. Lucas, *American Higher Education: A History* (New York, 1994); W. Norton Grubb and Martin Lazerson, *The Education Gospel: The Economic Power of Schooling* (Cambridge, MA, 2004), 158; Kent A. Phillippe and Leila Gonzalez Sullivan, *National Profile of Community Colleges: Trends & Statistics*, 4th ed. (Washington, DC, 2005), 70–73.

2. Lawrence R. Jacobs and Theda Skocpol, eds., *Inequality and American Democracy* (New York, 2005).

3. Peter F. Drucker, "The Age of Social Transformation," *The Atlantic* (Nov 1994), 7, 10.

4. Robert Reich, "The Lost Art of Democratic Narrative," *The New Republic* (March 2005); Deborah Stone, *Policy Paradox: The Art of Political Decision Making*, revised ed. (New York, 2002): 1–54.

5. These flippant criticisms are from a new television sitcom called *Community*, which debuted in fall 2009 on NBC. See "Poking Fun at Community Colleges," *Inside Higher Ed* (May 6, 2009). The "high school with ashtrays" comment was first quoted by Zwerling (1976). The Association of American Community College president has expressed an interest in influencing the themes of this sitcom and he hopes to persuade the producers to include "teachable moments" about real community college life. See "Presidents Report to the AACC Board of Directors," *AACC* (Aug 2009).

6. William Zumeta, "Public Policy and Accountability in Higher Education," Donald E. Heller, ed., *The States and Public Higher Education Policy* (Baltimore, 2001), 155, 161.

7. W. Norton Grubb and Marvin Lazerson, *Broken Promises* (Chicago, 1988), 58.

8. Ibid., 155–158. See also James G. Cibulka, "The Changing Role of Interest Groups in Education," *Educational Policy*, 15, no. 1 (2001): 12–40; Grubb and Lazerson, *Broken Promises*, 53–55; David Hursh, "Assessing No Child Left Behind and the Rise of Neoliberal Education Policies," *American Educational Research Journal*, 44, no. 3 (2007): 493–518; Tim L. Mazzoni, "State Policy-Making and School Reform: Influences and Influentials," Jay D. Scribner and Donald H. Layton, eds., *The Study of Educational Politics* (Washington, DC, 1995): 53–73; David Tyack and Larry Cuban, *Tinkering Toward Utopia* (Cambridge, 1995), 78–82; Aaron Wildavasky, *Speaking Truth to Power: The Art and Craft of Policy Analysis* (Boston, 1979).

9. Grubb and Lazerson, *Broken Promises*, 58.

10. Gert Biesta, "What 'What Works' Won't Work: Evidence Based Practice and the Democratic Deficit in Educational Research," *Educational Theory* 57, no. 1 (2007): 1–22; Grubb and Lazerson, *Broken Promises*, 53; Mazzoni, "State Policy-Making and School Reform"; Gerald E. Sroufe, "Politics of Education at the Federal Level," Jay D. Scribner and Donald H. Layton, eds., *The Study of Educational Politics* (Washington, DC, 1995): 75–88.

11. John L. Campbell, "Institutional Analysis and the Role of Ideas in Political Economy," John L. Campbell & Ove K. Pedersen, eds., *The Rise of Neoliberalism and Institutional Analysis* (Princeton, NJ, 2001), 159–189. See also Cibulka, "The Changing Role of Interest Groups in Education," 19; Mazzoni, "State Policy-Making and School Reform," 63–64.

12. Sandra Hollingsworth, Margaret A. Gallego, D. Jean Clandinin, Peter Morrell, Pedro Portes, Robert Rueda, and Olga Welch, eds., *Section on Social and Institutional Analysis: No Child Left Behind* [Special issue], *American Educational Research Journal*, 44, no. 3 (2001); Hursh, "Assessing No Child Left Behind and the Rise of Neoliberal Education Policies"; Sara Schwartz Chrismer, Shannon T. Hodge, and Debby Saintil, eds., *Assessing NCLB: Perspectives and Prescriptions* [Special issue]. *Harvard Educational Review*, 76, no. 4 (2006).

13. Spellings Commission, *A Test of Leadership: Charting the Future of U.S. Higher Education* (Washington, DC, 2006); Charles Miller and Geri Malandra, "Accountability/Assessment," *Issue Paper: A National Dialogue: The Secretary of Education's Commission on the Future of Higher Education* (Washington, DC, no date); National Center for Public Policy and Higher Education, *Measuring Up 2000* (San José, CA, 2000); Vanessa Smith Morest, Holly Moore, Sandra Ruppert, Kevin Dougherty, and James Jacobs, *Accountability and Learning Outcomes in Community Colleges*, Community College Research Center, Columbia University, New York, March 2002; George Kuh and Stanley Ikenberry, *More Than You Think, Less Than We Need: Learning Outcomes Assessment in American Higher Education*, National Institute for Learning Outcomes Assessment (Oct 2009).

14. David W. Breneman and Susan C. Nelson, *Financing Community Colleges: An Economic Perspective* (Washington DC, 1981); Alicia C. Dowd, "From Access to Outcome Equity," *Annals of the American Academy of Political and Social Science*, 586 (2003), 109; Kevin J. Dougherty and Esther Hong, "Performance Accountability as Imperfect Panacea," *Defending the Community College Equity Agenda*, Thomas Bailey and Vanessa Smith Morest, eds. (Baltimore, MD, 2006), 51–86; Thomas Byrne Edsall, "The Changing Shape of Power: A Realignment in Public Policy," *The Rise and Fall of the New Deal Order, 1930–1980*, Steve Fraser and Gary Gerstle, eds. (Princeton, NJ, 1989), 269–293; Peter H. Garland and S. V. Martorana, "The Interplay of Political Culture and Participant Behavior in Political Action to Enact Significant State Community College Legislation," *Community College Review*, 16, no. 2 (1988): 30–43; John S. Levin, *Globalizing the Community College* (New York, 2001), 64, 99, 111–113; James W. Thornton Jr., *The Community Junior College*, 3rd ed. (New York, 1972), 42, 91, 292; Sean Wilentz, *The Age of Reagan* (New York, 2008).

15. W. Norton Grubb and Associates, *Honored but Invisible* (New York, 1999), 245. See also Frankie Santos Laanan, "Accountability in Community Colleges." In *Community Colleges: Policy in the Future Context*, eds. Barbara K. Townsend & Susan B. Twombly (Westport, CT, 1999), 57–76. Grubb's book was intended as "criticism" of this institution in order to "help improve" it, not to "set off accountability policies," which was an indirect effect. Personal communication with author (Nov 2009).

16. League for Innovation in the Community College, *An Assessment Framework for the Community College: Measuring Student Learning and Achievement as a Means of Demonstrating Institutional Effectiveness*, Version 1.0 (Phoenix, AZ, 2004), 3–5, 10, 17.

17. Grubb and Associates, *Honored but Invisible*, 43; National Center for Public Policy and Higher Education, *Measuring Up 2000*, 23; Andreea M. Serban and Jack Friedlander, eds., *Developing and Implementing Assessment of Student Learning Outcomes, New Directions for Community Colleges*, 126 (San Francisco, 2004), 1.

18. Kevin J. Dougherty and Monica Reid, *Fifty States of Achieving the Dream: State Policies to Enhance Access to and Success in Community Colleges Across the United States*, Community College Research Center (New York, 2007), 25, 26.

19. Hursh, "Assessing No Child Left Behind and the Rise of Neoliberal Education Policies"; Levin, *Globalizing the Community College*, 64, 99, 111–113; Mazzoni, "State Policy-Making and School Reform"; Schwartz Chrismer et al., *Assessing NCLB*; Smith Morest et al., *Accountability and Learning Outcomes in Community Colleges*.

20. Raymond E. Callahan, *Education and the Cult of Efficiency* (Chicago, 1962); James G. Cibulka, "The Changing Role of Interest Groups in Education"; Herbert M. Kliebard, *The Struggle for the American Curriculum 1893–1958*, 3rd ed. (New York, 2004), 19–20; Tyack and Cuban, *Tinkering Toward Utopia*, 50–51.

21. On the lack of historical analysis on the community college see Kenneth Meier, *The Community College Mission: History & Theory, 1930–2000* (unpublished manuscript, 2008). On examples of recent historians neglect of community colleges see John Aubrey Douglas, *The California Idea and American Higher Education* (Stanford, 2000); John Aubrey Douglas, *The Conditions for Admission* (Stanford, CA, 2007); Lucas, *American Higher Education*; John R. Thelin, *A History of American Higher Education* (Baltimore, MD, 2004), 404.

22. Douglass C. North and Robert W. Fogel won the Nobel in 1993 for their work on economic history, although North's work specifically focused on institutionalism. Elinor Ostrom and Oliver Williamson won the Nobel in 2009 for institutionalism.

23. Vincent Ostrom and Elinor Ostrom, "Rethinking Institutional Analysis: An Interview with Vincent and Elinor Ostrom," Mercatus Center, George Mason University (Nov 7, 2003), 1; Anthony Giddens, *Capitalism and Modern Social Theory: An Analysis of the Writing of Marx, Durkheim, and Max Weber* (Cambridge, UK, 1971).

24. The term *political economy* was a rich term used in the 18th and 19th centuries by political theorists such as Adam Smith and Karl Marx. This term connotes

not only the political and economic sectors of a society but also the deep and complex interplay of social, cultural, political, and economic currents that infuse any politicized issue.

25. Peter L. Berger and Thomas Luckmann, *The Social Construction of Reality: A Treatise in the Sociology of Knowledge* (New York, 1966), 23; Paul J. DiMaggio and Walter W. Powell, "The Iron Cage Revisited: Institutional Isomorphism and Collective Rationality in Organizational Fields," *The New Institutionalism in Organizational Analysis,* Paul J. DiMaggio and Walter W. Powell, eds. (Chicago, 1991), 41–62; Giddens, *Capitalism and Modern Social Theory;* Ronald L. Jepperson, "Institutions, Institutional Effects, and Institutionalism," *The New Institutionalism in Organizational Analysis,* Ibid., 143; Douglas C. North, *Structure and Change in Economic History* (New York, 1981); John R. Searle, *The Construction of Social Reality* (New York, 1995).

26. On this debate see Isaiah Berlin, "Two Concepts of Liberty" and "The Counter-Enlightenment," *The Proper Study of Mankind* (New York, 2000).

27. DiMaggio and Powell, "The Iron Cage Revisited," 8; Roger Friedland and Robert R. Alford, "Bringing Society Back In: Symbols, Practices, and Institutional Contradictions," *The New Institutionalism in Organizational Analysis,* Ibid., 232–263; James Miller, *The Passion of Michel Foucault* (New York, 1993), 150; Searle, *The Construction of Social Reality.* On the debate over "free-will" and structural "determinism" see Isaiah Berlin, "Historical Inevitability," *The Proper Study of Mankind* (New York, 2000).

28. Berger and Luckmann, *The Social Construction of Reality,* 15; DiMaggio and Powell, "The Iron Cage Revisited," 20, 23, 26, 28; Andre Lecours, "New Institutionalism: Issues and Questions," *New Institutionalism: Theory and Analysis,* Andre Lecours, ed. (Toronto: University of Toronto Press, 2005), 3–25; John W. Meyer and Brian Rowan, "Institutionalized Organizations: Formal Structure as Myth and Ceremony," *The New Institutionalism in Organizational Analysis,* Ibid., 41, 44; Paul Pierson, *Politics in Time: History, Institutions, and Social Analysis* (Princeton, NJ, 2004), 20–21, 43, 51; Lynne G. Zucker, "The Role of Institutionalization in Cultural Persistence," *The New Institutionalism in Organizational Analysis,* Ibid., 85; Searle, *The Construction of Social Reality.*

29. Isaiah Berlin, "Historical Inevitability"; Giddens, *Capitalism and Modern Social Theory;* Miller, *The Passion of Michel Foucault,* 15, 150, 336.

30. James A. Berlin, "Postmodernism in the Academy"; *Rhetorics, Poetics, and Cultures* (West Lafayette, IN, 2003): 60–82; Friedland and Alford, "Bringing Society Back In," 232, 254; Jepperson, "Institutions, Institutional Effects, and Institutionalism," 145, 149, 151–52, 158; Walter W. Powell, "Expanding the Scope of Institutional Analysis," *The New Institutionalism in Organizational Analysis,* Ibid., 188, 194–195; Steven Brint and Jerome Karabel, "Institutional Origins and Transformations: The Case of American Community Colleges," *The New Institutionalism in Organizational Analysis,* Ibid., 337–360.

31. Sherry B. Ortner, *Anthropology and Social Theory: Culture, Power, and the Acting Subject* (Durham, 2006), 7, 18, 127, 130, 133, 139, 147, 152. On the relationship between institutions and agency see: Ludwig Wittgenstein, *Philosophical Investigations,* Trans. G. E. M. Anscombe (Oxford, UK, 2001), part I, 23. Paul Pierson argues

that the term *institutional change* is misleading because it is almost impossible to change institutions fundamentally. Instead, Pierson recommends *institutional development* as a more accurate description of how institutions change through time. See *Politics in Time*, 133, 137.

32. Ronald L. Jepperson and John W. Meyer, "The Public Order and the Construction of Formal Organizations," *The New Institutionalism in Organizational Analysis*, Ibid., 204–231; James March and Herbert Simon, *Organizations,* 2nd ed. (Oxford, 1993), 130; Meyer and Rowan, "Institutionalized Organizations"; Pierson, *Politics in Time*; W. Richard Scott, *Organizations: Rational, Natural, and Open Systems,* 3rd ed. (Englewood Cliffs, NJ, 1992).

33. Karl E. Weick, "Educational Organizations as Loosely Coupled Systems," *Administrative Science Quarterly*, 21, no. 1 (1976): 1–19; March and Simon, *Organizations,*157, 159; Michael D. Cohen and James G. March, "Leadership in an Organized Anarchy," *Organization and Governance in Higher Education,* 5th ed. M. C. Brown II, ed., (Boston, 2000), 16–35.

34. Meyer and Rowan, "Institutionalized Organizations"; W. Richard Scott and John M. Meyer, "The Organization of Societal Sectors: Propositions and Early Evidence," *The New Institutionalism in Organizational Analysis*, Ibid., 108–140; Theda Skocpol, "Bringing the State Back In," *Bringing the State Back In,* Peter B. Evans, Dietrich Rueschemeyer, and Theda Skocpol, eds. (Cambridge, UK, 1985), 3–37.

35. DiMaggio and Powell, "The Iron Cage Revisited," 66, 68; Meyer and Rowan, "Institutionalized Organizations," 41, 44–46, 48–50, 58, 60; Scott, *Organizations,*176; Scott and Meyer, "The Organization of Societal Sectors," 123–24; Powell, "Expanding the Scope of Institutional Analysis," 184.

36. Joel A. C. Baum and Jitendra V. Singh, "Organizational Hierarchies and Evolutionary Processes," *Evolutionary Dynamics of Organizations*, Joel A. C. Baum and Jitendra V. Singh, eds. (Oxford, UK, 1994), 5; DiMaggio and Powell, "The Iron Cage Revisited"; Friedland and Alford, "Bringing Society Back In"; Scott and Meyer, "The Organization of Societal Sectors," 137; Powell, "Expanding the Scope of Institutional Analysis."

37. Jepperson, "Institutions, Institutional Effects, and Institutionalism"; Doug McAdam and W. Richard Scott, "Organizations and Movements," *Social Movements and Organizational Theory*, Gerald F. Davis, Doug McAdam, W. Richard Scott, and Mayer N. Zald, eds. (Cambridge, UK, 2005), 4–40; Scott and Meyer, "The Organization of Societal Sectors," 117; Powell, "Expanding the Scope of Institutional Analysis"; Zucker, "The Role of Institutionalization in Cultural Persistence."

38. Friedland and Alford, "Bringing Society Back In," 232; McAdam and Scott, "Organizations and Movements"; Pierson, *Politics in Time;* Zucker, "The Role of Institutionalization in Cultural Persistence," 84.

39. Siobhan Harty, "Theorizing Institutional Change," *New Institutionalism: Theory and Analysis*, Ibid., 51–79.

40. Brint and Karabel, *The Diverted Dream* (see also "Institutional Origins and Transformations: The Case of American Community Colleges"); John H. Frye, *The Vision of the Public Junior College, 1900–1940* (New York, 1992); Meier, *The Community College Mission*; David F. Labaree, *How to Succeed in School Without Really*

Learning: The Credentials Race in American Education (New Haven, CT, 1997). I do not include Dougherty's *The Contradictory College* in this list because it includes no historical narrative and very little historical analysis; however, it does touch upon the history and institutionalization of the community college.

41. On practice theory see Ortner, *Anthropology and Social Theory*; Etienne Wenger, *Communities of Practice: Learning, Meaning, and Identity* (Cambridge, UK, 1998).

42. Burton R. Clark, *The Open Door College: A Case Study* (New York, 1960).

43. Brint and Karabel, *The Diverted Dream*, 5–19, 56, 59, 91, 205–32.

44. Ibid., 56, 59, 91, 205–32.

45. Brint and Karabel, "Institutional Origins and Transformations," 349.

Notes to Chapter 1

1. Arthur M. Cohen and Florence B. Brawer, *The American Community College*, 3d ed. (San Francisco: Jossey-Bass, 1996): 10, 25; Kevin J. Dougherty, *The Contradictory College: The Conflicting Origins, Impacts, and Futures of the Community College* (Albany, NY, 2001): Ch 2; Kevin J. Dougherty and Barbara K. Townsend, "Community College Missions: A Theoretical and Historical Perspective," *Community College Missions in the 21st Century, New Directions for the Community College* 136 (2006): 5–13; John H. Frye, "Educational Paradigms in the Professional Literature of the Community College," *Higher Education: Handbook of Theory and Research*, vol. 10, John C. Smart, ed. (New York, 1994); George L. Hall, "Behind the Bramble Bushes: A Mid-Century History of the Community College," *Community College Review* 2 (1974): 6–14; Christopher J. Lucas, *American Higher Education: A History* (New York, 1994): 221.

2. Norman F. Cantor, *The Civilization of the Middle Ages* (New York, 1993), 439–442; Lucas, *American Higher Education* (New York, 1994); Diarmaid MacCulloch, *The Reformation* (New York, 2003), 583–588; John R. Thelin, *A History of American Higher Education* (Baltimore, MD, 2004).

3. MacCulloch, *The Reformation*, 536–37, 664.

4. Daniel Walker Howe, *What Hath God Wrought: The Transformation of America, 1815–1848* (Oxford, UK, 2007), 457.

5. Lawrence A. Cremin, *American Education: The National Experience, 1783–1876* (New York, 1980).

6. Thelin, *A History of American Higher Education*, 52; Howe, *What Hath God Wrought*, 462.

7. Ibid., 26; Lucas, *American Higher Education*, 104.

8. Howe, *What Hath God Wrought*, 459, 462.

9. Cremin, *American Education*, 400–409; Thelin, *A History of American Higher Education*, 107.

10. Howe, *What Hath God Wrought*, 460–461.

11. Alan Dawley, *Struggles for Justice: Social Responsibility and the Liberal State* (Cambridge, MA, 1991); Richard Hofstadter, *The Age of Reform* (New York, 1955),

135–148; David Tyack and Elisabeth Hansot, *Managers of Virtue: Public School Leadership in America, 1820–1980* (New York, 1982); James Weinstein, *The Corporate Ideal in the Liberal State, 1900–1918* (Boston, 1968).

12. Cremin, *American Education*; Tyack and Hansot, *Managers of Virtue*.

13. Dawley, *Struggles for Justice*; Lucas, *American Higher Education*, 149, 175; Michael McGerr, *A Fierce Discontent: The Rise and Fall of the Progressive Movement in America, 1870–1920* (Oxford, UK, 2003); Thelin, *A History of American Higher Education*, 135–140, 146–50; Laurence R. Veysey, *The Emergence of the American University* (Chicago, 1965).

14. John D. Buenker, John C. Burnham, and Robert M. Crunden, *Progressivism* (Cambridge, MA, 1977); Dawley, *Struggles for Justice*.

15. Howe, *What Hath God Wrought*, 464.

16. Walter Crosby Eells, *Why Junior College Terminal Education?* (Washington DC, 1941), 48; Daniel Golden, *The Price of Admission* (New York, 2007); Jerome Karabel, *The Chosen* (New York, 2005); Dan A. Oren, *Joining the Club* (New Haven, CT, 1986); Thelin, *A History of American Higher Education*, 169, 171.

17. Jurgen Herbst, "Nineteenth-Century Normal Schools in the United States: A Fresh Look," *History of Education*, 9, no. 3 (1980): 219–227; David F. Labaree, *The Trouble with Ed Schools* (New Haven, CT, 2004), 26–28; David F. Labaree, *How to Succeed in School Without Really Learning* (New Haven, CT, 1997), 40; Jonathan Messerli, *Horace Mann: A Biography* (New York, 1972), 437–438.

18. Ray Lyman Wilbur, "Introduction," *The Junior College: Its Organization and Administration*, William Martin Proctor, ed. (Stanford, CA, 1927), ix–x.

19. William Rainey Harper, "The Small College–Its Prospects," *Proceedings of National Education Association* (Chicago, 1900), 67–87, quoted in Walter Crosby Eells, *The Junior College* (Boston, 1931), 60–61.

20. Chauncey Samuel Boucher, *The Chicago College Plan* (Chicago, 1935), ch 1 & 12; Lawrence A. Cremin, *American Education: The Metropolitan Experience, 1876–1980* (New York, 1988), 557–560; John Aubrey Douglas, *The California Idea and American Higher Education* (Stanford, CA, 2000), 114–116; Howard Erdman and William R. Ogden, "Reconsidering William Rainey Harper as 'Father' of the Junior College," *College Student Journal* 34, no. 3 (2000); William Warren Ferrier, *Ninety Years of Education in California, 1846–1936* (Berkeley, 1937), 352; Lucas, *American Higher Education*, 173–174, 180–182, 219–222; Hugh Ross, "University Influence in the Genesis and Growth of Junior Colleges in California," *History of Education Quarterly* 3, no. 3 (1963): 143–152; Thelin, *A History of American Higher Education*, 120–22, 250; James L. Wattenbarger and Allen A. Witt, "Origins of the California System," *Community College Review* 22, no. 4 (1995): 17–25.

21. Roy W. Cloud, *Education in California: Leaders, Organizations, and Accomplishments of the First Hundred Years* (Stanford, CA, 1952), 121, 130; Charles J. Falk, *The Development and Organization of Education in California* (New York, 1968), 47; M. E. Herriott, Elizabeth Sands, and Harry W. Stauffacher, "History and Objectives of Junior High Education in California," *National Association of Secondary School Principles Bulletin* 35, no. 9 (1951): 9–19; Herbert M. Kliebard, *The Struggle for the American Curriculum, 1893–1958*, 3rd ed. (New York, 2004): 7–8; Leonard V. Koos, *The American Secondary School* (Boston, 1927), 136; James L. Ratcliff, "'First'

Public Junior Colleges in an Age of Reform," *Journal of Higher Education* 58, no. 2 (1987): 151–180; James L. Ratcliff, "Seven Streams in the Historical Development of the Modern American Community College," *A Handbook on the Community College in America*, George A. Baker III, ed. (Westport, CT, 1994), 3–16; William J. Reese, *The Origins of the American High School* (New Haven, CT, 1995); David B. Tyack, *The One Best System: A History of American Urban Education* (Cambridge, MA, 1974): 182–184; Tyack and Hansot, *Managers of Virtue*.

22. Cohen and Brawer, *The American Community College*, Ch 1 & 2; Hall, "Behind the Bramble Bushes," 6–14; Kent A. Phillippe and Leila Gonzalez Sullivan, *National Profile of Community Colleges* (Washington, DC, 2005): 1–8, 23–24; Leonard V. Koos, "Recent Growth of the Junior College," *The School Review* 36, no. 4 (1928): 256–266.

23. Cloud, *Education in California*, 190; Cohen and Brawer, *The American Community College*, Ch 1; Lucas, *American Higher Education*, 220–222; Edmund J. Gleazer Jr., "Evolution of Junior Colleges into Community Colleges," *A Handbook on the Community College in America*, George A. Baker III, ed. (Westport, CT, 1994), 17–27; Eells, *The Junior College*, 75–80; Meier, *The Community College Mission*, Ch 1 & 2; George B. Vaughan, *The Community College Story*, 3rd ed. (Washington, DC, 2006); Frederick L. Whitney, "Present Standards for Junior Colleges," *The School Review* 36, no. 8 (1928): 593–603.

24. The *Junior College Journal* (1930–1972) was later named the *Community and Junior College Journal* (1973–1985), only to be later named the *Community, Technical, and Junior College Journal* (1985–1992), and presently it is called the *Community College Journal* (since 1992). Other histories of the community college have focused exclusively on this journal as primary source material (Frye, 1992; Meier, 2008). This study did not feel the need to replicate this scholarship. Also, this journal has been mostly a partisan booster of community colleges rather than a source for policy or scholarship; thus, it is a very limited source of data and analysis.

25. On progressivism as a national phenomenon see Buenker, Burnham, and Crunden, *Progressivism*; Dawley, *Struggles for Justice*; Arthur S. Link and Richard L. McCormick, *Progressivism* (Wheeling, IL, 1983); Nell Irvin Painter, *Standing at Armageddon* (New York, 1987); Robert H. Wiebe, *The Search for Order* (New York, 1967).

26. On educational progressivism see Lawrence A. Cremin, *The Transformation of the School: Progressivism in American Education, 1876–1957* (New York, 1961); Kliebard, *The Struggle for the American Curriculum*; Labaree, *How to Succeed in School Without Really Trying*; David B. Tyack, *The One Best System*; Tyack and Hansot, *Managers of Virtue*. I reject the analytical constructs of *administrative progressives* and *pedagogical progressives*, most notably developed by Tyack and Kliebard, although I recognize that these two terms do represent two distinct currents of educational thought during this era. I think the idea and actions of progressives, especially educational progressives, deserve a much more nuanced schematic, which will be the focus on my next book on the Americanization movement in education. While there are clear differences between the work of John Dewey and David Snedden, there is a murky gray area with the likes of Alexis F. Lange who used the democratic rhetoric of Dewey in the service of rationalizing a hierarchical educational system supported

by Snedden. There are also many similarities across the spectrum, including ethno-centrism, nationalism, technocraticism, and a moral high-mindedness.

27. Weick, "Educational Organizations as Loosely Coupled Systems," 1–19; March and Simon, *Organizations,*157, 159; Cohen and March, "Leadership in an Organized Anarchy," 16–35.

28. Friedland and Alford, "Bringing Society Back In," 232; McAdam and Scott, "Organizations and Movements"; Pierson, *Politics in Time;* Zucker, "The Role of Institutionalization in Cultural Persistence," 84.

29. Ortner, *Anthropology and Social Theory,* 7, 18, 127, 130, 133, 139, 147, 152.

30. Alexis F. Lange, "The Junior College–What Manner of Child Shall This Be?!," *School and Society,* 7 (1918): 211–216. Originally a speech at Junior College Section of the California Teachers' Association in 1917.

31. Leonard V. Koos, *The Junior-College Movement* (Boston, 1925), 16, 19–20, 28, 100, 121, 311; Koos, *The American Secondary School,* 236–242.

32. Koos, *The Junior-College Movement,* 116–117, 119–20, 162–163; Koos, *The American Secondary School,* 99–100.

33. Eells, *The Junior College,* xii, 5, 21, 40, 279–280, 289. Eells would condense elements from this book in an article in 1931 for the newly established *Junior College Journal.* Eells titled his article in homage to Alexis F. Lange's famous speech in 1917. See Walter Crosby Eells, "What Manner of Child Shall This Be?," *Junior College Journal,* 1 (1931): 309–328.

34. Bureau of Education, *Cardinal Principles of Secondary Education,* Bulletin No. 35 (Washington DC, 1918), 22, quoted in Frye, *Vision of the Public Junior College,* 24–27. See also Frye, Ibid., 7, 39, 46, 53, 130–133.

35. DiMaggio and Powell, "The Iron Cage Revisited," 66, 68; Meyer and Rowan, "Institutionalized Organizations," 41, 44–46, 48–50, 58, 60; Scott, *Organizations,*176; Scott and Meyer, "The Organization of Societal Sectors," 123–124; Powell, "Expanding the Scope of Institutional Analysis," 184.

36. James Rowland Angell, "Problems Peculiar to the Junior College," *The School Review* 25, no. 6 (1917): 385–397; Cohen and Brawer, *The American Community College,* Ch 1; Frye, *The Vision of the Public Junior College,* 119; Gleazer, "Evolution of Junior Colleges into Community Colleges," 19; Alexis F. Lange, "The Junior College as an Integral Part of the Public-School System," *The School Review* 25, no. 7 (1917): 456–479; Lucas, *American Higher Education,* 220–222; Ratcliff, "Seven Streams in the Historical Development of the Modern American Community College"; Whitney, "Present Standards for Junior Colleges"; George F. Zook, "Is the Junior College a Menace or a Boom," *The School Review* 37, no. 6 (1929): 415–425.

37. David F. Labaree, "From Comprehensive High School to Community College," *Research in Sociology of Education and Socialization,* 9 (Greenwich, CT, 1990): 203–240. See also Grubb and Lazerson, *The Education Gospel;* Kliebard, *The Struggle for the American Curriculum;* Labaree, *How to Succeed in School Without Really Learning;* Tyack, *The One Best System;* Tyack and Hansot, *Managers of Virtue.*

38. Philo Hutcheson, "The 1947 President's Commission on Higher Education and the National Rhetoric on Higher Education Policy," *History of Higher Education Annual,* 22 (2002): 92–93, footnote 13.

39. Eells, *The Junior College,* 289, 310; Walter Crosby Eells, *Why Junior College Terminal Education?*

40. Eells, *Why Junior College Terminal Education?,* 1, 6–7, 11, 22–23, 26, 29.

41. Ibid.; Edward F. Mason, "New Aims for Junior Colleges," in *Why Junior College Terminal Education?,* Ibid., 267–276; William Henry Snyder, "Philosophy of Semiprofessional Education," in *Why Junior College Terminal Education?,* Ibid., 256–266. For a critique of junior college leader ideology as a socially conservative movement desiring "social stability, not social change" see Gregory L. Goodwin, A *Social Panacea: A History of the Community-Junior College Ideology,* ERIC Document No. ED 093 427 (1973), 15. On early human capital theory see Theodore W. Schultz, "Investment in Human Capital," *The American Economic Review,* 51, no. 1 (1961): 1–17; Gary S. Becker, *Human Capital* (New York, 1964). On FDR social programs and expanding the economy see Dawley, *Struggles for Justice.*

42. Hutcheson, "The 1947 President's Commission on Higher Education and the National Rhetoric on Higher Education Policy"; Julie A. Reuben and Linda Perkins, "Introduction: Commemorating the Sixtieth Anniversary of the President's Commission Report," *History of Education Quarterly* 47, no. 3 (2007): 265–276; Dongbin Kim and John L. Rury, "The Changing Profile of College Access: The Truman Commission and Enrollment Patterns in the Postwar Era," *History of Education Quarterly* 47, no. 3 (2007): 302–327.

43. The spelling of community college is inconsistent within the literature on this subject. It began as a term in all lower case, but by the 1970s some authors began to capitalize it. Around this time, the California Community College system, the largest state system of community colleges in the United States, institutionalized the capitalization as it became the proper name of one of the official state segments of higher education. In this study, community college refers to the general institution.

44. Quentin J. Bogart, "The Community College Mission," *A Handbook on the Community College in America,* Ibid., 60–73; Brint and Karabel, *The Diverted Dream,* 68–71; John H. Frye, "The Rhetoric of Professional Educators and the Definition of Public Junior Colleges from 1900 to 1940," *Community College Review* 20 (1993): 5–16; Edmund J. Gleazer Jr., *This Is the Community College* (Boston, 1968): 28; Gleazer, "Evolution of Junior Colleges into Community Colleges"; Martin S. Quigley and Thomas W. Bailey, *Community College Movement in Perspective: Teachers College Responds to the Truman Commission* (Lanham, MD, 2003).

45. Cohen and Brawer, *The American Community College,* Ch 1; Hall, "Behind the Bramble Bushes," 6–14; Meier, *The Community College Mission,* Ch 2 & 3.

46. Jesse Bogue, *The Community College* (New York, 1950), 21; Carnegie Commission on Higher Education, *The Open Door Colleges* (New York, 1970): 2; Cohen and Brawer, *The American Community College,* Ch 1; Hall, "Behind the Bramble Bushes," 6–14; Meier, *The Community College Mission,* Ch 2 & 3; George F. Zook, "The Next Twenty Years," *Why Junior College Terminal Education?,* Ibid., 277–284.

47. Leland L. Medsker, *The Junior College: Progress and Prospect* (New York, 1960), 16, 18, 20, 22, 66. In relation to the open-door policy and remedial education, Medsker makes an argument that many critics would later use to criticize the de facto American policy of "college for all": "It is also argued that so long as junior

colleges admit virtually everybody, the high school student is not encouraged to perform at optimum capacity because he knows that his deficiencies can be made up in junior college" (67). For a contemporary revision of this argument see James E. Rosenbaum, *Beyond College for All: Career Paths for the Forgotten Half* (New York, 2001).

48. Medsker, *The Junior College,* 23–24.

49. Ibid. Medsker noted the ideal of social mobility through the meritocracy of the educational system, but he seemed ambivalent to any attempt to address the inequality of postsecondary educational access, especially access to the bachelor's degree. Medsker wrote, "[The junior college] may now, so far as its preparatory function is concerned, become a screening agency for the four-year colleges. The extent to which this becomes true will depend on how selective society allows higher education to become and to what degree the survival of the fittest should come to apply to the attainment of a baccalaureate degree" (317). On the critique of American meritocracy see Josh M. Beach, "Ideology of the American Dream: Two Competing Philosophies in Education, 1776–2006," *Educational Studies* 41, no. 2 (2007): 148–164; Samuel Bowles and Herbert Gintis, "Schooling in Capitalist America Revisited," *Sociology of Education,* 75, no. 1 (2002): 1–18; Labaree, *How to Succeed in School Without Really Learning.*

50. Ibid., 25–26, 41, 90–94, 113, 317. Medsker argued, "A great burden is placed on the junior college to motivate capable students from lower social groups to continue in college and to perform at an acceptable academic level" (42–43, 142).

51. Burton R. Clark, "The 'Cooling Out' Function in Higher Education," *The American Journal of Sociology* 65, no. 6 (1960): 569–76; John Aubrey Douglass, *The California Idea and American Higher Education* (Stanford, CA, 2000); Medsker, *The Junior College,* 112–116; Labaree, "From Comprehensive High School to Community College," 215–216; Wattenbarger and Witt, "Origins of the California System."

52. Burton R. Clark, *The Open Door College* (New York, 1960), 2, 5, 39, 41–42.

53. Ibid., 41–46, 48, 71–77, 83, 146. The idea that junior colleges cooled out overly ambitious students could also be applied to high school as well, given that most American high schools grouped students into academic and vocational tracts long before they were able to get to the junior college. In this respect, the cooling-out function of the junior college was an extension of its roots in the high school.

54. Ibid., viii, 159–161.

55. Clyde E. Blocker, Robert H. Plummer, and Richard C. Richardson Jr., *The Two-Year College: A Social Synthesis* (Englewood Cliffs, NJ, 1965), 2–3, 6, 18, 35, 69, 269, 272–74, 282, 286–287.

56. Cohen and March, "Leadership in an Organized Anarchy," 16–35.

57. Ibid., 2–3, 6, 18, 35, 69, 269, 272–74, 282, 286–287.

58. Gleazer Jr., *This Is the Community College,* 14, 16, 27, 32–33; Labaree, "From Comprehensive High School to Community College," 219–221.

59. Ibid., 28, 31, 96.

60. Ibid., 28, 46, 48, 50, 53, 86; Leland L. Medsker and Dale Tillery, *Breaking the Access Barriers: A Profile of Two-Year Colleges* (New York, 1971), 71. See also Bogart, "The Community College Mission"; Albert L. Lorenzo, "The Mission and

Functions of the Community College," *A Handbook on the Community College in America,* Ibid., 111–122.

61. Carnegie Commission on Higher Education, *The Open-Door Colleges: Policies for Community Colleges* (New York, 1970), 1–3, 10–11, 15, 18. Arthur M. Cohen, "Governmental Policies affecting Community Colleges: A Historical Perspective." *Community Colleges: Policy in the Future Context,* Barbara K. Townsend & Susan B. Twombly, eds. (Westport, CT, 1999), 3–22.

62. Ibid., 5–6, 54–57. For more on the "social efficiency" goals of the Carnegie Corporation see Labaree, *How to Succeed in School without Really Learning,* ch 5; Ellen Condliffe Lagemann, *The Politics of Knowledge: The Carnegie Corporation, Philanthropy, and Public Policy* (Middletown, CT, 1989).

63. Gary Orfield, Mark D. Bachmeier, David R. James, and Tamela Eide, *Deepening Segregation in American Public Schools,* Harvard Project on School Desegregation (Boston, 1997).

64. Hurley H. Doddy, "The Progress of the Negro in Higher Education," *The Journal of Negro Education* 32 (1963), 487.

65. As late as 1965, Blocker, Plummer, and Richardson's *The Two-Year College: A Social Synthesis* included a wealth of data on 2-year college students in terms of education, age, class, employment, and even gender, but there is not a single word on race or ethnicity (107–133). See also Meier, *The Community College Mission,* ch 3.

66. James D. Anderson, *The Education of Blacks in the South, 1860–1935* (Chapel Hill, SC, 1988), 1–2, 279; Regina Werum, "Sectionalism and Racial Politics: Federal Vocational Policies and Programs in the Predesegregation South," *Social Science History,* 21, no. 3 (1997): 399–453.

67. Horace Mann Bond, "Education in the South," *Journal of Educational Sociology* 12 (1939): 264–274.

68. Koos, *The American Secondary School,* 136, 354.

69. Eells, *The Junior College,* 22, 37.

70. "Current Events of National Importance in Negro Education," *The Journal of Negro Education,* 1, no. 1 (1932): 91–97; Nick Aaron Ford, "The Negro Junior College," *The Journal of Negro Education,* 5, no. 4 (1936): 591–594; David A. Lane Jr., "The Junior College Movement Among Negroes," *The Journal of Negro Education,* 2, no. 3 (1933): 272–283.

71. Ford, "The Negro Junior College," 591–594. On progressivism and black educators see Derrick P. Alridge, "Of Victorianism, Civilizationism, and Progressivism: The Educational Ideals of Anna Julia Cooper and W. E. B. DuBois, 1892–1940," *History of Education Quarterly,* 47, no. 4 (2007): 416–446; Anderson, *The Education of Blacks in the South*; David Levering Lewis, *W. E. B. DuBois, 1868–1919* (New York, 1993).

72. Davison M. Douglas, *Jim Crow Moves North: The Battle over Northern School Segregation, 1865–1954* (Cambridge, UK, 2005); Peter Irons, *Jim Crow's Children: The Broken Promise of the* Brown *Decision* (New York, 2002; James T. Patterson, Brown v. Board of Education: *A Civil Rights Milestone and its Troubled Legacy* (Oxford, UK, 2001).

73. Meier, *The Community College Mission,* Ch 3; Rufus E. Clement, "The Present and Future Role of Private Colleges for Negroes," *Phylon* 10, no. 4 (1949):

323–327; Carroll L. Miller, "The Negro Publicly-Supported Junior College," *The Journal of Negro Education* 31, no. 3 (1962): 386–395; George H. Walker Jr. and David W. Hazel, "Integration in the Junior College," *The Journal of Negro Education* 29, no. 2 (1960): 204–206.

74. Carnegie Commission, *The Open-Door Colleges*, Appendix A, Table 1; Cohen, "The Process of Desegregation"; Gibson and Jung, *Historical Census Statistics*, Table 24; Miller, "The Negro Publicly-Supporting Junior College," 389–391; Medsker, *The Junior College*, 214–216.

75. Cohen, "The Process of Desegregation."

76. Carnegie Commission, *The Open-Door Colleges*, Appendix A, Table 1; Gibson and Jung, *Historical Census Statistics on Population*, Tables 15, 28, 37. The population percentages are estimates that are skewed because of a lack of data on Latino/Latinas in the United States before 1970. Until 1970 the U.S. census only collected demographic information by race on whites, blacks, American Indians, Asians and Pacific Islanders, and Other. For a discussion of race and ethnicity as social scientific and political categories in relation to the U.S. census see David A. Hollinger, *Postethnic America: Beyond Multiculturalism*, 10th anniversary edition (New York, 2005).

77. Medsker and Tillery, *Breaking the Access Barriers*, 76–77.

78. Mark A. Chesler and James Crowfoot, *Racism in Higher Education*. Center for Research on Social Organization, PCMA Working Paper #21, CRSO Working Paper #412 (Ann Arbor, 1989); Sylvia Hurtado, Jeffrey F. Milem, Alma R. Clayton-Padersen, and Walter R. Allen, "Enhancing Campus Climates for Racial/Ethnic Diversity: Educational Policy and Practice," *The Review of Higher Education*, 21, no. 3 (1998): 279–302; Watson Scott Swail, Kenneth E. Redd, and Laura W. Perna, *Retaining Minority Students in Higher Education*. ASHE-ERIC Higher Education Report 30, no. 2 (San Francisco, 2003), 57–61; Thelin, *A History of American Higher Education*, 304–305.

79. Medsker and Tillery, *Breaking the Access Barriers*, 69. See also Gerald Graff, *Beyond the Culture Wars* (New York, 1992); James Davison Hunter, *Culture Wars* (New York, 1991), ch 8; Lawrence W. Levine, *The Opening of the American Mind: Canons, Culture, and History* (Boston, 1996).

80. Antoine M. Garibaldi, "Four Decades of Progress . . . and Decline: An Assessment of African American Educational Attainment," *The Journal of Negro Education*, 66, no. 2 (1997): 105–120; Swail, Redd, and Perna, *Retaining Minority Students in Higher Education*, 1–30.

81. Richardson and Bender defined *underrepresented minorities* as blacks and Hispanics. Asians are acknowledged as minorities, but they were not underrepresented in public institutions of higher education. Native Americans were also acknowledged as minorities, but they were not largely enrolled in public, urban institutions of higher education, which was the focus of this study (15).

82. Richard C. Richardson Jr. and Louis W. Bender, *Fostering Minority Access and Achievement in Higher Education: The Role of Urban Community Colleges and Universities* (San Francisco, 1987), 1–3, 5, 18, 28, 34, 36, 44, 49, 64, 98, 134, 178, 202.

83. Berger and Luckmann, *The Social Construction of Reality*, 15; DiMaggio and Powell, "The Iron Cage Revisited," 20, 23, 26, 28; Lecours, "New Institutionalism: Issues and Questions," 3–25; Meyer and Rowan, "Institutionalized Organizations:

Formal Structure as Myth and Ceremony," 41, 44; Pierson, *Politics in Time*, 20–21, 43, 51; Zucker, "The Role of Institutionalization in Cultural Persistence," 85; Searle, *The Construction of Social Reality.*

84. DiMaggio and Powell, "The Iron Cage Revisited," 8; Friedland and Alford, "Bringing Society Back In, 232–263; Miller, *The Passion of Michel Foucault,* 150; Searle, *The Construction of Social Reality.*

85. Medsker and Tillery, *Breaking the Access Barriers.*

86. David W. Breneman and Susan C. Nelson, *Financing Community Colleges: An Economic Perspective* (Washington, DC, 1981); Carnegie Commission, *The Open-Door Colleges*; John A. Douglas, "The Carnegie Commission and Council on Higher Education," Center for Studies in Higher Education (Berkeley, CA, 2005); Gleazer, "Evolution of Junior Colleges into Community Colleges," 20–26; Labaree, "From Comprehensive High School to Community College," 221–22; Michael Mumper, "The Paradox of College Prices: Five Stories with No Clear Lesson," *The States and Public Higher Education Policy,* Donald E. Heller, ed. (Baltimore, MD, 2001), 47; Richard C. Richardson Jr. and Larry L. Leslie, *The Impossible Dream? Financing Community College's Evolving Mission* (Washington, DC, 1980). On the political-economic environment see Sean Wilentz, *The Age of Reagan: A History, 1974–2008* (New York, 2008), 35.

87. Dale Tillery and William L. Deegan, "The Evolution of Two-Year Colleges Through Four Generations," *Renewing the American Community College,* William L. Deegan and Dale Tillery, eds. (San Francisco, 1985), 3–33.

88. Medsker and Tillery, *Breaking the Access Barriers,* 3, 17, 53, 136; James W. Thornton Jr., *The Community Junior College,* 3rd ed. (New York, 1972), 4, 33, 63, 81, 84, 151, 290.

89. K. Patricia Cross, "Community Colleges on the Plateau," *The Journal of Higher Education* 52, no. 2 (1981): 113–123; K. Patricia Cross, "Determining Missions and Priorities for the Fifth Generation," *Renewing the American Community College,* Ibid., 34–50.

90. Anne-Marie McCartan, "The Community College Mission: Present Challenges and Future Visions," *The Journal of Higher Education,* 54, no. 6 (1983): 676–692.

91. Breneman and Nelson, *Financing Community Colleges,* 3, 19, 39, 54, 92, 195, 199, 201; Richardson and Leslie, *The Impossible Dream?*; Tillery and Deegan, "The Evolution of Two-Year Colleges through Four Generations," 18–19, 23.

92. John S. Levin, Susan Kater, and Richard L. Wagoner, *Community College Faculty: At Work in the New Economy* (New York, 2006), ch 6; John E. Roueche, Suanne D. Roueche, and Mark D. Milliron, *Strangers in Their Own Land: Part-Time Faculty in American Community Colleges* (Washington, DC, 1995), vii, 3, 5.

93. Richard C. Richardson Jr., Elizabeth C. Fisk, and Morris A. Okun, *Literacy in the Open-Access College* (San Francisco, 1983), x–xiii, 62, 72; Earl Seidman, *In the Words of the Faculty: Perspectives on Improving Teaching and Educational Quality in Community Colleges* (San Francisco, 1985), 9–11, 249, 268.

94. Alan Pifer, "Community College and Community Leadership," *Community and Junior College Journal,* 44, no. 8 (1974): 23–26; Roger Yarrington, "Assessing the Community Base," *Community and Junior College Journal,* 46, no. 3 (1975): 9–11;

Ervin L. Harlacher and James F. Gollatscheck, eds., *Implementing Community Based Education. New Directions for Community Colleges*, 21 (San Francisco, 1978).

95. Edmund J. Gleazer Jr., *The Community College: Values, Vision, and Vitality* (Washington, DC, 1980), 4, 10–11, 67, 91, 100, 110–111, 116.

96. Commission on the Future of Community Colleges, *Building Communities: A Vision for a New Century* (Washington, DC, 1988).

97. Darrel A. Clowes and Bernard H. Levin, "Community, Technical, and Junior Colleges: Are They Leaving Higher Education?" *The Journal of Higher Education*, 60, no. 3 (1989): 349–355.

98. Judith S. Eaton, "The Fortunes of the Transfer Function: Community Colleges and Transfer 1900–1990," *A Handbook on the Community College in America*, Ibid., 28–40; Judith S. Eaton, *Strengthening Collegiate Education in Community Colleges* (San Francisco, 1994); Howard B. London, *The Culture of a Community College* (New York, 1978); Dennis McGrath and Martin B. Spear, *The Academic Crisis of the Community College* (Albany, NY, 1991); Richardson, Fisk, and Okun, *Literacy in the Open-Access College*, x–xiii, 2, 6, 62, 72, 88; John E. Roueche and George A. Baker III, *Access and Excellence: The Open Door College* (Washington, DC, 1987), 33–36; John E. Roueche and Suanne D. Roueche, *High Stakes, High Performance: Making Remedial Education Work* (Washington, DC, 1999).

99. McGrath and Spear, *The Academic Crisis of the Community College*, 12, 15, 93, 139, 142, 155–158.

100. George B. Vaughan, "The Community College Perspective," *Thinking About American Higher Education: The 1990s and Beyond*, J. Wade Gilley, ed. (New York, 1991), 89–98.

101. Ibid., 91, 93–94, 97; Labaree, "From Comprehensive High School to Community College."

Notes to Chapter 2

1. Daniel Bell, *The End of Ideology*, rev. ed. (Cambridge, MA, 1988), 423–433; Todd Gitlin, *The Sixties* (New York, 1987); Peter Novick, *That Noble Dream: The "Objectivity Question" and the American Historical Profession* (Cambridge, UK, 1988), ch 13 & 14; Theodore Roszak, *The Making of a Counter Culture* (New York, 1969).

2. There were many New Left critics who published influential scholarship on education: Michael B. Katz, Colin Greer, Clarence Karier, Paul Violas, Joel Spring, Walter Feinberg, Samuel Bowles, Herbert Gintis, Jerome Karabel, Fred L. Pincus, and L. Steven Zwerling. See Gary B. Nash, Charlotte Crabtree, and Ross E. Dunn, *History on Trial: Culture Wars and the Teaching of the Past* (New York, 2000), ch 4; Diane Ravitch, *The Revisionists Revised: A Critique of the Radical Attack on the Schools* (New York, 1978); Fred L. Pincus, "How Critics View the Community College's Role in the Twenty-First Century," *A Handbook on the Community College in America*, Ibid., 624–636; L. Steven Zwerling, ed., *The Community College and Its Critics, New Directions for Community Colleges*, 54 (San Francisco, 1986).

3. Pincus, "How Critics View the Community College's Role in the Twenty-First Century," 625–626, 633.

4. L. Steven Zwerling, *Second Best: The Crisis of the Community College* (New York: McGraw Hill, 1976), xix, 9, 30–35, 76, 83, 98, 159, 161, 164, 174.

5. Howard B. London, *The Culture of a Community College* (New York, 1978), xv, 81, 91–93, 152–153; Willard Waller, *The Sociology of Teaching* (1932; reprint, New York, 1961), 8–12.

6. Lois Weis, *Between Two Worlds: Black Students in an Urban Community College* (Boston, 1985), 7, 13, 27, 56, 133, 166–69.

7. Fred L. Pincus, "The False Promises of Community Colleges: Class Conflict and Vocational Education." *Harvard Educational Review* 50, vol. 3 (1980): 332–361; Fred L. Pincus, "Contradictory Effects of Customized Contract Training in Community Colleges," *Critical Sociology* 16, vol. 1 (1989): 77–93.

8. Brint and Karabel, *The Diverted Dream*, 5–19, 56, 59, 91, 205–232. See also Jerome Karabel, "Community Colleges and Social Stratification," *Harvard Educational Review*, 42, no. 4 (1972): 521–562; Steven Brint and Jerome Karabel, "The Community College and Democratic Ideals," *Community College Review* 17 (1989): 9–19; Brint and Karabel, "Institutional Origins and Transformations: The Case of American Community Colleges," *The New Institutionalism in Organizational Analysis*, Ibid., 337–360.

9. Ibid. See also Steven Brint, "Few Remaining Dreams: Community Colleges Since 1985," *Annals of the American Academy of Political and Social Science* 586 (2003): 16–37; Clark, *The Open Door College*; Dougherty, *The Contradictory College*; Frye, "The Rhetoric of Professional Educators and the Definition of Public Junior Colleges from 1900 to 1940," 5–16; Kathleen M. Shaw, Sara Goldrick-Rab, Chistopher Mazzeo, and Jerry A. Jacobs, *Putting Poor People to Work: How the Work-First Idea Eroded College Access for the Poor* (New York, 2006).

10. Labaree, "From Comprehensive High School to Community College," 226–227, 230–32, 235; Ernest T. Pascarella and Patrick T. Terenzini, *How College Affects Students: Findings and Insights from Twenty Years of Research* (San Francisco, 1991), 372–373, 590.

11. Dougherty, *The Contradictory College*; Christine Kelly-Kleese, "Community College Scholarship and Discourse," *Community College Review* 32, no 1 (2004): 52–68; John S. Levin, Susan Kater, and Richard L. Wagoner, *Community College Faculty* (New York, 2006); Richard L. Wagoner, "*Plus Ça Change:* Toward a Professional Identity for Community College Faculty in the 21st Century," California Community College Collaborative Symposium, Riverside, CA, June 7, 2007.

12. Brint, "Few Remaining Dreams"; Arthur M. Cohen, "The Case for the Community College," *American Journal of Education* 98, no. 4 (1990), 426–442; Cohen and Brawer, *The American Community College*, Ch 14; Frye, "Educational Paradigms in the Professional Literature of the Community College," 199–204; W. Norton Grubb and Marvin Lazerson, *The Education Gospel: The Economic Power of Schooling* (Cambridge, MA, 2004), p. 85; Lucas, *American Higher Education*, 221–222. Meier offers a critique of early community college defenders, which could also be applied to contemporary defenders such as Cohen and Brawer: "The community-junior college as a mass educational movement *cum* institution emerged as a vehicle

of educational democracy meeting the status aspirations of the American middle and working classes and only secondarily as an adjunct to economic modernization. The consensus social movement challenged neither capitalism nor state legitimacy; it employed conventional democratic rhetoric without questioning significantly the prevailing civil *status quo*. Public community colleges inserted themselves into the interstices between secondary and higher education and the community and the state while conflating equality of opportunity with efficient adaptation of citizens to the labor market." See *The Community College Mission*, Ch 3.

13. Dougherty, *The Contradictory College*, 7, 15–36.

14. Ibid., 7, 9–13, 67, 89, 106, 155–173, 183–88, 273–286. Dougherty summarized his critique in these words: "On closer examination, the community college appears to be much less functional to the economy than either side claims. Like the sorcerer's apprentice, the community college has been a willing, but unreliable, instrument of the invisible hand" (44–45).

15. Joanne Cooper and Ken Kempner, "Lord of the Flies Community College: A Case Study of Organizational Disintegration." *The Review of Higher Education*, 16, no. 4 (1993): 419–437; W. Norton Grubb and Associates, *Honored but Invisible*, 2, 11, 27, 49, 251, 280, 335, 366.

16. Robert M. Pirsig, *Zen and the Art of Motorcycle Maintenance* (1974; reprint, San Francisco, 1999), 145.

17. Professor X, "In the Basement of the Ivory Tower," *The Atlantic* (June 2008): 68–73. This paragraph also draws from my own experiences as a community college instructor, from many conversations with community college faculty, and from my own research on the pass rates in California community colleges.

18. Ernest T. Pascarella and Patrick T. Terenzini, *How College Affects Students: A Third Decade of Research* (San Francisco, 2005), 376–381.

19. Marlene Griffith and Ann Connor, *Democracy's Open Door: The Community College in America's Future* (Portsmouth, VA, 1994), xii–xiii, 30, 48, 85, 99, 104–105.

20. John E. Roueche, Lynn Sullivan Taber, and Suanne D. Roueche, eds., *The Company We Keep: Collaboration in the Community College* (Washington, DC, 1995).

21. Edmund J. Gleazer Jr., "Introduction," Ibid., 3–22; Robert McCabe, "Community Is Our Middle Name," Ibid., 59–79; Roueche, Taber, & Roueche, "Striking a Balance: Creating the Collaborative Mosaic," Ibid., 345–371; Lynn Sullivan Taber, "Chapter and Verse: How We Came to Be Where We Are," Ibid., 25–37.

22. John S. Levin and John D. Dennison, "Responsiveness and Renewal in Canada's Community Colleges," *The Canadian Journal of Higher Education*, 19, no. 2 (1989): 41–57.

23. Thomas R. Bailey and Irina E. Averianova, "Multiple Missions of Community Colleges: Conflicting or Complementary?" *Community College Research Center Brief* 1 (1999), 1–6; Patrick M. Callan, "Reframing Access and Opportunity: Problematic State and Federal Higher Education Policy in the 1990s," *The States and Public Higher Education Policy*, Ibid., 85; John S. Levin, "The Revised Institution: The Community College Mission at the End of the Twentieth Century," *Community College Review*, 28, no. 1 (2000), 1–25.

24. Barbara K. Townsend and Kristin B. Wilson, "The Transfer Mission: Tried and True, but Troubled?," *Community College Missions in the 21st Century, New*

Directions for the Community College 136 (2006): 33–41. Thomas R. Bailey and Irina E. Averianova argued in 1999 that the "primacy" of the transfer mission had been "lost." See Bailey and Averianova, "Multiple Missions of Community Colleges," Ibid., 2.

25. D. Franklin Ayers, "Neoliberal Ideology in Community College Mission Statements," *The Review of Higher Education,* 28, no. 4 (2005): 527–549; Levin, "The Revised Institution," Ibid., 1, 9; John S. Levin, *Globalizing the Community College* (New York, 2001): xviii–xx, 1–3, 58–62; Levin, Kater, and Wagoner, *Community College Faculty,* ch 2 & 7.

26. Levin, *Globalizing the Community College,* 9, 40–41, 50–51, 64–67, 83, 87, 159, 165, 170.

27. Kevin J. Dougherty and Marianne F. Bakia, *The New Economic Development Role of the Community College,* Community College Research Center (Nov 1999), 61. See also Sherrie L. Kantor, ed., *A Practical Guide to Conducting Customized Work Force Training. New Directions for Community Colleges* 85 (San Francisco, 1994); Pincus, "Contradictory Effects of Customized Contract Training in Community Colleges."

28. Levin, "The Revised Institution"; Levin, *Globalizing the Community College,* 70–78.

29. James Davison Hunter, *Culture Wars* (New York, 1991); Samuel P. Huntington, *Who Are We? The Challenges to America's National Identity* (New York, 2004); Nash, Crabtree, and Dunn, *History on Trial*; Arthur M. Schlesinger Jr., *The Disuniting of America: Reflections on a Multicultural Society,* rev. ed. (New York, 1998); Joel Westheimer, ed., *Pledging Allegiance: The Politics of Patriotism in America's Schools* (New York, 2007); Jonathan Zimmerman, *Whose America? Culture Wars in the Public Schools* (Cambridge, MA, 2002).

30. James Valadez, "Cultural Capital and Its Impact on the Aspirations of Nontraditional Community College Students," *Community College Review* 21, no. 3 (1993), 30–43.

31. Penelope E. Herideen, *Policy, Pedagogy, and Social Inequality: Community College Student Realities in Post-Industrial America* (Westport, CT, 1998), 82–83; Rosalind Latiner Raby, "International, Intercultural, and Multicultural Dimensions of Community Colleges in the United States," *Dimensions of the Community College: International, Intercultural, and Multicultural Perspectives,* Rosalind Latiner Raby and Norma Tarrow, eds. (New York, 1996), 9–36; Laura I. Rendon, "Toward a New Vision of the Multicultural Community College for the Next Century," *Community Colleges as Cultural Texts,* Kathleen M. Shaw, James R. Valadez, and Robert A. Rhoads, eds. (Albany, NY, 1999), 195–204; Robert A. Rhoads, "The Politics of Culture and Identity: Contrasting Images of Multiculturalism and Monoculturalism," *Community Colleges as Cultural Texts,* Ibid., 103–124; Robert A. Rhoads and James R. Valadez, *Democracy, Multiculturalism, and the Community College* (New York, 1996), 10, 18, 23, 79–81, 85, 100; Naomi Okumura Story, "Weaving the American Tapestry: Multicultural Education in Community Colleges," *Dimensions of the Community College,* Ibid., 79–110; Cornelia H. van der Linde, "The Role of the Community College in Countering Conflict in Multicultural Societies," *Dimensions of the Community College,* Ibid., 239–258; Berta Vigil Laden, "Celebratory Socialization of

Culturally Diverse Students Through Academic Programs and Support Services," *Community Colleges as Cultural Texts*, Ibid., 173–194.

32. John S. Levin, "The Community College as a Baccalaureate-Granting Institution," *The Review of Higher Education* 28, no. 1 (2004): 1–22; Deborah L. Floyd, "The Community College Baccalaureate in the United States," *The Community College Baccalaureate*, Deborah L. Floyd, Michael L. Skolnik, and Kenneth P. Walker, eds. (Sterling, VA, 2005), 25–47; Barbara K. Townsend, "A Cautionary View," *The Community College Baccalaureate*, Ibid., 179–190; Kenneth P. Walker, "History, Rationale, and the Community College Baccalaureate Association," *The Community College Baccalaureate*, Ibid., 9–23.

33. Rhoads and Valadez, *Democracy, Multiculturalism, and the Community College*, xv, 45; Kathleen M. Shaw, "Defining the Self: Constructions of Identity in Community College Students," *Community Colleges as Cultural Texts,* Ibid., 153–171; Kathleen Shaw, "Remedial Education as Ideological Battleground: Emerging Remedial Education Policies in the Community College," *Educational Evaluation and Policy Analysis* 19, no. 3 (1997), 284–296; Kathleen M. Shaw and Howard B. London, "Culture and Ideology in Keeping Transfer Commitment: Three Community Colleges," *The Review of Higher Education* 25, no. 1 (2001), 91–114; Kathleen M. Shaw, James R. Valadez, and Robert A. Rhoads, "Community Colleges as Cultural Texts: A Conceptual Overview," *Community Colleges as Cultural Texts,* Ibid., 1–13.

34. James G. Cibulka, "Policy Analysis and the Study of the Politics of Education," *The Study of Educational Politics*, Ibid., 105–125; Herideen, *Policy, Pedagogy, and Social Inequality*, 17, 25; Deborah Stone, *Policy Paradox*.

35. Thomas Bailey and Vanessa Smith Morest, "Introduction: Defending the Community College Equity Agenda," *Defending the Community College Equity Agenda*, Thomas Bailey and Vanessa Smith Morest, eds. (Baltimore, MD, 2006), 1–27; Vanessa Smith Morest, "Double Vision: How the Attempt to Balance Multiple Missions Is Shaping the Future of Community Colleges," *Defending the Community College Equity Agenda,* Ibid., 28–50.

36. Bailey and Smith Morest, "Introduction;" Debra D. Bragg, "Community College Access, Mission, and Outcomes." *Peabody Journal of Education* 76, no. 1 (2001): 93–116; Smith Morest, "Double Vision"; Grubb and Lazerson, *The Education Gospel*.

37. Alicia C. Dowd, "From Access to Outcome Equity: Revitalizing the Democratic Mission of the Community College," *Annals of the American Academy of Political and Social Science* 586 (2003): 92–119. Alicia C. Dowd and Tatiana Melguizo, "Socioeconomic Stratification of Community College Transfer Access in the 1980s and 1990s," *The Review of Higher Education* 31, no. 4 (2008): 377–400; Tatiana Melguizo, Linda Serra Hagedorn, and Scott Cypers, "Remedial/Developmental Education and the Cost of Community College Transfer: A Los Angeles County Sample," *The Review of Higher Education* 31, no. 4 (2008): 401–431.

38. Ibid. There has been empirical evidence of higher socioeconomic status students enrolling in the academic transfer curriculum from at least 1969. K. Patricia Cross, *The Junior College's Role in Providing Postsecondary Education for All* (Washington DC, 1969).

39. Ibid. See also Alexander W. Astin and Leticia Oseguera, "The Declining 'Equity' of American Higher Education," *The Review of Higher Education* 27, no. 3 (2004): 321–341; Brint and Karabel, "The Community College and Democratic Ideals."

40. Brint, "Few Remaining Dreams"; Brint and Karabel, *The Diverted Dream.*

41. W. Norton Grubb, "The Convergence of Educational Systems and the Role of Vocationalism," *Comparative Education Review* 29, no. 4 (1985): 526–548; Pascarella and Terenzini, *How College Affects Students* (1991), 530.

42. Dougherty, *The Contradictory College,* 66, 75–82; David Stern, Neal Finkelstein, James R. Stone, John Latting, and Carolyn Dornsife, *School to Work* (London, 1995), 98, 103, 106; Pascarella and Terenzini, *How College Affects Students* (2005); David G. Whitaker and Ernest T. Pascarella, "Two-Year College Attendance and Socioeconomic Attainment," *The Journal of Higher Education* 65, no. 2 (1994): 194–210.

43. W. Norton Grubb, *Working in the Middle: Strengthening Education and Training for the Mid-Skilled Labor Force* (San Francisco, 1996), 12–14.

44. Ibid., 13–17, 19–28, 45–47.

45. Ibid., 86, 93–108, 169, 212. In 1999 Grubb revisited many of his conclusions and he demonstrated the general economic viability of the associate's degree, but he stressed that the full economic potential of this credential could only be realized if individuals enroll in certain occupational/technical-oriented programs, complete a degree, and find employment related to their field of study. There is little evidence that many community college students can complete all three of these steps. See W. Norton Grubb, *Learning and Earning in the Middle: The Economic Benefits of Sub-Baccalaureate Education,* Community College Research Center (New York, 1999).

46. W. Norton Grubb, *Learning to Work: The Case for Reintegrating Job Training and Education* (New York, 1996), 6,7, 35, 38, 42–3, 45, 48–49, 73, 90.

47. Ibid., 91.

48. Ibid., 105–122. For contrasting views see Sherrie L. Kantor, ed., *A Practical Guide to Conducting Customized Work Force Training;* Pincus, "Contradictory Effects of Customized Contract Training in Community Colleges." For a good overview of the issue of work first programs see Shaw et al., *Putting Poor People to Work: How the Work-First Idea Eroded College Access for the Poor.*

49. Grubb, *Learning and Earning in the Middle;* Jorge R. Sanchez and Frankie Santos Laanan, eds., *Determining the Economic Benefits of Attending Community College. New Directions for Community Colleges* 104 (San Francisco, 1998). For warnings against generalizations see Grubb, *Working in the Middle.*

50. Michael B. Paulsen, "The Economics of Human Capital and Investment in Higher Education," *The Finance of Higher Education,* Michael B. Paulsen and John C. Smart, eds. (New York, 2001), 55–94. Paulsen reiterates the standard characterization of nontraditional students enrolled in community colleges: work while enrolled, low socioeconomic status, high percentage from nonwhite minority groups, locally bound, part-time students, typically older than 18–22, and often academically unprepared. For nontraditional students in the community college see Alyssa N. Bryant, "Community College Students: Recent Findings and Trends," *Community College Review* 29, no. 3 (2001): 77–93; Sara Goldrick-Rab, *Promoting Academic Momentum*

at Community Colleges, Community College Research Center (New York, 2001); John S. Levin, *Nontraditional Students and Community Colleges* (New York, 2007).

51. Gregory S. Kienzl, "The Triple Helix of Education and Earnings: The Effect of Schooling, Work, and Pathways on the Economic Outcomes of Community College Students" (PhD diss., Columbia University, 2004); Lawrence Mishel, Jared Bernstein, and Sylvia Allegretto, *The State of Working America 2006/2007* (Ithaca, NY, 2007), 150, 201–202. See also Paul E. Barton, "How Many College Graduates Does the United States Labor Force Really Need?" *Change* 40, no. 1 (2008): 16–21.

52. Grubb, "The Convergence of Educational Systems and the Role of Vocationalism"; Grubb, *Working in the Middle*; Grubb, *Learning to Work*; W. Norton Grubb and Marvin Lazerson, *The Education Gospel*; Harvey A. Kantor, *Learning to Earn: School, Work, and Vocational Reform in California, 1880–1930* (Madison, WI, 1988); Herbert M. Kliebard, *Schooled to Work: Vocationalism and the American Curriculum, 1876–1946* (New York, 1999); Rosenbaum, *Beyond College for All*; Stern et al., *School to Work*.

53. Grubb, *Learning to Work*; Grubb and Lazerson, *The Education Gospel*; Grubb, *Learning and Earning in the Middle*; Rosenbaum, *Beyond College for All*; Stern et al., *School to Work*.

54. Grubb, "The Convergence of Educational Systems and the Role of Vocationalism"; Grubb, *Working in the Middle*; Grubb, *Learning to Work*; W. Norton Grubb and Marvin Lazerson, *The Education Gospel*.

55. Debra D. Bragg and Russell E. Hamm, *Linking College and Work: Exemplary Policies and Practices of Two-Year College Work-Based Learning Programs*, National Center for Research in Vocational Education (Berkeley, CA, 1996); Grubb, "The Convergence of Educational Systems and the Role of Vocationalism"; Grubb, *Working in the Middle*; Grubb, *Learning to Work*; Grubb, *Learning and Earning in the Middle*; W. Norton Grubb and Marvin Lazerson, *The Education Gospel*; Katherine L. Hughes and Melinda Mechur Karp, "Strengthening Transitions by Encouraging Career Pathways: A Look at State Policies and Practices," *Community College Research Brief 30* (2006): 1–4; Herbert M. Kliebard, *Schooled to Work*; Ann M. Milne, ed., *National Assessment of Vocational Education* (Washington, DC, 1998); Rosenbaum, *Beyond College for All*; Stern et al., *School to Work*.

56. Grubb, *Working in the Middle*, 21.

57. Ibid.

58. On sociopolitical and economic inequality see Cal Jillson, *Pursuing the American Dream* (Lawrence, KS, 2004); Lawrence R. Jacobs and Theda Skocpol, eds., *Inequality and American Democracy* (New York, 2005). On inequality and higher education see Brint and Karabel, *The Diverted Dream*; Labaree, *How to Succeed in School without Really Learning*. On inequality and vocational education see Richard D. Lakes and Patricia A. Carter, "Disciplining the Working Classes: Neoliberal Designs in Vocational Education," *Pedagogies* 4, no. 2 (2009): 139–152.

59. Stu Woo and Sudeep Reddy, "Jobless Rates Climb in 46 States," *Wall Street Journal* (April 18, 2009); Catherine Rampell, "Teenage Unemployment Rate Reaches Record High," *New York Times* (Sept 5, 2009); Conor Dougherty, "Recession Takes Heavy Toll on US," Wall Street Journal (Sept 10, 2009); Carmen Denavas-Walt, Bernadette D. Proctor, and Jessica C. Smith, *Income, Poverty, and Health*

Insurance Coverage in the United States: 2008, U.S. Census Bureau (Sept 2009); "Not So Colour-Blind," *The Economist* (Dec 5, 2009), 36.

60. John Richard Schrock, "US Jobs Prospects Plummet," *University World News* (April 12, 2009); Gerry Shih, "Downturn Dims Prospects Even at Top Law Schools," *New York Times* (Aug 26, 2009); Gerry Shih, "Unpaid Work, but They Pay for Privilege," *New York Times* (Aug 9, 2009).

61. Dennis Carter, "Campuses Adjust to Enrollment Spikes," *E Campus News* (July 22, 2009); Steven Greenhouse, "At Sinclair Community College, Focus Is Jobs," *New York Times* (Aug 15, 2009).

62. Barak Obama, "Remarks by the President on the American Graduation Initiative," Office of the Press Secretary (July 14, 2009), http://www.whitehouse. gov/the_press_office; Jim Rutenberg, "Obama Attacks on Economy and Seeks Billions for Community Colleges," *New York Times* (July 15, 2009); Joseph E. Aoun, "Millions More Going to College?" *The Boston Globe* (July 16, 2009).

63. Berger and Luckmann, *The Social Construction of Reality,* 15; DiMaggio and Powell, "The Iron Cage Revisited," 20, 23, 26, 28; Lecours, "New Institutionalism: Issues and Questions," 3–25; Meyer and Rowan, "Institutionalized Organizations: Formal Structure as Myth and Ceremony," 41, 44; Pierson, *Politics in Time,* 20–21, 43, 51; Zucker, "The Role of Institutionalization in Cultural Persistence," 85; Searle, *The Construction of Social Reality.*

64. DiMaggio and Powell, "The Iron Cage Revisited," 66, 68; Meyer and Rowan, "Institutionalized Organizations," 41, 44–46, 48–50, 58, 60.

65. Ortner, *Anthropology and Social Theory,* 7, 18, 127, 130, 133, 139, 147, 152.

66. Isaiah Berlin, "The Pursuit of the Ideal," *The Proper Study of Mankind* (New York, 2000), 4, 16.

Notes to Chapter 3

1. On K–12 public schools see Roy W. Cloud, *Education in California: Leaders, Organizations, and Accomplishments of the First Hundred Years* (Stanford, CA, 1952); Charles J. Falk, *The Development and Organization of Education in California* (New York, 1968); William Warren Ferrier, *Ninety Years of Education in California, 1846–1936* (Berkeley, CA, 1937). On issues of segregation and vocationalization see: Irving G. Hendrick, *Public Policy toward the Education of Non-White Minority Group Children in California, 1849–1970,* National Institute of Education Project, no. NE-G-00–3-0082 (Riverside, CA, 1975); Harvey A. Kantor, *Learning to Earn: School, Work, and Vocational Reform in California, 1880–1930* (Madison, WI, 1988); Charles M. Wollenberg, *All Deliberate Speed: Segregation and Exclusion in California Schools, 1855–1975* (Berkeley, CA, 1976). On higher education see William Warren Ferrier, *Origin and Development of the University of California* (Berkeley, CA, 1930); Verne A. Stadtman, *The University of California, 1868–1968* (New York, 1970); Donald R. Gerth and James O. Haehn, *An Invisible Giant: The California State Colleges* (San Francisco, 1971); Howard Ball, *The Bakke Case: Race, Education and Affirmative Action* (Lawrence, 2000); John Aubrey Douglas, "Californians and Public Higher Education," *History of Higher Education Annual* 16 (1996): 71–104; John Aubrey

Douglas, *The California Idea and American Higher Education* (Stanford, 2000); John Aubrey Douglas, *The Conditions for Admission: Access, Equity, and the Social Contract of Public Universities* (Stanford, 2007); Brian Pusser, *Burning Down the House: Politics, Governance, and Affirmative Action at the University of California* (Albany, NY, 2004).

2. The first attempt to chronicle the history of California junior colleges was made by Walter Crosby Eells. He devoted a chapter to "Historical Development: California," in *The Junior College*. Recent histories include Steven Brint and Jerome Karabel, *The Diverted Dream* (Oxford, UK, 1989); Hugh Ross, "University Influence in the Genesis and Growth of Junior Colleges in California," *History of Education Quarterly* 3, no. 3 (1963): 143–152; James L. Wattenbarger and Allen A. Witt, "Origins of the California System: How the Junior College Movement Came to California," *Community College Review*, 22, no. 4 (1995): 17–25.

3. Burton R. Clark, *The Open Door College* (New York, 1960), 39, 84–85.

4. Wollenberg, *All Deliberate Speed*, 178. For segregation in the North and West see: Davison M. Douglas, *Jim Crow Moves North: The Battle over Northern School Segregation, 1865–1954* (Cambridge, UK, 2005).

5. The California legislature actually passed what was called the Caminetti Act in 1891, which authorized high schools to offer college classes meant to prepare students for entry to the University of California, but this act was repealed that same year because of the issue of paying teachers from the grammar school fund for conducting high school duties. By 1903 the California legislature had approved Article IX, Section 9, which allowed high schools to offer university prep courses. Cloud, *Education in California*, 89, 130; W. J. Cooper, "The Junior-College Movement in California," *The School Review* 36, no. 6 (1928): 409–422; John Aubrey Douglas, *The California Idea and American Higher Education*, 120–124; John Aubrey Douglas, *The Conditions for Admission*, 11, 35–39; Falk, *The Development and Organization of Education in California*, 43; Edward A. Gallagher, "Jordan and Lange: The California Junior College as Protector of Teaching," *Working Papers in Education*, The Hoover Institution, Stanford University (Stanford, CA, 1994); A. A. Gray, "The Junior College in California," *The School Review* 23, no. 7 (1915): 465–473; Ross, "University Influence in the Genesis and Growth of Junior Colleges in California"; Wattenbarger and Witt, "Origins of the California System."

6. Cooper, "The Junior-College Movement in California"; Douglas, *The California Idea and American Higher Education*, 120–24, 126; Douglas, *The Conditions for Admission*, 11, 35–39; Falk, *The Development and Organization of Education in California*, 46–47; Ferrier, *Ninety Years of Education in California*, 353; Gray, "The Junior College in California," 467; Vaughan, *The Community College Story*; Ross, "University Influence in the Genesis and Growth of Junior Colleges in California"; Wattenbarger and Witt, "Origins of the California System."

7. Cloud, *Education in California*, 218; Cooper, "The Junior-College Movement in California"; Douglas, "Californians and Public Higher Education," 71; Douglas, *The California Idea and American Higher Education*, 120–124; Douglas, *The Conditions for Admission*, 11, 35–39, 45; Ross, "University Influence in the Genesis and Growth of Junior Colleges in California."

8. Falk, *The Development and Organization of Education in California*, 47.

9. Douglas, "Californians and Public Higher Education," 83.

10. Brint and Karabel, *The Diverted Dream*, 23–66; Arthur G. Coons, *Crisis in California Higher Education: Experience under the Master Plan and Problems of Coordination, 1959 to 1968* (Los Angeles, 1968), 24–25; Cooper, "The Junior-College Movement in California"; Eells, *The Junior College Movement*, ch 4; William Martin Proctor, ed., *The Junior College: Its Organization and Administration* (Stanford, CA, 1927).

11. David Starr Jordan, "Letter to Andrew White," quoted in John Aubrey Douglas, *The California Idea and American Higher Education*, 117.

12. Alexis F. Lange, *The Lange Book,* quoted in Cooper, "The Junior-College Movement in California."

13. Alexis F. Lange, "Report," California Teachers Association Annual Meeting, San Francisco, California, 1916, cited in Roy W. Cloud, *Education in California*, 130; Brint and Karabel, *The Diverted Dream*, 24; Douglas, "Californians and Public Higher Education," 81. See also Alexis F. Lange, "The Junior College as an Integral Part of the Public-School System," *The School Review* 25, no. 7 (1917): 456–479.

14. Cloud, *Education in California*, 188.

15. Ferrier, *Ninety Years of Education in California*, 354.

16. Merton E. Hill, *The Functioning of the California Public Junior College: A Symposium* (Berkeley, CA, 1938), 15.

17. Brint and Karabel, *The Diverted Dream*, 23–66; Clark, *The Open Door College*; Douglas, *The California Idea and American Higher Education*, 117, 124–125; Douglas, *The Conditions for Admission*, 35–39, 45; Gallagher, "Jordan and Lange"; Kantor, *Learning to Earn*; David F. Labaree, "From Comprehensive High School to Community College: Politics, Markets, and the Evolution of Educational Opportunity," *Research in Sociology of Education and Socialization* 9 (Greenwich, CT, 1990): 203–240; Meier, *The Community College Mission*, Ch 2.

18. In *The California Idea and American Higher Education*, John Aubrey Douglas argues for the liberal qua progressive motivations of Wheeler, Lange, and other junior college leaders. Douglas claims that these leaders "intended to buttress economic development. However, the intent was not to sustain a stagnant class system based on social and economic status. Rather, the goal, which reflected their powerful, if at times romantic, sense that California could be a bold democratic experiment, was to reinvent and create a new, inclusive class structure based more fully on merit. In their paternal view, there were tremendous benefits for *all* [italics added] in this emerging structure of higher education" (p. 125). Edward A. Gallagher, a colleague of Douglas's at Stanford and a member of the conservative think tank the Hoover Institution at the university, has also argued for a more forgiving reading of Lange and Jordan. Gallagher argues that early junior college leaders in California were "more anti-elitist than elitist" (p. 2). Gallagher defends this argument by noting that Stanford was not an "elitist" research university because it allowed an open curriculum and it allowed junior college students to transfer to the institution. He also notes that Lange and Jordan were concerned about the quality of undergraduate teaching (pp. 5, 6, 9–10). Gallagher's argument is not very strong by any stretch of the imagination, new use of primary sources notwithstanding. Both Gallagher and Douglas are correct in focusing on the progressive platforms and concerns of the

early leaders, however, both authors reveal an utter ignorance of three decades' worth of research on U.S. progressives, progressivism, and progressive reform, which has brought to the fore the deep inconsistency, if not hypocrisy, of many progressives when it came to issues of class, race, religion, and democracy (i.e., most progressives wanted rule and reform by white, Christian middle-class experts). See Douglas, *The California Idea,* Ch 1, footnotes 8, 10, 11, 13, 21, 22 for references on this subject; Gallagher, "Jordan and Lange."

19. Brint and Karabel, *The Diverted Dream,* 79–101; Cooper, "The Junior-College Movement in California"; CJCA Committee on Institutional Research, *Critical Problems and Needs of California Junior Colleges,* California Junior College Association (Sacramento, CA, 1965), 2–3; Coons, *Crisis in California Higher Education,* 20; Douglas, *The Conditions for Admission,* 36; Ferrier, *Ninety Years of Education in California,* 356; Gray, "The Junior College in California"; Ross, "University Influence in the Genesis and Growth of Junior Colleges in California"; *A Report of a Survey of the Needs of California in Higher Education* (Sacramento, CA, 1948), 61.

20. Coordinating Council for Higher Education, *A Consideration of Issues Affecting California Public Junior Colleges* (Sacramento, CA, 1965), 23; Linda L. West, *Meeting the Challenge: A History of Adult Education in California from the Beginnings to the 1990s* (Sacramento, CA, 1995), 6, 11–12, 23, 31, 33–34.

21. The first attempt to coordinate postsecondary education in California was made in 1919 by a Joint Legislative Committee, which looked at public higher education and argued for an increase role for state normal schools, but this committee did not seem to successfully affect state policy. The Suzzalo Report was the result of a second legislative commission formed in 1931, which was able to more comprehensive evaluate postsecondary policy in the state of California and it helped initiate a state planning body, the State Council for Educational Planning and Coordination, which was active until 1941.

22. Cloud, *Education in California,* 174–175; *Report of the Special Legislative Committee on Education,* Sacramento, CA, 1920, quoted in Cooper, "The Junior-College Movement in California," 418; Commission for the Review of the Master Plan for Higher Education, *Background Papers: The Master Plan Renewed* (Sacramento, CA, August 1987), 2; Douglas, "Californians and Public Higher Education," 84–86; Labaree, *How to Succeed in School without Really Trying,* 114–115. See also Brint and Karabel, *The Diverted Dream,* 79–101.

23. Brint and Karabel, *The Diverted Dream,* 79–87; William H. Chafe, *The Unfinished Journey: America Since World War II,* 2nd ed. (Oxford, UK, 1991); Coons, *Crisis in California Higher Education,* 11–17; Douglas, *The California Idea and American Higher Education,* 233–235; James T. Patterson, *Grand Expectations: The United States, 1945–1974* (Oxford, UK, 1996).

24. *A Report of a Survey of the Needs of California in Higher Education;* Douglas, "Californians and Public Higher Education," 90.

25. *A Report of a Survey of the Needs of California in Higher Education,* 11–13, 78–79, 124; Commission for the Review of the Master Plan for Higher Education, *Background Papers: The Master Plan Renewed* (Sacramento, CA, August 1987), 2–3.

26. Ibid.

27. Robert G. Sproul, Foreword, in Merton E. Hill, *The Functioning of the California Public Junior College*, 2.

28. Hill, *The Functioning of the California Public Junior College*, 5–15; J. H. McNeedly, *College Student Mortality*, Bulletin No. 11 (Washington DC, 1937), quoted in Walter Crosby Eells, *Why Junior College Terminal Education?* 49. On California high school enrollments and junior college transfer rates see Walter Crosby Eells, *Why Junior College Terminal Education?* 53, 60.

29. Ibid.

30. Ibid. On high school graduation rates see: Eells, *Why Junior College Terminal Education?*, 44, 46.

31. Clark, *The Open Door College*, 42–43, 47.

32. Ibid., 63–65, 68–67, 71, 77, 84–85.

33. CJCA Committee on Institutional Research, *Critical Problems*, 1–2; Coons, *Crisis in California Higher Education*, 28–29; Douglas, *The California Idea and American Higher Education*, 176–187, 257, 298–313; Douglas, *The Conditions for Admission*, ch 4.

34. Brint and Karabel, *The Diverted Dream*, 86–89; California State Department of Education, *A Master Plan for Higher Education in California, 1960–1975* (Sacramento, CA, 1960), 30–31, 34, 76; CJCA Committee on Institutional Research, *Critical Problems*, 1–2; Coons, *Crisis in California Higher Education*, 29, 48; Falk, *The Development and Organization of Education in California*, 201–202; Douglas, *The California Idea and American Higher Education*, 176–187, 257, 298–313; Douglas, *The Conditions for Admission*, ch 4; Thelin, *A History of American Higher Education*, 286–90.

35. Burton R. Clark, "The 'Cooling Out' Function in Higher Education," *The American Journal of Sociology* 65, no. 6 (1960): 569–576; Clark, *The Open Door College*, 2, 5, 39, 41–46, 48, 71–77, 83, 146.

36. Coons, *Crises in California Higher Education*, 177, 180–82, 184–85.

37. Frederick L. Whitney, "Present Standards for Junior Colleges," *The School Review* 36, no. 8 (1928): 593–603.

38. Howard Erdman and William R. Ogden, "Reconsidering William Rainey Harper as 'Father' of the Junior College," *College Student Journal* 34, no. 3 (2000); *New York Times*, 24 June 1902; *New York Times*, 31 July 1902; *New York Times*, 1 Feb 1904. In 1931 Walter Crosby Eells stated that the majority of junior colleges were coeducational; however, there were many sex-segregated private junior colleges in the East and South. Eells, *The Junior College*, 4, 31.

39. Clara S. Foltz was denied access in 1879 to Hastings College of Law in San Francisco because she was a women. But because the college had been recently redesignated as part of the University of California in 1878 Clara Foltz won her case before the State Supreme Court in November 1879, which ruled that female students had a right to attend any school within the University of California. *Article IX of California's New Constitution of 1879*, quoted in Cloud, *Education in California*, 70, 82, 261; Douglas, *The Conditions for Admission*, 21.

40. Davison M. Douglas, *Jim Crow Moves North*; Irons, *Jim Crow's Children*; Patterson, *Brown v. Board of Education*.

41. James D. Anderson, *The Education of Blacks in the South, 1860–1935* (Chapel Hill, SC, 1988), 1–2, 279; Regina Werum, "Sectionalism and Racial Politics: Federal Vocational Policies and Programs in the Predesegregation South," *Social Science History* 21, no. 3 (1997): 399–453. Walter Crosby Eells included the equivalent of one page on black junior colleges out of over 800 pages in his textbook *The Junior College*. Eells reported that the AAJC directory only listed 14 out of the 33 known black institutions to Eells because of, as he explained, "a lack of definite information regarding their present existence and status." Eells, *The Junior College,* 22. See also: Ford, "The Negro Junior College"; Lane, "The Junior College Movement among Negroes."

42. State Superintendent Andrew J. Moulder wrote in 1859: "It is not desirable that such children [Africans, Chinese, and Diggers be brought up in ignorance and heathenism. Any district may establish a separate school for the benefit of the interior races and apply a certain portion of the public funds to its support, provided the citizens do not object, which it is presumed they will not do, unless for cogent reasons." Cloud, *Education in California,* 38, 42, 44–45; Davison M. Douglas, *Jim Crow Moves North,* 28–29, 67–68; Charles M. Wollenberg, *All Deliberate Speed, 23.* See also John Aubrey Douglas, *The Conditions for Admission;* Irving G. Hendrick, *Public Policy toward the Education of Non-White Minority Group Children in California.*

43. Davison M. Douglas, *Jim Crow Moves North,* 105; Wollenberg, *All Deliberate Speed,* 25. See also Hendrick, *Public Policy toward the Education of Non-White Minority Group Children in California.*

44. Wollenberg, *All Deliberate Speed,* 26.

45. George J. Sanchez, *Becoming Mexican American: Ethnicity, Culture and Identity in Chicano Los Angeles, 1900–1945* (Oxford, UK, 1993), 87–107; Wollenberg, *All Deliberate Speed,* 96–97. For discussion or Americanization, citizenship, and sociopolitical exclusion see Edward George Hartmann, *The Movement to Americanize the Immigrant* (New York, 1967); Gary Gerstle, *American Crucible: Race and Nation in the Twentieth Century* (Princeton, 2001); Desmond King, *Making Americans: Immigration, Race, and the Origins of the Diverse Democracy* (Cambridge, MA, 2000); John F. McClymer, *War and Welfare: Social Engineering in America, 1890–1925* (Westport, CT, 1980), ch 4 & 5; Noah Pickus, *True Faith and Allegiance: Immigration and American Civic Nationalism* (Princeton, NJ, 2005); Rogers M. Smith, *Civic Ideals: Conflicting Visions of Citizenship in U.S. History* (New Haven, CT, 1997).

46. Geraldine Joncich Clifford, "No Shade in the Golden State: School and University in Nineteenth-Century California," *History of Higher Education Annual* 12 (1992): 42.

47. Thomas J. Archdeacon, *Becoming American: An Ethnic History* (New York, 1983); Alan M. Kraut, *The Huddled Masses: The Immigrant in American Society, 1880–1921,* 2nd ed. (Wheeling, 2001); James P. Shenton and Kevin Kenny, "Ethnicity and Immigration," in *The New American History,* Eric Foner, ed., 2nd ed. (Philadelphia, 1997): 353–373; Starr, *California,* 178–179, 225.

48. John Modell, *The Economics and Politics of Racial Accommodation: The Japanese of Los Angeles, 1900–1942* (Urbana, IL, 1977), 36–37, 41, 45; Kevin Starr, *Embattled Dreams: California in War and Peace, 1940–1950* (Oxford, UK, 2002), 37, 40,

42–50, 89, 94–95; Wollenberg, *All Deliberate Speed,* 54, Ch 2 & 3; David K. Yoo, *Growing Up Nisei: Race, Generation, and Culture among Japanese Americans of California, 1924–49* (Urbana, IL, 2000).

49. Wollenberg, *All Deliberate Speed,* 125–135. See also Hendrick, *Public Policy toward the Education of Non-White Minority Group Children in California.*

50. In writing about segregation in California, historian Kevin Starr wrote: "Jim Crow was a well-known figure to Mexican, African, and Japanese Americans in the first half of the twentieth century. Even the so-called Okies were targets of ethnic prejudice. They were white people, true, but they were also racialized." Devra Weber points out that even though lower-class whites like the Okies could be racialized, they still often felt superior to blacks and Mexicans and often struggled to maintain racial distinctions. Starr, *California,* 306; Devra Weber, *Dark Sweat, White Gold: California Farm Workers, Cotton, and the New Deal* (Berkeley, CA, 1994), 148.

51. Davison M. Douglas, *Jim Crow Moves North,* 136–137; Starr, *California,* 178–179, 232, 234.

52. Campbell Gibson and Kay Jung, *Historical Census Statistics on Population Totals by Race, 1790 to 1990, and by Latino Origin, 1970 to 1990, for the United States, Regions, Divisions, and States,* Population Division, U.S. Bureau of the Census, Working Paper 56 (Washington, DC, 2002), Table 19.

53. Davison M. Douglas, *Jim Crow Moves North,* 228; Matt S. Meier and Feliciano Ribera, *Mexican Americans/American Mexicans: From Conquistadors to Chicanos* (New York, 1993), 154–155, 194–195; Ricardo Romo, *East Los Angeles: History of a Barrio* (Austin, TX, 1983), 162–165; Sanchez, *Becoming Mexican American,* 34, 87–105, 210; U.S. Commission on Civil Rights, *The 50 States Report* (Washington, DC, 1961), 43–46.

54. Ibid. While there were over 600,000 Mexicans and Mexican Americans in the United States by 1930, this was a highly unstable population composed mostly of young men who planed to return to Mexico. In California Mexicans had the lowest rates of naturalization of any ethnic group. The population of Mexicans in the United States dropped considerably in the 1930s because of the Depression, as U.S. and Mexican officials conducted a widespread, and often forced, repatriation effort to send Mexicans back across the border. Over 350,000 Mexicans repatriated during the 1930s and legal immigration into the United States was severely curtailed until these restrictions were lifted during World War II because of the need for cheap labor for the war effort.

55. John Aubrey Douglas, *The Conditions for Admission,* 68; Wollenberg, *All Deliberate Speed,* 137–139. Interestingly, junior college sports teams in California seemed to have been racially integrated since at least the 1940s. In fact, Jones Junior College of Ellisville, Mississippi, almost withdrew from the junior college Little Rose Bowl in 1955 because the opposing team, Compton College, fielded black students. But the majority of teams were coached by whites until the early 1970s, and some black student athletes at University of California, Berkeley, in 1968 spoke of racial discrimination by coaches and officials. Gendered integration of junior college sports teams in California did not take place until 1973. "Race Issue Touches Little Rose Bowl," *Los Angeles Times,* 4 Dec 1955, B7; "Pasadena, San Diego Grids Clash," *Los Angeles Times,* 23 Sept 1948, C3; Dwight Chapin, "Conflict at Cal: Negroes Give

Their View," *Los Angeles Times,* 29 Jan 1968, C3; Sue Avery, "Girls Enter College Sports; Turmoil Begins," *Los Angeles Times,* 8 Apr 1973, GF1.

56. Brint and Karabel, *The Diverted Dream*; Douglas, *The Conditions for Admission*, ch 3.

57. Coordinating Council for Higher Education, *Increasing Opportunities in Higher Education for Disadvantaged Students* (Sacramento, CA, July 1966), 14–22; Coordinating Council for Higher Education, *California Higher Education and the Disadvantaged* (Sacramento, CA, March 1968), 1–2.

58. Douglas, *The Conditions for Admission*, 70, 72–73.

59. "CDC Accuses Police of Attacking Civil Rights," *Los Angeles Times,* 13 April 1964, 2; Modell, *The Economics and Politics of Racial Accommodation,* 128.

60. Collier-Thomas and Franklin, *My Soul Is a Witness,* 42, 61.

61. Carter and Hickerson, "A California Citizens' Committee Studies Its Schools and De Facto Segregation," 102.

62. California Advisory Committee to the U.S. Commission on Civil Rights, *Fair and Open Environment? Bigotry and Violence on College Campuses in California* (Washington, DC, June 1991). According to this study, which cautioned that it was not an "exhaustive review," during the 1988–89 school year in Los Angeles County there were 2,265 "hate incidents." From 1985 to 1988 there were 178 "racial/ethnic incidents" between all University of California campuses. For studies on the racial climates in institutions of higher education see Chesler and Crowfoot, "An Organizational Analysis of Racism in Higher Education"; Hurtado, Milem, Clayton-Pedersen, and Allen, "Enhancing Campus Climates for Racial/Ethnic Diversity."

63. Collier-Thomas and Franklin, *My Soul Is a Witness,* 104.

64. Turpin, Dick, "Negro Group Requests Non-Technical College," *Los Angeles Times,* 1 April 1966, A8; "Board Refuses State Loan on Junior College," *Los Angeles Times,* 30 Sept 1966, 29; "Southwest Jr. College: Teacher Group Disapproves," *Los Angeles Times,* 28 Jan 1967, B4; Jack McCurdy, "Board Plans to Give Priority to South L.A. Area College," *Los Angeles Times,* 13 Oct 1967, SG1; Jack McCurdy, "Educational Board Unit Ends Integration Study," *Los Angeles Times,* 24 Oct 1967, A8; John Dart, "Race Issue Explanation Is Candidate's Purpose," *Los Angeles Times,* 29 Jun 1968, 19.

65. Yoo, *Growing Up Nisei,* 4, 26, 27, 50, 109.

66. Douglas, *The Conditions for Admission,* 98; Jack McCurdy, "Junior Colleges Charged with Lagging in Minority Education," *The Los Angeles Times,* 1 Nov 1968, A12.

67. Carnegie Commission, *The Open-Door Colleges,* Appendix A, Table 1; Gibson and Jung, *Historical Census Statistics on Population,* Tables 19.

68. The Carnegie Commission on Higher Education, *The Open-Door Colleges* (New York, 1970), 2, 5, 10–11.

69. Coordinating Council for Higher Education, *California Higher Education and the Disadvantaged* (Sacramento, CA, March 1968), 1–2.

70. California Postsecondary Education Commission (CPEC), *Planning for Postsecondary Education in California,* 21; CPEC, *The Role of the California Postsecondary Education Commission in Achieving Educational Equity in California,* 4, 5.

71. Joint Committee on Higher Education of the California legislature, *The Challenge of Achievement* (Sacramento, CA, 1969); Commission for the Review of the Master Plan for Higher Education, *Background Papers: The Master Plan Renewed* (Sacramento, CA, August 1987), 6–7.

72. CPEC, *Planning for Postsecondary Education in California: A Five Year Plan Update, 1979* (Sacramento, CA, 1978), 1–4, 7–8; CPEC, *The Role of the California Postsecondary Education Commission in Achieving Educational Equity in California* (Sacramento, CA, Sept 1988); Commission for the Review of the Master Plan for Higher Education, *Background Papers: The Master Plan Renewed*, 7; State of California, *California Constitution*, Article 13A, Official California Legislative Information, http://www.leginfo.ca.gov/.const/.article_13A; The John Vasconcellos Legacy, The John Vasconcellos Project, June 1, 2008, hrrp://www.politicsoftrust.net

73. CPEC, *Through the Open Door: A Study of Patterns of Enrollment and Performance in California's Community Colleges* (Feb 1976), 5. The other four reports were *Through the Open Door: Sources and Selected Characteristics of Students* (June 1973); *Through the Open Door: 32,000 Students in 32 Colleges* (Oct 1973); *Through the Open Door: The Other Side of Persistence* (Feb 1974); and *Through the Open Door: A Limited View of Performance* (July 1974).

74. Ibid., i, 2–3, 17. The collection of racial and ethnic student data was in a transition period. Requiring students to submit such data and recording it had been against state law, but in 1968 the federal government began to require colleges and universities to report such data, which put institutions of higher education in the state in a difficult situation. But by the late 1960s more and more institutions began to comply with federal requirements (p. 19).

75. Ibid., ii, vi–vii, 2, 6, D1.

76. Ibid., 23–25, 32, 49.

77. In a 1985 report the CPEC complained, "No rates of transfer can be computed and no statement can be made about changes in such a rate over the past two decades, since there is no agreed-upon pool of potential transfers to use in computing a rate." CPEC, *Reaffirming California's Commitment to Transfer: Recommendations for Aiding Student Transfer from the California Community Colleges to the California State University and the University of California* (March 1985), 48; CPEC, *Planning for Postsecondary Education in California,* 21; CPEC, *Plan for Obtaining Community College Transfer Student Information* (March 1980); CPEC, *Toward Educational Equity* (Jan 1989), 28; CPEC, *Update of Community College Transfer Student Statistics 1988–89* (Aug 1989), 12; CPEC, *Student Transfer in California Postsecondary Education* (June 2005). For national transfer issues see Ellen M. Bradburn and David G. Hurst, "Community College Transfer Rates to 4-Year Institutions Using Alternative Definitions of Transfer," *Education Statistics Quarterly* 3, no. 3 (2001), National Center for Education Statistics. From 1982 to 1991, CPEC released yearly reports called *Update of Community College Transfer Student Statistics.* From 1995 to 2001, these reports became *New Community College Transfer Students at California's Public Universities.* Finally, these reports were given a new name in 2002, *Student Transfer in California Postsecondary Education.*

78. Ibid.

79. CPEC, *Background Papers to a Prospectus for California Postsecondary Education, 1985–2000* (March 1985), 133–35, 140, 184; Commission for the Review of the Master Plan for Higher Education, *Background Papers: The Challenge of Change* (March 1986), 125.

80. Commission for the Review of the Master Plan, *Background Papers*, 44, 126; Commission for the Review of the Master Plan, *The Challenge of Change: A Reassessment of the California Community College* (March 1986), 1–2, 5, 7; Russell G. Fischer, "California Community Colleges: On the Road to Reform?" *Community College Review* 15, no. 1 (1987): 13–20; Peter Schrag, "California Screamin': Proposition 13 Cuts Deep," *The New Republic* (23 June 1986): 14–16.

81. Commission for the Review of the Master Plan, *The Challenge of Change*, 7, 12, 21, 25, 126.

82. Commission for the Review of the Master Plan, *Background Papers*, 30–31.

83. Commission for the Review of the Master Plan, *The Master Plan Renewed: Unity, Equity, Quality, and Efficiency in California Postsecondary Education* (July 1987), 1–3.

84. Ibid., 3–4.

85. Ibid., 4, 10–14.

86. Ibid., 4, 10–14.

87. While money is necessary to equitable and efficient outcomes, it is not sufficient. See W. Norton Grubb, *The Money Myth: School Resources, Outcomes, and Equity* (New York, 2009).

88. Coordinating Council for Higher Education, *A Consideration of Issues*, 50–53; California Postsecondary Commission, *Developments in Community College Finance* (Sacramento, CA, Dec 1987).

89. California Postsecondary Commission, *Developments in Community College Finance*; California Postsecondary Commission, *Statewide Fees in the California Community Colleges* (Sacramento, CA, Feb 1987). See also W. Norton Grubb and Marvin Lazerson, *Broken Promises* (Chicago, 1988), 84.

90. Ibid.; California Postsecondary Commission, *Implementation of the California Community Colleges Course Classification System* (Sacramento, CA, April 1982); California Postsecondary Commission, *Principles for Community College Finance* (Sacramento, CA, March 1983).

91. California Postsecondary Commission, *A Special Report to the California Postsecondary Education Commission on State Support of California Community Colleges* (Sacramento, CA, April 1984).

92. CPEC, *Who Will Take Responsibility for the Future of California Higher Education: A Statement by Clark Kerr* (Oct 1993), 1–4, 6; CPEC, *Restabilizing Higher Education: Moderating the Impact on California's College Students and the State's Future from Cutting State Support for Higher Education by $1.4 Billion Over the Past Three Years. Report of the Executive Director of the California Postsecondary Education Commission* (December 1993).

93. CPEC, *The Master Plan, Then and Now: Policies of the 1960–1975 Master Plan for Higher Education in Light of 1993 Realities* (April 1993), 25.

94. CPEC, *A Dream Deferred: California's Waning Higher Education Opportunities* (June 1993). On the issue of institutional funding see Grubb, *The Money Myth: School Resources, Outcomes, and Equity*.

95. CPEC, *A Bridge to the Future: Higher Education Planning for the Next Century* (Sept 1999), 5–6, 8–9.

96. Ibid., 13.

97. Ibid., 33, 37; W. Norton Grubb and Marvin Lazerson, *The Education Gospel.*

98. Ryan Phillips, *Public Education and the Construction of American Identity: The Role of the Foreign.* MA Dissertation, University of Bristol (Sept 2004), ch 2.

99. CPEC, The Performance of California Higher Education: Annual Reports to California's Governor, Legislature, and Citizens in Response to Assembly Bill 1808 (Chapter 741, Statues of 1991). Later renamed Performance Indicators of California Higher Education (Dec 1994), (Feb 1996), (April 1998), (Dec 1998), (Feb 2000), (April 2002).

100. CPEC, The Performance of California Higher Education: Annual Reports to California's Governor, Legislature, and Citizens in Response to Assembly Bill 1808 (Chapter 741, Statues of 1991). Later renamed Performance Indicators of California Higher Education (Dec 1994), (Feb 1996), (April 1998), (Dec 1998), (Feb 2000), (April 2002).

101. Ibid.

102. Joint Committee to Develop a Master Plan for Education, *The California Master Plan for Education* (Sacramento, CA, 2002), 77–79. Gert Biesta argues that education is "non causal and normative," therefore, educators must make "normative judgments," not technocratically based efficiency judgments because educational conflicts can never be solved, only normatively resolved. See Biesta, "What 'What Works' Won't Work," 20.

103. Biesta, "What 'What Works' Won't Work"; James Davison Hunter, *Culture Wars: The Struggle to Define America*; Gary B. Nash, Charlotte Crabtree, and Ross E. Dunn, *History on Trial: Culture Wars and the Teaching of the Past*; Jonathan Zimmerman, *Whose America? Culture Wars in the Public Schools.*

104. Daniel Bell, *The Cultural Contradictions of Capitalism* (New York, 1978), 26.

105. Joint Committee, *The California Master Plan for Education*, 83, 85–88.

106. Ibid., 64, 68.

107. Ibid.

108. CPEC, *Prospectus: Developing a Framework for Accountability in California's Higher Education System* (Sept 2004); CPEC, *Recommendation for a Higher Education Accountability Framework* (March 2005).

109. Chancellor's Office of California Community Colleges, *Accountability Reporting for the Community Colleges: Draft Report* (Sacramento, CA, Jan 2007).

110. Ibid.

111. CPEC, *California Higher Education Accountability: Goal—Student Success Measure: California Community College Students' Degrees and Certificates Awarded and Successful Transfers* (March 2007).

112. John S. Levin, Josh M. Beach, and Carrie B. Kisker, "Short-Term Credentials and the California Community College Curriculum, 1993–2006," California Community College Collaborative (April 2007), http://www.cccc.ucr. This report calls into question the recommendation made by Moore and Shulock for structuring programs "to encourage completion of shorter-term credentials along the pathway to longer-term credentials." See *Beyond the Open Door*, ix.

113. Nancy Shulock and Colleen Moore, *Rules of the Game: How State Policy Creates Barriers to Degree Completion and Impedes Student Success in the California Community Colleges*, Institute for Higher Education Leadership and Policy (Feb 2007); Colleen Moore and Nancy Shulock, *Beyond the Open Door: Increasing Student Success in the California Community Colleges*, Institute for Higher Education Leadership and Policy (Aug 2007). A look at the raw data on enrolled students from 2002 to 2007 reveals a 26 to 28 percent persistence rate between the first- and second-years. CPEC, *Custom Data Reports.*

114. Moore and Shulock, *Beyond the Open Door*, v–vi; Nancy Shulock and Colleen Moore, *Invest in Success: How Finance Policy Can Increase Student Success at California's Community Colleges*, Institute for Higher Education Leadership and Policy (Oct 2007), 3, 7, 11, 46; Nancy Shulock, Colleen Moore, Jeremy Offenstein, and Mary Kirlin, *It Could Happen: Unleashing the Potential of California's Community Colleges to Help Students Succeed and California Thrive*, Institute for Higher Education Leadership and Policy (Feb 2008), 12.

115. For student outcomes data before 1950 see Cooper, "The Junior-College Movement in California"; Gray, "The Junior College in California"; Hill, *The Functioning of the California Public Junior College*; Whitney, "Present Standards for Junior Colleges." On student evaluation data before 1950 see J. Fletchner Wellemeyer, "The Junior College as Viewed by Its Students," *School Review* 34 (1926): 760–67; Walter Crosby Eells and R. Romayne Brand, "Student Opinion in Junior Colleges in California," *The School Review* 38, no. 3 (1930): 176–190. For student outcomes data from 1950s to 1960s see Clark, *The Open Door College*; Medsker and Tillery, *Breaking the Access Barriers*. For student outcomes data from 1970s to present see CPEC reports as referenced above. For recent statistics see Moore and Shulock, *Beyond the Open Door*; Shulock and Moore, *Invest in Success*. I have tabulated all the known student outcomes data for California community colleges over the past century in a spreadsheet, as well as in charts and graphs, which are available on my website at http://www.jmbeach.com.

116. On pedagogy see Grubb and Associates, *Honored but Invisible*. On developmental education see Jan M. Ignash, ed., *Implementing Effective Policies for Remedial and Development Education, New Directions for Community Colleges* 100 (San Francisco, 1997). On organizational change see John S. Levin, ed., *Organizational Change in the Community College: A Ripple or a Sea Change? New Directions for Community Colleges* 102 (San Francisco, 1998).

117. I draw upon my own experiences as a California community college instructor. See also Breneman and Nelson, *Financing Community Colleges*, 55; Ken Buckman, "What Counts as Assessment in the 21st Century?" *Thought & Action* 23 (2007): 29–37; David Clemens, "Exposing the Big Lies about SLOs: Professor Contents SLOs Have Disastrous Consequences for Students and Faculty," *CCA Advocate* (June 2008): 5; Patrick Sullivan, "Measuring 'Success' at Open Admissions Institutions: Thinking Carefully about This Complex Question," *College English* 70, no. 6 (2008): 618–632.

118. Nancy Shulock, one of the principle authors of these studies, was shocked that community college administrators felt blamed by these reports as Shulock intended the blame to be placed on state policies, not administrators. However,

the reports make it abundantly clear that California community colleges are not functioning well, largely because of current policies, but implicitly, if not explicitly, this critique extends to the administrators who embody institutions and state policies (Shulock, 2007). For administrator reaction see Smith, 2007. Dennis R. Smith, "Letter to Hon. Anthony Portantino: California Community College Student Success Response to *Rules of the Game*," Testimony given to California Assembly Higher Education Committee, Sacramento, CA, Feb 27, 2007, Retrieved Jan 30, 2008, from http://www.faccc.org/whatsnew/whatsnew_files/2007/Final%20Copy_RulesResponse .pdf.

119. Thomas R. Bailey, D. Timothy Leinbach, and Davis Jenkins, *Is Student Success Labeled Institutional Failure? Student Goals and Graduation Rates in the Accountability Debate at Community Colleges,* Community College Research Center (New York, 2006); Duane E. Leigh and Andrew M. Gill Leigh, *Do Community Colleges Respond to Local Needs? Evidence from California* (Kalamazoo, MI, 2007), 25–45,84– 85, 99–106; Grubb and Associates, *Honored but Invisible,* 321–23.

120. "CCA/CTA Organizes to Restore Millions in Budget Cuts to Higher Education," *CCA Advocate* 43, no. 4 (June 2008): 1; Scott Lay, "League Budget Update #22: Governor Proposes $322 Million Cut to Community Colleges," *Community College League of California* (Nov 2, 2008), http://www.ccleague.org; Geoff Maslen, "US: Waiting for the Worst," *University World News* (2 Nov 2008), http://www.uni versityworldnews.com; "California's Budget Crisis," *The Economist* (July 11 2009); "California's Universities in Trouble," *The Economist* (Aug 8 2009); Stu Woo and Ryan Knutson, "Budget Agreement Deepens California's Pain," *Wall Street Journal* (July 22 2009); Larry Gordon, "UC Panel Approves 11 to 26 Furlough Days," *Los Angeles Times* (July 16 2009); Larry Gordon and Amina Khan, "UC Regents Approve Fee Hike Amid Loud Student Protests," *Los Angeles Times* (Nov 19 2009).

121. Nanette Asimov, "More Eligible Students, Fewer College Slots," *San Francisco Chronicle* (Dec 10 2008), http://www.sfgate.com.

122. "Keynes in Reverse," *The Economist* (Dec 5, 2009), 36–37.

123. Martin Zimmerman, Marc Lifsher, and Andrea Chang, "California Budget Crisis Could Bring Lasting Economic Harm," *The Los Angeles Times* (May 23 2009); Mitchell Landsberg, "Budget to Reshape the Golden State," *The Los Angeles Times* (July 22 2009); Sarah King Head, "California's Higher Education Apocalypse," *University World News* (Aug 30, 2009). Douglas quoted in Head article.

Notes to Chapter 4

1. Grubb and Lazerson, *The Education Gospel,* 164.

2. Jeremy Atack and Peter Passell, *A New Economic View of American History,* 2nd ed. (New York, 1994), 19.

3. Atack and Passell, *A New Economic View of American History,* 522, 533; Claudia Goldin, *Understanding the Gender Gap: An Economic History of American Women* (Oxford, UK, 1990); Roger L. Ransom and Richard Sutch, *One Kind of Freedom: The Economic Consequences of Emancipation,* 2nd ed. (Cambridge, UK, 2001), 165; David R. Roediger, *The Wages of Whiteness,* rev ed. (London, 2003).

4. Atack and Passell, *A New Economic View of American History*, 539; Richard Edwards, *Contested Terrain: The Transformation of the Workplace in the Twentieth Century* (New York, 1979); Nell Irvin Painter, *Standing at Armageddon*.

5. Jeanne Boydston, *Home & Work: Housework, Wages, and the Ideology of Labor in the Early Republic* (Oxford, UK, 1990); Goldin, *Understanding the Gender Gap*.

6. Atack and Passell, *A New Economic View of American History*, 529, 543.

7. Edwards, *Contested Terrain*, 26, 31; Kliebard, *Schooled to Work*, 52.

8. Dawley, *Struggles for Justice*; Edwards, *Contested Terrain*; Nelson Lichtenstein, *State of the Union: A Century of American Labor* (Princeton, NJ, 2002).

9. Claudia Golden and Lawrence F. Katz, *The Race Between Education and Technology* (Cambridge, MA, 2009).

10. Theodore W. Schultz, "Investment in Human Capital," *The American Economic Review* 51, no. 1 (1961): 2–5, 11.

11. Kern Alexander, "The Value of an Education" (1976), *ASHE Reader on Finance in Higher Education*, D. W. Breneman, L. L. Leslie, and R. E. Anderson, eds. (Needham Heights, MA, 1996), 85–86, 88, 89; Michael B. Paulsen, "The Economics of Human Capital and Investment in Higher Education," *The Finance of Higher Education*, Ibid., 60, 74.

12. For expansive economic usage see Alexander, "The Value of an Education"; Grubb and Lazerson, *The Education Gospel*; Amartya Sen, *Development as Freedom* (New York, 1999). For narrow economic usage see David Breneman, "The Outputs of Higher Education," *Ford Policy Forum 2001* (Cambridge, MA, 2001); Stacy Berg Dale and Alan B. Krueger, *Estimating the Payoff to Attending a More Selective College*, National Bureau of Economic Research (Cambridge, MA, 1999); Larry L. Leslie and Paul T. Brinkman, *The Economic Value of Higher Education* (New York, 1988); Paulsen, "The Economics of Human Capital and Investment in Higher Education."

13. Breneman, "The Outputs of Higher Education"; Leslie and Brinkman, *The Economic Value of Higher Education*.

14. W. Norton Grubb, "The Economic Returns to Baccalaureate Degrees: New Evidence from the Class of 1972," *The Review of Higher Education* 15, no 2 (1992): 213–231; Grubb, *Learning and Earning in the Middle*; Grubb and Lazerson, *The Education Gospel*, 160; Paulsen, "The Economics of Human Capital and Investment in Higher Education," 65, 74–76; Rosenbaum, *Beyond College for All*.

15. Breneman, "The Outputs of Higher Education," 8; Dale and Krueger, *Estimating the Payoff to Attending a More Selective College*, 30; Dey and Hill, *Behind the Pay Gap*; Grubb, "The Economic Returns to Baccalaureate Degrees"; Grubb and Lazerson, *The Education Gospel*, 158; Mishel, Bernstein and Allegretto, *The State of Working America 2006/2007*; Paulsen, "The Economics of Human Capital and Investment in Higher Education," 76; Devah Pager, *Marked: Race, Crime, and Finding Work in an Era of Mass Incarceration* (Chicago, 2007); Rosenbaum, *Beyond College for All*, 68–81; Bruce Western, *Punishment and inequality in America* (New York, 2006).

16. American Council on Education, *Minorities in Higher Education 2008* (Washington DC, 2008); Katherine Magnuson and Jane Waldfogel, eds., *Steady*

Gains and Stalled Progress: Inequality and the Black-White Test Score Gap (New York, 2008).

17. Na'ilah Suad Nasir and Victoria M. Hand, "Exploring Sociocultural Perspectives on Race, Culture, and Learning," *Review of Educational Research* 76, no. 4 (2006): 456.

18. Samuel Bowles and Herbert Gintis, "*Schooling in Capitalist America* Revisited," *Sociology of Education* 75, no. 2 (2001): 1–18; Gloria Ladson-Billings, "From the Achievement Gap to the Education Debt: Understanding Achievement in U.S. Schools," *Educational Researcher* 35, no. 7 (2006): 3–12; John R. Logan and Deirdre Oakley, *The Continuing Legacy of the Brown Decision*; Lewis Mumford Center for Comparative Urban and Regional Research (Albany, NY, 2004); Samuel Roundfield Lucas, *Tracking Inequality: Stratification and Mobility in American High Schools* (New York, 1999); Gary Orfield and John T. Yun, *Resegregation in American Schools*, Harvard Civil Rights Project (Cambridge, MA, 1997); Gary Orfield and Chungmei Lee, *Brown at 50*, Harvard Civil Rights Project (Cambridge, MA, 2004); Gary Orfield, *Why Segregation Matters: Poverty and Educational Inequality*, Harvard Civil Rights Project (Cambridge, MA, 2005).

19. Bowles and Gintis, "*Schooling in Capitalist America* Revisited"; Brantlinger, *The Politics of Social Class in Secondary School*; Cabrera and La Nasa, "On the Path to College, 121; John Aubrey Douglas and Gregg Thomson, "The Poor and the Rich: A Look at Economic Stratification and Academic Performance Among Undergraduate Students in the United States," Center for Studies in Higher Education (Stanford, CA, 2008); Linda Darling-Hammond, "Securing the Right to Learn," *Educational Researcher* 35, no. 7 (2006): 13–4; Darling-Hammond, "The Flat Earth and Education," *Educational Researcher* 36, no. 6 (2007): 318–334; Gloria Ladson-Billings, "From the Achievement Gap to the Education Debt"; Lucas, *Tracking Inequality*; Magnuson and Waldfogel, *Steady Gains and Stalled Progress: Inequality and the Black-White Test Score Gap*; Greg Wiggan, "Race, School Achievement, and Educational Inequality," *Review of Educational Research* 77, no. 3 (2007): 310–333.

20. Jennifer L. Hochschild and Nathan Scovronick, *The American Dream and the Public Schools* (Oxford, UK, 2003); Cal Jillson, *Pursuing the American Dream* (Lawrence, KS, 2004), 286.

21. Robert N. Bellah, Richard Madsen, William M. Sullivan, Ann Swidler, and Steven M. Tipton, *The Good Society* (New York, 1991), 289, 306.

22. Barack Obama, *The Audacity of Hope: Thoughts on Reclaiming the American Dream* (New York, 2006), 92.

23. Bellah, et al., *The Good Society*, 5.

24. Ortner, *Anthropology and Social Theory*.

25. Isiah Berlin, "Does Political Theory Still Exist?" *The Proper Study of Mankind* (New York, 2000).

26. Most if not all policy reports urging more stringent use of student outcomes assessment do not investigate the history, political motivations, or controversy surrounding this issue. For example, see George Kuh and Stanley Ikenberry, *More Than You Think, Less Than We Need: Learning Outcomes Assessment in American Higher Education*, National Institute for Learning Outcomes Assessment (Oct 2009).

27. Breneman and Nelson, *Financing Community Colleges,* 55–59; Callahan, *Education and the Cult of Efficiency*; Grubb and Lazerson, *Broken Promises*, 99, 57; Dougherty and Hong, "Performance Accountability as Imperfect Panacea," 52; Zumeta, "Public Policy and Accountability in Higher Education," 172, 185–186.

28. "The Pedagogy of the Privileged," *The Economist* (Sept 26, 2009), 72.

29. For a discussion of this philosophical issue see Isaiah Berlin, "Two Concepts of Liberty," *The Proper Study of Mankind* (New York, 2000), 191–242.

30. On policy see James G. Cibulka, "Policy Analysis and the Study of the Politics of Education," *The Study of Educational Politics*; Lawrence A. Cremin, "Education as Politics," *Popular Education and Its Discontents* (New York, 1989); Debra Stone, *Policy Paradox*. On school reform see Peter Schrag, "Schoolhouse Crock: Fifty Years of Blaming America's Educational System for Our Stupidity," *Harper's Magazine* (Sept 2007): 36–44; Tyack and Larry Cuban, *Tinkering Toward Utopia,* 135.

31. Zumeta, "Public Policy and Accountability in Higher Education," 185.

32. Joseph Stiglitz, Amaryta Sen, Jean-Paul Fitoussi, and associates, *Report by the Commission on the Measurement of Economic Performance and Social Progress* (Sept 2009), http://www.stiglitz-sen-fitoussi.fr/en/documents.htm.

33. Chris M. Anson, "Closed Systems and Standardized Writing Tests," In Assessment Symposium, *College Composition and Communication 60*, no. 1 (2008): 122. See also: Grubb and Lazerson, *The Education Gospel*, 102. Grubb and Lazerson argue that community colleges "should strive to be as good as they can be *in their own terms*" [emphasis in original].

34. Tyack and Larry Cuban, *Tinkering Toward Utopia,* 135.

35. Isaiah Berlin, "Two Concepts of Liberty," 238.

36. John S. Levin, Elizabeth M. Cox, Carrie Kisker, Christine Cerven, Yueh-Ching Chang, Josh M. Beach, Jennifer Silverman, and Shaila Mulholland, "Community College Literature Reviews: Basic Skills, Counseling, ESL, Transfer, Vocational Education," *C4 eJournal,* II (2008), http://repositories.cdlib.org/cgi/viewcontent.cgi?article = 1000&context = ucr_c4. See also Grubb and Associates, *Honored but Invisible*; Ignash, *Implementing Effective Policies for Remedial and Development Education;* Levin, *Organizational Change in the Community College.*

37. Richard J. Bernstein, "Democratic Hope," *The Hedgehog Review* 10, no. 1 (2008): 36–50; Biesta, "What 'What Works' Won't Work"; Robert A. Dahl, *On Democracy* (New Haven, 1998); Amy Gutmann, *Democratic Education* (Princeton, NJ, 1987); Alexis F. Lange, "The Junior College as an Integral Part of the Public-School System," 466–67.

38. Callahan, *Education and the Cult of Efficiency,* 121; Aaron Wildavasky, *Speaking Truth to Power: The Art of Craft of Policy Analysis* (Boston, 1979), 131, 148, 309. On education being made into the "fall guy," see also Grubb and Lazerson, *The Education Gospel.*

39. Berlin, "The Pursuit of the Ideal," *The Proper Study of Mankind,* 15.

SELECTED BIBLIOGRAPHY

Astin, Alexander W., and Leticia Oseguera. "The Declining 'Equity' of American Higher Education." *The Review of Higher Education* 27, no. 3 (Spring 2004): 321–341.

Ayers, D. Franklin. "Neoliberal Ideology in Community College Mission Statements: A Critical Discourse Analysis." *The Review of Higher Education* 28, no. 4 (Summer 2005): 527–549.

Bailey, Thomas, and Vanessa Smith Morest, eds. *Defending the Community College Equity Agenda.* Baltimore, MD: Johns Hopkins University Press, 2006.

Bailey, Thomas R., and Irina E. Averianova. "Multiple Missions of Community Colleges: Conflicting or Complementary?" *Community College Research Center Brief* 1 (May 1999): 1–6.

Bailey, Thomas R., D. Timothy Leinbach, and Davis Jenkins. *Is Student Success Labeled Institutional Failure? Student Goals and Graduation Rates in the Accountability Debate at Community Colleges.* Community College Research Center, Working Paper No. 1. New York: Teachers College, Columbia University, 2006.

Beach, J. M. (2009). A critique of human capital formation in the United States and the economic returns to sub-baccalaureate credentials. *Educational Studies,* 45(1), 24 1/n 38.

Biesta, Gert. "What 'What Works' Won't Work: Evidence Based Practice and the Democratic Deficit in Educational Research." *Educational Theory* 57, no. 1 (2007): 1–22.

Blocker, Clyde E., Robert H. Plummer, and Richard C. Richardson, Jr. *The Two-Year College: A Social Synthesis.* Englewood Cliffs, NJ: Prentice-Hall, 1965.

Bogart, Quentin J. "The Community College Mission." In *A Handbook on the Community College in America: Its History, Mission, and Management,* edited by George A. Baker III. Westport, CT: Greenwood Press, 1994.

Bogue, Jesse. *The Community College.* New York: McGraw-Hill, 1950.

Bradburn, Ellen M., and David G. Hurst. "Community College Transfer Rates to 4-Year Institutions Using Alternative Definitions of Transfer." *Education Statistics Quarterly* 3, no. 3 (2001). National Center for Education Statistics, Report 2001–197.

Bragg, Debra D. "Community College Access, Mission, and Outcomes: Considering Intriguing Intersections and Challenges." *Peabody Journal of Education,* 76, no. 1 (2001): 93–116.

Breneman, David W., and Susan C. Nelson. *Financing Community Colleges: An Economic Perspective.* Washington, DC: The Brookings Institution, 1981.

Brint, Steven. "Few Remaining Dreams: Community Colleges Since 1985." *Annals of the American Academy of Political and Social Science* 586 (2003, March): 16–37.

Brint, Steven, and Jerome Karabel. "The Community College and Democratic Ideals." *Community College Review* 17 (1989): 9–19.

———. *The Diverted Dream: Community Colleges and the Promise of Educational Opportunity in America, 1900–1985.* Oxford: Oxford University Press, 1989.

———. "Institutional Origins and Transformations: The Case of American Community Colleges," In The *New Institutionalism in Organizational Analysis,* edited by Paul J. DiMaggio and Walter W. Powell. Chicago: The University of Chicago Press, 1991.

Bryant, Alyssa N. "Community College Students: Recent Findings and Trends." *Community College Review* 29, no. 3 (Winter 2001): 77–93.

Carnegie Commission on Higher Education. *The Open-Door Colleges: Policies for Community Colleges.* New York: McGraw Hill, 1970.

Clark, Burton R. "The 'Cooling Out' Function in Higher Education." *The American Journal of Sociology* 65, no. 6 (May 1960): 569–576.

———. *The Open Door College: A Case Study.* New York: McGraw Hill, 1960.

Cohen, Arthur M. "The Case for the Community College." *American Journal of Education* 98, no. 4 (Aug 1990), 426–442.

———. "Governmental Policies affecting Community Colleges: A Historical Perspective." In *Community Colleges: Policy in the Future Context,* edited by Barbara K. Townsend & Susan B. Twombly. Westport, CT: Ablex, 1999.

———. "The Process of Desegregation: A Case Study." *The Journal of Negro Education* 35, no. 4 (Autumn 1966): 445–451.

Cohen, Arthur. M., and Florence B. Brawer. *The American Community College.* 3d ed. San Francisco: Jossey-Bass, 1996.

Cooper, Joanne, and Ken Kempner. "Lord of the Flies Community College: A Case Study of Organizational Disintegration." *The Review of Higher Education* 16, no. 4 (1993, Summer): 419–437.

Cross, K. Patricia. "Community Colleges on the Plateau." *The Journal of Higher Education* 52, no. 2 (March/April 1981): 113–123.

———. "Determining Missions and Priorities for the Fifth Generation." In *Renewing the American Community College: Priorities and Strategies for Effective Leadership,* edited by William L. Deegan and Dale Tillery. San Francisco, CA: Jossey-Bass, 1985.

———. *The Junior College's Role in Providing Postsecondary Education for All.* Washington DC: U.S. Office of Education, 1969.

Dougherty, Kevin J. *The Contradictory College: The Conflicting Origins, Impacts, and Futures of the Community College.* 1994. Reprint. Albany, NY: State University of New York Press, 2001.

Dougherty, Kevin J., and Marianne F. Bakia. *The New Economic Development Role of the Community College.* Community College Research Center, Teachers College, Columbia University. New York: author, Nov 1999.

Dougherty, Kevin J., and Esther Hong. "Performance Accountability as Imperfect Panacea." In *Defending the Community College Equity Agenda,* edited by Thomas Bailey and Vanessa Smith Morest. Baltimore, MD: The Johns Hopkins University Press, 2006.

Dougherty, Kevin J., and Monica Reid. *Fifty States of Achieving the Dream: State Policies to Enhance Access to and Success in Community Colleges Across the United States.* Community College Research Center, Teachers College, Columbia University. New York: author, April 5, 2007.

Dougherty, Kevin J., and Barbara K. Townsend. "Community College Missions: A Theoretical and Historical Perspective." In *Community College Missions in the 21st Century, New Directions for the Community College* 136 (Winter 2006): 5–13.

Douglas, John Aubrey. *The California Idea and American Higher Education, 1850 to the 1960 Master Plan.* Stanford, CA: Stanford University Press, 2000.

————. *The Conditions of Admission: Access, Equity, and the Social Contract of Public Universities.* Stanford, CA: Stanford University Press, 2007.

Douglas, John Aubrey, and Gregg Thomson. "The Poor and the Rich: A Look at Economic Stratification and Academic Performance among Undergraduate Students in the United States." Center for Studies in Higher Education. Occasional Papers Series, 15. 2008.

Dowd, Alicia C. "From Access to Outcome Equity: Revitalizing the Democratic Mission of the Community College." *Annals of the American Academy of Political and Social Science,* 586 (2003, March): 92–119.

Dowd, Alicia C., and Tatiana Melguizo. "Socioeconomic Stratification of Community College Transfer Access in the 1980s and 1990s: Evidence from HS&B and NELS." *The Review of Higher Education* 31, no. 4 (Summer 2008): 377–400.

Eaton, Judith S. "The Fortunes of the Transfer Function: Community Colleges and Transfer 1900–1990." in *A Handbook on the Community College in America: Its History, Mission, and Management,* edited by George A. Baker III. Westport, CT: Greenwood Press, 1994.

————. *Strengthening Collegiate Education in Community Colleges.* San Francisco, CA: Jossey-Bass, 1994.

Eells, Walter Crosby. *The Junior College.* Boston: Houghton Mifflin Co., 1931.

————. "What Manner of Child Shall This Be?" *Junior College Journal* 1 (Feb 1931): 309–328.

————. *Why Junior College Terminal Education?* Terminal Education Monograph no. 3. Washington DC: American Association of Junior College, 1941.

Floyd, Deborah L. "The Community College Baccalaureate in the U.S." In *The Community College Baccalaureate: Emerging Trends and Policy Issues,* edited by Deborah L. Floyd, Michael L. Skolnik, and Kenneth P. Walker. Sterling, VA: Stylus, 2005.

Frost, Susan. H. *Academic Advising for Student Success: A System of Shared Responsibility.* ASHE-ERIC Higher Education Report No. 3. Washington, DC: The

George Washington University, School of Education and Human Development, 1991.

Frye, John H. "Educational Paradigms in the Professional Literature of the Community College." In *Higher Education: Handbook of Theory and Research*, vol. 10, edited by John C. Smart. New York: Agathon Press, 1994.

———. "The Rhetoric of Professional Educators and the Definition of Public Junior Colleges from 1900 to 1940." *Community College Review* 20 (1993): 5–16.

———. *The Vision of the Public Junior College, 1900–1940: Professional Goals and Popular Aspirations*. New York: Greenwood Press, 1992.

Gleazer, Edmund J. Jr., *The Community College: Values, Vision, and Vitality*. Washington, DC: American Association of Community and Junior Colleges, 1980.

———. "Evolution of Junior Colleges into Community Colleges." In *A Handbook on the Community College in America: Its History, Mission, and Management*, edited by George A. Baker III. Westport, CT: Greenwood Press, 1994.

———. *This Is the Community College*. Boston: Houghton Mifflin, 1968.

Golden, Daniel. *The Price of Admission: How America's Ruling Class Buys Its Way into Elite Colleges—and Who Gets Left Outside the Gates*. New York: Three Rivers Press, 2007.

Griffith, Marlene, and Ann Connor. *Democracy's Open Door: The Community College in America's Future*. Portsmouth, NH: Boynton/Cook, 1994.

Grubb, W. Norton. "The Convergence of Educational Systems and the Role of Vocationalism." *Comparative Education Review* 29, no. 4 (Nov 1985): 526–548.

———. "The Economic Returns to Baccalaureate Degrees: New Evidence from the Class of 1972." *The Review of Higher Education* 15, no. 2 (1992): 213–231.

———. *Learning and Earning in the Middle: The Economic Benefits of Sub-Baccalaureate Education*. Community College Research Center. Teachers College, Columbia University. New York: author, 1999.

———. *Learning to Work: The Case for Reintegrating Job Training and Education*. New York: Russell Sage Foundation, 1996.

———. *The Money Myth: School Resources, Outcomes, and Equity*. Russell Sage: New York, 2009.

———. *Working in the Middle: Strengthening Education and Training for the Mid-Skilled Labor Force*. San Francisco: Jossey-Bass, 1996.

Grubb, W. Norton, and Associates. *Honored but Invisible: An Inside Look at Teaching in Community Colleges*. New York: Routledge, 1999.

Grubb, W. Norton, and Marvin Lazerson. *Broken Promises: How Americans Fail Their Children*. Chicago: University of Chicago Press, 1988.

———. *The Education Gospel: The Economic Power of Schooling*. Cambridge, MA: Harvard University Press, 2004.

Hall, George L. "Behind the Bramble Bushes: A Mid-Century History of the Community College." *Community College Review* 2 (1974): 6–14.

Herideen, Penelope E. *Policy, Pedagogy, and Social Inequality: Community College Student Realities in Post-Industrial America.* Westport, CT: Bergin & Garvey, 1998.

Ignash, Jan M., ed. *Implementing Effective Policies for Remedial and Development Education. New Directions for Community Colleges* 100 (Winter 1997).

Karabel, Jerome. "Community Colleges and Social Stratification." *Harvard Educational Review* 42, no. 4 (1972): 521–562.

Koos, Leonard V. *The American Secondary School.* Boston: Ginn & Co., 1927.

———. *The Junior-College Movement.* Boston: Ginn & Co., 1925.

Laanan, Frankie Santos. "Accountability in Community Colleges: Looking toward the 21st Century." In *Community Colleges: Policy in the Future Context,* edited by Barbara K. Townsend and Susan B. Twombly. Westport, CT: Ablex, 1999.

Labaree, David F. "From Comprehensive High School to Community College: Politics, Markets, and the Evolution of Educational Opportunity." *Research in Sociology of Education and Socialization: A Research Annual* 9 (Greenwich, CT: JAI Press, 1990): 203–240.

———. *How to Succeed in School without Really Learning: The Credentials Race in American Education.* New Haven, CT: Yale University Press, 1997.

Leigh, Duane E., and Andrew M. Gill. *Do Community Colleges Respond to Local Needs? Evidence from California.* Kalamazoo, MI: Upjohn Institute for Employment Research, 2007.

Levin, John S. "The Community College as a Baccalaureate-Granting Institution." *The Review of Higher Education* 28, no. 1 (Fall 2004): 1–22.

———. *Globalizing the Community College: Strategies for Change in the Twenty-First Century.* New York: Palgrave, 2001.

———. *Nontraditional Students and Community Colleges: The Conflict of Justice and Neoliberalism.* New York: Palgrave Macmillan, 2007.

———. "The Revised Institution: The Community College Mission at the End of the Twentieth Century." *Community College Review* 28, no. 1 (2000): 1–25.

Levin, John S., Josh M. Beach, and Carrie B. Kisker. "Short-Term Credentials and the California Community College Curriculum, 1993–2006." California Community College Collaborative. Riverside, CA: Author, April 2007.

Levin, John S., Susan Kater, and Richard L. Wagoner. *Community College Faculty: At Work in the New Economy.* New York: Palgrave Macmillan, 2006.

London, Howard B. *The Culture of a Community College.* New York: Praeger Publishers, 1978.

Lorenzo, Albert L. "The Mission and Functions of the Community College: An Overview." In *A Handbook on the Community College in America: Its History, Mission, and Management,* edited by George A. Baker III. Westport, CT: Greenwood Press, 1994.

Lucas, Christopher J. *American Higher Education: A History.* New York: St. Martin's Griffin, 1994.

Magnuson, Katherine, and Jane Waldfogel, eds. *Steady Gains and Stalled Progress: Inequality and the Black-White Test Score Gap.* New York: Russell Sage, 2008.

Medsker, Leland L. *The Junior College: Progress and Prospect.* New York: McGraw Hill, 1960.

McCartan, Anne-Marie. "The Community College Mission: Present Challenges and Future Visions." *The Journal of Higher Education* 54, no. 6 (Nov/Dec 1983): 676–692.

McGrath, Dennis, and Martin B. Spear. *The Academic Crisis of the Community College.* Albany, NY: State University of New York Press, 1991.

Medsker, Leland L., and Dale Tillery. *Breaking the Access Barriers: A Profile of Two-Year Colleges.* New York: McGraw-Hill, 1971.

Meier, Kenneth. *The Community College Mission: History and Theory, 1930–2000.* Chico, CA: Unpublished manuscript, 2008.

Miller, Carroll L. "The Negro Publicly-Supported Junior College." *The Journal of Negro Education* 31, no. 3 (Summer 1962): 386–395.

Moore, Colleen, and Nancy Shulock. *Beyond the Open Door: Increasing Student Success in the California Community Colleges.* Institute for Higher Education Leadership & Policy. Sacramento, CA: author, August 2007.

Orfield, Gary. *Why Segregation Matters: Poverty and Educational Inequality.* Harvard Civil Rights Project. Cambridge, MA: Author, 2005.

Pascarella, Ernest T., and Patrick T. Terenzini. *How College Affects Students: A Third Decade of Research.* San Francisco, CA: Jossey-Bass, 2005.

———. *How College Affects Students: Finding and Insights from Twenty Years of Research.* San Francisco: Jossey-Bass, 1991.

Phillippe, Kent A., and Leila Gonzalez Sullivan. *National Profile of Community Colleges: Trends & Statistics,* 4th ed. Washington, DC: The American Association of Community Colleges, 2005.

Pincus, Fred L. "Contradictory Effects of Customized Contract Training in Community Colleges." *Critical Sociology,* 16, vol. 1 (1989, Spring): 77–93.

———. "The False Promises of Community Colleges: Class Conflict and Vocational Education." *Harvard Educational Review,* 50, vol. 3 (1980): 332–361.

———. "How Critics View the Community College's Role in the Twenty-First Century." In *A Handbook on the Community College in America: Its History, Mission, and Management,* edited by George A. Baker III. Westport, CT: Greenwood Press, 1994.

Proctor, William Martin, ed. *The Junior College: Its Organization and Administration.* Stanford University Press, 1927.

Raby, Rosalind Latiner. "International, Intercultural, and Multicultural Dimensions of Community Colleges in the United States." In *Dimensions of the Community College: International, Intercultural, and Multicultural Perspectives,* edited by Rosalind Latiner Raby and Norma Tarrow. New York: Garland, 1996.

Ratcliff, James L. "'First' Public Junior Colleges in an Age of Reform." *Journal of Higher Education* 58, no. 2 (March/April 1987): 151–180.

————. "Seven Streams in the Historical Development of the Modern American Community College." In *A Handbook on the Community College in America: Its History, Mission, and Management*, edited by George A. Baker III. Westport, CT: Greenwood Press, 1994.

Rhoads, Robert A., and James R. Valadez. *Democracy, Multiculturalism, and the Community College.* New York: Routledge, 1996.

Rhomberg, Chris. *No There There: Race, Class, and Political Community in Oakland.* Berkeley, CA: University of California Press, 2004.

Richardson, Richard C. Jr., and Louis W. Bender. *Fostering Minority Access and Achievement in Higher Education: The Role of Urban Community Colleges and Universities.* San Francisco, CA: Jossey-Bass, 1987.

Richardson, Richard C. Jr., and Larry L. Leslie. *The Impossible Dream? Financing Community College's Evolving Mission.* Washington, DC: American Association of Community and Junior Colleges, 1980.

Richardson, Richard C. Jr., Elizabeth C. Fisk, and Morris A. Okun. *Literacy in the Open-Access College.* San Francisco, CA: Jossey-Bass, 1983.

Rosenbaum, James E. *Beyond College for All: Career Paths for the Forgotten Half.* New York: Russell Sage Foundation, 2001.

Roueche, John E., and George A. Baker III. *Access and Excellence: The Open Door College.* Washington, DC: Community College Press, 1987.

Roueche, John E., and Suanne D. Roueche. *High Stakes, High Performance: Making Remedial Education Work.* Washington, DC: Community College Press, 1999.

Roueche, John E., Suanne D. Roueche, and Mark D. Milliron. *Strangers in Their Own Land: Part-Time Faculty in American Community Colleges.* Washington, DC: Community College Press, 1995.

Sacks, Peter. "Class Rules: The Fiction of Egalitarian Higher Education." *The Chronicle Review in the Chronicle of Higher Education* 49, no. 46 (July 25, 2003): B7 +.

————. "How College Perpetuates Inequality." *The Chronicle Review in the Chronicle of Higher Education* 53, no. 19 (January 12 2007): B9 +.

Sanchez, Jorge R., and Frankie Santos Laanan, eds. *Determining the Economic Benefits of Attending Community College. New Directions for Community Colleges,* 104 (Winter 1998).

Seidman, Earl. *In the Words of the Faculty: Perspectives on Improving Teaching and Educational Quality in Community Colleges.* San Francisco, CA: Jossey-Bass, 1985.

Shaw, Kathleen. "Remedial Education as Ideological Battleground: Emerging Remedial Education Policies in the Community College." *Educational Evaluation and Policy Analysis* 19, no. 3 (Fall 1997), 284–296.

Shaw, Kathleen M. "Defining the Self: Constructions of Identity in Community College Students." In *Community Colleges as Cultural Texts,* edited by Kathleen M. Shaw, James R. Valadez, and Robert A. Rhoads. Albany, NY: State University of New York Press, 1999.

Shaw, Kathleen M., and Howard B. London. "Culture and Ideology in Keeping Transfer Commitment: Three Community Colleges." *The Review of Higher Education* 25, no. 1 (Fall 2001), 91–114.

Shaw, Kathleen M., Sara Goldrick-Rab, Christopher Mazzeo, and Jerry A. Jacobs. *Putting Poor People to Work: How the Work-First Idea Eroded College Access for the Poor.* New York: Russell Sage Foundation, 2006.

Shaw, Kathleen M., James R. Valadez, and Robert A. Rhoads. *Community Colleges as Cultural Texts.* Albany, NY: State University of New York Press, 1999.

Shulock, Nancy, and Colleen Moore. *Invest in Success: How Finance Policy Can Increase Student Success at California's Community Colleges.* Institute for Higher Education Leadership & Policy. Sacramento, CA: Author, October 2007.

Shulock, Nancy, and Colleen Moore. *Rules of the Game: How State Policy Creates Barriers to Degree Completion and Impedes Student Success in the California Community Colleges.* Institute for Higher Education Leadership & Policy. Sacramento, CA: Author, February 2007.

Shulock, Nancy, Colleen Moore, Jeremy Offenstein, and Mary Kirlin. *It Could Happen: Unleashing the Potential of California's Community Colleges to Help Students Succeed and California Thrive.* Institute for Higher Education Leadership and Policy. Sacramento, CA: Author, Feb 2008.

Swail, Watson Scott, Kenneth E. Redd, and Laura W. Perna. *Retaining Minority Students in Higher Education: A Framework for Success.* ASHE-ERIC Higher Education Report 30, no. 2. San Francisco, CA: Jossey-Bass, 2003.

Thelin, John R. *A History of American Higher Education.* Baltimore, MD: Johns Hopkins University Press, 2004.

Thornton, James W. Jr., *The Community Junior College,* 3rd ed. New York: John Wiley & Sons, 1972.

Tillery, Dale, and William L. Deegan. "The Evolution of Two-Year Colleges Through Four Generations." In *Renewing the American Community College: Priorities and Strategies for Effective Leadership,* edited by William L. Deegan and Dale Tillery. San Francisco, CA: Jossey-Bass, 1985.

Townsend, Barbara K. "A Cautionary View." In *The Community College Baccalaureate: Emerging Trends and Policy Issues,* edited by Deborah L. Floyd, Michael L. Skolnik, and Kenneth P. Walker. Sterling, VA: Stylus, 2005.

Townsend, Barbara K., and Kristin B. Wilson. "The Transfer Mission: Tried and True, but Troubled?" In *Community College Missions in the 21st* Century. *New Directions for the Community College* 136 (Winter 2006): 33–41.

Valadez, James. "Cultural Capital and its Impact on the Aspirations of Nontraditional Community College Students." *Community College Review* 21, no. 3 (1993): 30–43.

Vaughan, George B. "The Community College Perspective." In *Thinking about American Higher Education: The 1990s and Beyond,* edited by J. Wade Gilley. New York: Macmillan, 1991.

Weick, Karl E. "Educational Organizations as Loosely Coupled Systems." *Administrative Science Quarterly* 21, no. 1 (March 1976): 1–19.

Weis, Lois. *Between Two Worlds: Black Students in an Urban Community College.* Boston, MA: Routledge & Kegan Paul, 1985.

Whitaker, David G., and Ernest T. Pascarella. "Two-Year College Attendance and Socioeconomic Attainment: Some Additional Evidence." *The Journal of Higher Education* 65, no. 2 (March/April 1994): 194–210.

Zumeta, William. "Public Policy and Accountability in Higher Education: Lessons from the Past and Present for the New Millennium." In *The States and Public Higher Education Policy: Affordability, Access, and Accountability,* edited by Donald E. Heller. Baltimore, MD: Johns Hopkins University Press, 2001.

Zwerling, L. Steven. *The Community College and Its Critics* 54 (June 1986).

———, ed. *Second Best: The Crisis of the Community College.* New York: McGraw Hill, 1976.

ABOUT THE AUTHOR

J. M. Beach has advanced degrees in English, History, Philosophy, and Education. He has been a teacher and educational administrator for over fifteen years. He has been a Lecturer at Oregon State University and the University of California, and an Instructor at several community colleges in Southern California. For a time, Beach was a Research Associate at the California Community College Collaborative, focusing on promising practices in community colleges and vocational education. Outside of higher education, Beach has been a teacher and school administrator. Beach has taught an array of subjects to a broad range of students, from pre-school all the way to high school, in both public and private schools. Beach has also taught English as a Second Language in South Korea. Beach's scholarly research includes *Studies in Poetry: The Visionary* (2004) and *Studies in Ideology: Essays on Culture and Subjectivity* (2005). Beach has written a textbook, *Educating for Democracy* (2008), and he is a poet. His collection of selected poetry is *Living into Words: Poetry in a Time of Killing* (2007). Beach is currently working on two projects on education in its broader sense: a philosophy of education and a history of the Americanization movement. Email at jmbeach@jmbeach.com or browse through his research on his website at www.jmbeach.com

INDEX

AAJC. *See* American Association of Junior
    Colleges
academic instruction
    1900–1949, 9–10
    CPEC on, 100
    Grubb on, xiv–xv
access to education, xvii
    1950–1969, 16–24
    issues in, xix–xx, xxxiv
    myths on, xix
    See also race
accountability, xiv, xxi–xxii
    California and, 69, 103–119
    issues in, 111, 133
    term, 107
administrative progressives, 141n26
    Grubb on, xvi
administrators of community colleges
    1900–1949, 8
    1970–1989, 35
    Grubb on, xi
    and neoliberalism, xxxiv
adult education, California and, 76–77
African Americans
    in California, 88, 92–93
    enrollment of, 38
    junior colleges for, 25–26
    New Left on, 43
    and progressivism, 26–27
    and unemployment, 66
age, and unemployment, 66
agency, and institutionalization, xxvii–xxviii
Alexander, Kern, 122–123
Alford, Robert R., xxvii
Alien Land Laws, 87
Allegretto, Sylvia, 64
ambiguity
    institutionalization of, 47

of legacy, 120–132
of mission, 41
American Association of Junior Colleges
    (AAJC), 8, 14, 22, 26, 36, 86
American Indians. *See* Native Americans
Anson, Chris, 131
Asian Americans
    in California, 86–88, 93
    enrollment of, 38
    and unemployment, 66
assessment movement, xxii–xxiii
    California and, 95
associate's degree
    California and, 72
    economic return on, 64–65
attrition, in California, 80–81
Averianova, Irina E., 53
Ayers, D. Franklin, 53

baccalaureate degree, 50–51
    attainment of, xvii
    community colleges and, 53–56
    return on investment for, 124
Bailey, Thomas R., 53, 57
Ballard Act, 72
Bell, Daniel, 110
Bellah, Robert N., 128–129
Bender, Louis W., 29–30
Berlin, Isaiah, 132
Bernstein, Jared, 65
Biesta, Gert, 165n102
blacks. *See* African Americans
Blocker, Clyde E., 21–22
Bogue, Jesse, 17
Bond, Horace Mann, 25
Brawer, Florence B., 47
Breneman, David W., 34, 123
Brint, Steven, xxx, xxxii–xxxiii, 45–47

Also available from Stylus

Community College Leadership
http://stylus.styluspub.com/Orders/AddToCart.aspx?ISBN=9781579224165
A Multidimensional Model for Leading Change
Pamela L. Eddy
Foreword by George R. Boggs

"Pamela Eddy has done seminal work in creating a multidimensional model for leading change in the community college. This is an excellent resource for all aspiring community college leaders as well as those serving as senior leaders in our institutions. The book is well written and contains an exceptional combination of theory to practice ideas and thoughts. It is sure to become required reading in community college leadership development programs."—**Larry H. Ebbers**, *Community College Leadership Programs, Iowa State University*

"The author has raised the bar on our thinking about community college leadership."—**Nan Ottenritter**, *Director of Professional Development for the Virginia Community College System, and former manager of AACC's "Leading Forward" initiative*

The Community College Baccalaureate
http://stylus.styluspub.com/Orders/AddToCart.aspx?ISBN=9781579221300
Emerging Trends and Policy Issues
Edited by Deborah L. Floyd, Michael L. Skolnik , and Kenneth P. Walker

". . . an important contribution to our understanding of what is sure to become a major policy issue . . . a must read for state policy makers and community college leaders contemplating adding the baccalaureate. Leaders of four-year colleges and universities, particularly in states where the community college baccalaureate is, or is likely to become a reality, will also find this book very helpful."—*Journal of Applied Research in the Community College*

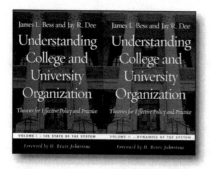

"An important point to make early in this review is that the editors have taken care to present both supporting and opposing views to this trend. This comprehensive perspective is one of the strengths of this work, as all individuals concerned with the community college baccalaureate can use the book to consider both sides of the issue. This book…will contribute greatly towards future research and policy decisions regarding the mission and role of the community college."—*Community College Journal of Research and Practice*

Understanding College and University Organization
http://stylus.styluspub.com/Orders/AddToCart.aspx?ISBN=9781579221973
Theories for Effective Policy and Practice / Two Volume Set
James L. Bess and Jay R. Dee
Foreword by D. Bruce Johnstone

This two-volume work is intended to help readers develop powerful new ways of thinking about organizational principles, and apply them to policy-making and management in colleges and universities.

The book is written with two audiences in mind: administrative and faculty leaders in institutions of higher learning, and students (both doctoral and Master's degree) studying to become upper-level administrators, leaders, and policy makers in higher education.

"Quite simply a *tour de force*. Not only have the authors written by far the broadest and deepest theoretical analysis of college and university organization I've seen, but they have clearly organized a complex topic, and written it engagingly. This will be seen as a landmark work in the field. It should be required reading for all who claim to understand higher education institutions and the behavior that goes on inside and around them."—**David W. Leslie**, *Chancellor Professor of Education, The College of William and Mary*

22883 Quicksilver Drive
Sterling, VA 20166-2102

Subscribe to our e-mail alerts: www.Styluspub.com